THE MITCHELL BEAZLEY

Red Wine Guide

A complete introduction to
choosing red wines

Written by Jim Ainsworth

**Fully updated and revised by
Simon Woods**

The Mitchell Beazley Red Wine Guide

by Jim Ainsworth, fully updated and revised
by Simon Woods

First published in Great Britain in 1990
by Mitchell Beazley, an imprint of Octopus
Publishing Group Ltd, 2–4 Heron Quays,
London E14 4JP.

Revised editions 1999.

A CIP catalogue record for this book is
available from the British Library.

ISBN 1 84000 196 8

The author and publishers will be grateful
for any information which will assist them
in keeping future editions up to date.
Although all reasonable care has been
taken in the preparation of this book,
neither the publishers nor the author can
accept any liability for any consequences
arising from the use thereof or the
information contained therein.

Commissioning Editor: Rebecca Spry
Managing Editor: Hilary Lumsden
Editor: Gill Pitts
Design: Lovelock & Co
Production Controller: Karen Farquhar

Typeset in Stone Serif, MetaPlus.

Printed and bound by Toppan Printing
Company in China.

Contents

Top left: Old bush vines in South Australia produce world-class red wines
Top right: Picturesque landscape of intertwined vineyards and orchards in Burgundy, France
Bottom: The vast vineyards of central Spain produce good-value, fruity red wines

Introduction

When the first edition of this book came out in 1990, red wine wasn't good for us. That all changed in 1991 when the American programme *Sixty Minutes* broadcast an item about a small part of rural France. The inhabitants ate a high-fat diet and often smoked large numbers of Gauloises, but the incidence of heart disease was tiny – thanks, researchers found, to the high consumption of red wine. So don't think of this book as merely a wine guide. It's a health manual, the natural follow-on to the *Hip and Thigh Diet.*

This guide also gives an overview of what is currently happening on the red wine scene, which again is very different to that of 1990. Several California Cabernet Sauvignons now regularly sell for higher prices than first-growth claret. Washington State makes some of the world's finest Merlot and New Zealand some of the best Pinot Noir. Chile has finally emerged as a major red wine producer, and neighbouring Argentina is following suit.

Languedoc-Roussillon still provides plenty of dross for the European wine lake but can now boast dozens of fine wine estates with more appearing every year. New life has been breathed into Portugal, southern Italy and Spain. Perhaps most remarkable of all, the well-known British off-licence chain, Oddbins, has done a major promotion on the wines of – wait for it – Greece! Even where progress has been less noticeable, the average standard of the wines is much higher, and the number of bad red wines we taste each year gets smaller and smaller.

However, the worldwide popularity of red wine has meant that it is increasingly difficult to find certain wines in the shops. When you do manage to locate them, you might find that they are considerably more expensive than when you last bought them. In that case, this book will come to your rescue by recommending many alternatives which you might not have considered from other places around the world. And the good news is that, unlike back in 1990, *all* of them are now good for your health.

How to use this book

The book is organised in an A–Z fashion, giving details of all the major red wine styles, regions and grapes. Wine-producing countries are described in a separate section. Rosé and sparkling wines can be found in the companion *White Wine Guide*, along with wines such as Liqueur Muscat which, though dark, is made from white grapes. In the next few pages you will find simple guides to matching wine with food.

Each entry in the directory follows a similar pattern, beginning with a brief resumé. A regional listing gives the best-known wines, the main grape varieties and the general style of the wines; a grape variety listing gives the general style of the wines and the regions where the variety is grown; a specific wine listing gives the region of origin, the grape varieties used and a brief description of the typical flavour. Where relevant, the entry will also have a quality/price rating as follows:

	Quality		Price
*	Mediocre	£	£4
**	Simple Quaffer	££	£4–6
***	Good	£££	£6–10
****	Excellent	££££	£10–15
*****	The Best	£££££	£15+

The quality bands assess each wine on a worldwide, rather than a regional, scale of worth. The price bands reflect approximately the retail cost of a wine, rather than its cost in a restaurant, where it will usually rise in price to a higher band.

Following the main body of the entry, where relevant there are details of the tastes to expect from the wine/grape/region/country. In addition, where relevant there is a box of recommended producers and, in certain cases, entries for the larger countries also give details of the main wine laws.

At the end of each entry is a subsection entitled "Where next?" This suggests taste paths to follow, directing the reader towards other entries in the directory – highlighted in bold – where information on similar styles of wine can be found. The recommended wines might be slightly lighter or heavier, a little oakier or less oaky, cheaper or more expensive, but each recommendation is designed to encourage confident experimentation.

Wine with food

Entire volumes have been written about matching food and wine, as if the subject were a precise science. It isn't, it never will be and it only makes wine unnecessarily complicated. If people concentrated on serving wine they love with food they love, they would be happy 99 per cent of the time. Having said that, here are ten guidelines which will either increase your pleasure or help you avoid the few disastrous combinations that do exist.

1   **Body talk** Weighty food needs weighty wine and light food needs light wine. So Aussie Shiraz with your steak-and-kidney pie, and Muscadet with your oysters.

2   **Who is showing off?** Meaning which is more important to you: the dish you're making or ordering in a restaurant or the bottle of wine you're going to have with it? Whichever comes first, the other should be content to play a minor role. Great food, uncomplicated wine; great wine, uncomplicated food. Uncomplicated in either case doesn't mean tasteless. A first-class leg of lamb, simply roasted, is an excellent choice with a fine, mature red from any part of the world. Similarly, Beaujolais will never be the world's greatest red wine, but fine examples can happily partner a variety of ornate dishes.

3   **The acid test** Acidity is what keeps a wine fresh, and all wines have it to some degree. Sweet wines often have a very high level to prevent cloying. If a wine is lower in acidity than the food it's served with, it will seem flabby. This is seldom a problem as, apart from fruit, there are few foods which are high in acidity. If you find yourself with a wine that is just too acidic for the food, try sprinkling a little vinegar or lemon juice on the dish and the wine will calm down and behave better. Acidity in a wine is useful for counterbalancing the richness of fatty foods.

4   **Sweets for my sweet** If a wine isn't as sweet as the food it's served with, it can seem bitter, acidic and astringent. There's not much you can do about this except take note of it for next time. Remember that certain

vegetables such as carrots and onions are actually sweet, and this character is especially noticeable after long, slow cooking. With savoury dishes and even lighter desserts, you don't have to go for something which is out-and-out sweet, providing it has plenty of ripe, fruity flavour.

5   **The Italian job** If in doubt, try a bottle of Italian wine. High acidity and not much flavour is a hallmark of many Italian whites, but it means you won't have any disastrous clashes.

6   **Sauce for the goose** If a dish has a strongly flavoured sauce, it's more important to think of this than the meat/fish/whatever underneath. If you've used wine in the sauce, serve a similar wine with the dish.

7   **Bun fight at the Oaky Corral** Too much oak in a wine is a killer, unless you have some smoked fish or meat on hand.

8   **Red or white?** Is red wine really better with meat and white wine with fish? Swap them around and see for yourself. You'd be surprised how well rich Chardonnays go with steaks and how less full-bodied reds such as Pinot Noir and lighter Chiantis partner salmon.

9   **Say cheese** Cheese and wine is supposed to be a classic combination, but which wine and which cheese? If you do some experimenting with a selection of cheeses – hard, soft, goat's, blue and smoked – you'll be surprised how unpalatable some of the combinations are. Red wine is what many would choose for the entire cheeseboard, but you might find that whites, especially sweet wines, perform better. Serving just one very good cheese with an appropriate wine may be the best solution.

10   **Bread and water** Occasionally, some combinations are either truly vile – Chianti with chocolate profiteroles – or simply do no favours to either the food or wine: for example, mature red burgundy and Brie. Okay, we all make mistakes. Have a drink of water, nibble a piece of bread in between mouthfuls and remember for next time.

The 11th guideline is to ignore any or all of the above if it conflicts with your own experience. Put a variety of wines and plates in front of a panel of "expert" tasters and at the end of the nibbling and sipping, there will often be little agreement as to which are the best combinations. So if you do find that Chianti with profiteroles is your thing, then go for it – just don't invite us to your dinner parties.

A–Z of red wine

Adelaide Hills

Not just for whites
Grape varieties Pinot Noir, Cabernet Sauvignon,
Cabernet Franc, Merlot
Style Ripe, berry-and-plum Pinot Noir, fairly high acidity
Quality/Price ***·····⟩****/£££·····⟩£££££

It's no coincidence that the Adelaide Hills, which show promise for Pinot Noir, is also the source of some of Australia's finest Sauvignon Blancs. Bordeaux varieties are also grown, and Nepenthe even makes an impressive Zinfandel. It's cool here, even by European standards, so a long, slow ripening period results in more intense flavours in the grapes. The wines made so far have been good rather than great, but as producers progress in their techniques for making Pinot Noir they should get even better.

The Adelaide Hills taste The Pinots are fine, with ripe, earthy, plum-and berry-fruit, but they do seem to show high acidity and lack the lush texture of great Pinot Noir. Bordeaux varietals often show leafy hints, as if the fruit had not ripened fully, but the best are elegant, with plum and cassis fruit.

Where next? Pinot from **Yarra Valley**, **Victoria** and **Western Australia**.

Alentejo

Alcoholic fomentation
Best-known wines Mouchão, Tinto da Anfora
Grape varieties Periquita (aka Castelhão Francês), Moreto,
Trincadeira, Aragonez, Alicante Bouschet
Style Rich, leathery, dark-berry fruit
Quality/Price *·····⟩****/£·····⟩£££££

The Alentejo, an area of cork oaks and wheat fields spreading south and east from the capital of Lisbon, is Portugal's most southerly winemaking region. Well, the

Algarve is, really, but nobody counts that. It is becoming increasingly apparent that a bit of money and know-how can transform the wonderful grapes of the region – principally Periquita (aka Castelhão Francês), Moreto, Trincadeira and Aragonez – into some of Portugal's best red wines. Prices for these are creeping up, but they've still not reached extortionate levels. And with an injection of winemaking knowledge, some of Portugal's finest co-ops are also able to turn out gutsy, good-value reds in large quantities.

The region is sub-divided into smaller demarcated areas which may be indicated on the label – Borba, Granja, Portalegre, Redondo, Reguengos and Vidigueira – although you are more likely to find a good bottle if you look for the name of the producer.

The Alentejo taste The local grapes provide good colour, aroma, some tannin and rich damson, plum and berry fruit flavours that can develop into leathery, tarry, cedary, swirly, smoky complexity over about five years. They still have a swashbuckling, rustic feel about them, and good structure, but they appeal because they have not sold out to international tastes, even when new oak is used. They show that Portugal can not only produce good wine, but can also reflect something distinctively Portuguese at the same time. Long may it continue.

Where next? Compare the wines with those from **Dão**, **Bairrada** and the **Douro**. And if you want to look outside **Portugal**, bypass Spain and head for the wines of central and southern **Italy**.

Some of Portugal's best wines are produced in the expansive Alentejo region

Alsace

No longer just pale and interesting
Grape varieties Pinot Noir
Style Light and spicy, with red-fruit flavours
Quality/Price **⋯⟩***/£££⋯⟩££££

Alsace, one of France's great white wine regions, also makes red wine and rosé from Pinot Noir. Traditionally it has been difficult to tell the reds from the rosés, but with better vinification techniques and more care in the vineyard, some surprisingly deep-coloured wines with no shortage of flavour and character have resulted. Yet, as is so often the case with red wines from white wine producing areas, prices can be high.

The town of Riquewihr sits nestled among vines which stretch as far as the eye can see

The Alsace taste Alsatian Pinot Noir offers a pleasant aroma and simple, spicy, strawberry and cherry flavours; try wines from Paul Blanck, Marcel Deiss, Hugel et fils and Zind Humbrecht. Not burgundy, but not bad.

Where next? Alsace **Pinot Noir** makes an interesting comparison with the Pinot Noirs of **Sancerre** and **Germany**; in **Burgundy** itself, Côte de Beaune villages such as Savigny or Santenay provide greater complexity, without adding notably greater weight.

RECOMMENDED PRODUCERS
De Bablut
Clos Rougèard
Des Deux Roches (Germain)
Filliatreau
Du Hureau
Langlois-Château
De Montgilet
Ogereau
Pierre-Bise (Clos du Coulaine)
Richou
Caves des Vignerons de Saumur
De Villeneuve

Anjou-Saumur

Life after rosé
Best-known wines Saumur-Champigny
Grape varieties Cabernet Franc, Gamay, Cabernet Sauvignon, Pineau d'Aunis
Style Crisp, earthy, blackcurrant-leaf flavours
Quality/Price *⋯⟩****/££⋯⟩£££££

Anjou-Saumur sprawls across the River Loire to the east of Muscadet and to the west of Touraine. The region, like the Loire Valley as a whole, is best known for its great white wines and rather less great rosés, but it also produces some excellent reds. Cabernet Sauvignon is a permitted variety in the region, while Anjou Rouge may include Pineau d'Aunis and Anjou

Gamay is 100 per cent Gamay. However, by and large the wines are based on Cabernet Franc. Anjou Rouge is the catch-all appellation for the region, with 46 of the best villages entitled to use the Anjou-Villages appellation. The best wines come from Saumur and Saumur-Champigny, which are situated west of Chinon, across the River Loire from Bourgueil.

The Anjou-Saumur taste Cabernet Franc is not everybody's cup of tea, but these wines can be juicily delicious with an earthy rawness and a lively, edgy bite in youth that makes them invigorating. In poor years they can be a bit rasping, but in good years they can be remarkably soft, and will age happily for five years or more – although they are excellent when young (and ever-so-lightly chilled).

In Saumur-Champigny, many growers bottle a young, easy, Anjou-style wine and a more serious *vin de garde*, occasionally aged in new-oak *barriques*. This second style can be substantial stuff, providing the fruit is ripe enough to sustain the oak.

Where next? For more **Loire Cabernet Franc**, try the neighbouring produce of **Chinon**, **Bourgueil** and St-Nicolas-de-Bourgueil. Or take a look at the **Cabernet Franc** entry to see how it fares in other countries.

Apulia

Well heeled
Best-known wines Castel del Monte
Grape varieties Negroamaro, Primitivo,
Uva di Troia, Malvasia Nera
Style Ripe, spicy berry fruit, becoming more
impressive each vintage
Quality/Price *⋯⟩****/£⋯⟩££££

RECOMMENDED PRODUCERS
Candido
Càntele
Leone de Castris
CS di Copertino
Rivera
Taurino
Torrevento
Vallone

Apulia, the heel of Italy's boot, usually comes first or second in the league table of Italy's provinces where production levels are concerned. Traditionally, most of the wine has been of a low standard, useful for adding a bit of colour to some more anaemic northern brews, but certainly not what anyone with a taste bud would get excited about. Fortunately, that situation is changing. Even though only about two per cent of what is made here sees the inside of a bottle, there are some great-value wines to be found, as well as a few with rather loftier ambitions. And behind the wines are some excellent local grapes.

Negroamaro – "black and bitter" – is used to good effect with Malvasia Nera in Copertino, Brindisi and Salice Salentino. Primitivo, suspected to be California's Zinfandel, forms the bulk of Gioia del Colle and is the only grape in Primitivo di Manduria (dry and sweet). Uva di Troia's claim to fame is Castel del Monte, while Aleatico is used throughout the region to make a rich, red dessert wine. Apulia can also claim two of Italy's most delightfully named wines: Squinzano and Cacc'e Mmittee di Lucera.

The Apulia taste Taste the best wines made from Primitivo and you can see something of the spicy berry flavour of Zinfandel shining through. Uva di Troia, at its best in Castel del Monte, produces rich, soft, juicy wines with cherry fruit, some of which don't mind five years' ageing. Negroamaro is possibly the best of the trio, making reds whose flavours include cherries, damsons, liquorice, chocolate, cinnamon and cloves, underpinned by a characteristic bitterness.

Where next? Sicily, **Sardinia** and Campania first, then head for **California** for the Primitivo/**Zinfandel** comparison. After that, see how the Greeks and Portuguese are succeeding with their indigenous varieties.

RECOMMENDED PRODUCERS
Goldwater Estate
Peninsula
Providence
St Jerome
Stonyridge
Te Motu

Auckland

Bordeaux look-alikes at Bordeaux prices
Grape varieties Cabernet Sauvignon, Merlot, Cabernet Franc, Pinot Noir
Style Elegant, powerful and long-lived reds
Quality/Price **····⟩****/££····⟩£££££

Auckland is the hub for a number of small regions dotted around the north end of New Zealand's North Island. There's a wide variation in climates, with some parts being warmer and drier than others. The star region is Waiheke Island, 2–3 °C (4–6 °F) warmer than Auckland, and the source of some of New Zealand's finest and most expensive Bordeaux-style reds. Around Matakana, to the north of Auckland, there are a couple of wineries that would dispute both titles.

The high rainfall hampers Henderson's potential for making wine, as does encroaching suburbia, however, the area remains important because it is where Babich, Collards, Corbans and Delegat's have their headquarters. The Waimauku-Huapai-Kumeu region to the north of Auckland also has medium to large wineries such as Cooper's Creek, Matua Valley, Nobilo and Selaks, which use grapes from other regions together with local fruit.

The Auckland taste Waiheke reds are intensely fruity, with ripe, berry and blackcurrant flavours and a firm, tannic structure. There's none of the green meanies which can afflict other Kiwi reds, and they'll happily keep for ten years, becoming more and more claret-like as they age.

Where next? Hawke's Bay is Waiheke's main competition in New Zealand for the Bordeaux-style crown. Try wines from both regions against those from cooler Australian spots such as the Yarra Valley and Margaret River.

Bairrada

A real Baga of a wine

Region Central Portugal
Grape varieties Baga, Castelhão Francês, Tinto Pinheira
Flavour Gutsy, with blackcurrant, plum and tobacco hints
Quality/Price *····⟩****/£····⟩££££

RECOMMENDED PRODUCERS
Bright Brothers
Caves Aliança
Luis Pato
Casa de Saima
Caves São João
Sogrape

Like so many wines in Portugal, those of Bairrada are making the transition from tough and tannic old numbers to strong, flavoursome, fruit-filled styles, which, if not exactly gainly, are certainly not the kind of wines we can ignore. They have potential written all over them.

Baga is the main grape variety, making up 80 per cent or more of a typical wine. It's a sturdy, thick-skinned variety with heaps of colour and flavour. However, traditional winemaking techniques have produced wines that can make cold stewed tea taste soft and appealing. Yet, with a bit of TLC in the press-house, and ageing in stainless steel or new oak instead of a lengthy stay in big old barrels, the wines can be very good – without sacrificing their Portuguese identity. Luis Pato leads the way, taking Baga to new heights with his single-vineyard wines Vinha Barrosa and Vinha Pan. Others are now following his example.

The Bairrada taste Baga makes wines with deep, intense colours, and rich plum, tobacco and blackcurrant flavours, spiked with a swirl of black pepper. Unoaked versions are fresh, just slightly jammy and perfect barbecue fodder. The best wines add in flavours of cherries and savoury hints, all wrapped up in a tannic shroud which can take five years to loosen its grip, and then preserve the wine for ten years more after that.

Where next? Dão, Douro and Alentejo all can compete with the best Bairrada. See also Touriga Nacional – a great red variety.

Bandol

RECOMMENDED PRODUCERS

Bunan (Mas de la Rouvière)
De Pibarnon
Pradeaux
Ray Jane
Ste Anne
Tempier

Serious wine in sensibly shaped bottles

Region Provence

Grape varieties Mourvèdre, Grenache, Cinsault, Syrah, Carignan

Style Savoury, herby, plum and blackcurrant flavours

Quality/Price **····⟩****/£££····⟩££££

Tourists in Provence who stick to indifferent and overpriced whites and rosés in silly bottles are missing out on one of the unsung greats of French wine. The heroic Bandol, made from a minimum of 50 per cent Mourvèdre and often considerably more, comes from coastal vineyards to the east of Marseilles. The Mediterranean sun teases complex feral characters out of the grape, and the result is a wine of complexity and amazing longevity.

The Bandol taste Bandol is a savoury, meaty wine, which in its youth can have aromas of – let's be polite now – the farmyard. These fade with time, revealing a rich, spicy wine packed with plummy, blackcurrant flavours and hints of vanilla and tobacco. The best will safely keep for ten years or more, indeed, they often need that amount of time to show at their best.

Where next? See the Mourvèdre entry for other regions using this underrated variety.

Banyuls

RECOMMENDED PRODUCERS

De la Casa Blanca
L'Etoile
Du Mas Blanc
De la Rectorie
De la Tour Vieille
Vial Magnères

Beautiful port, beautiful "port"

Region Languedoc-Roussillon

Grape varieties Minimum of 50 per cent Grenache

Style Tawny port look-alike

Quality/Price **····⟩****/£££····⟩£££££

Travel any further along the Mediterranean coastline from the precipitous terraced vineyards in the appellation of Banyuls and you'll find yourself in Spain. The main town of the region is the picturesque port of Collioure, which gives its name to still wine of the area. Jolly good it is too, with producers making great wine at great prices.

Banyuls itself is a *vin doux naturel*, and is perhaps the nearest France comes to producing port. It must be made from at least 50 per cent Grenache, with that proportion rising to 75 per cent for Banyuls *grand cru*. The *grand cru* wines must spend at least 30 months in cask before bottling, although many spend much more. There are no such limitations on Banyuls, and a few producers choose to bottle it early. However, lengthy ageing either in cask or glass *bonbonnes* – with or without a stopper – is the norm.

The Banyuls taste This depends largely on when the wine was bottled. Early bottlings mature rather like vintage port: young and vigorously fruity with spicy, berry flavours, acquiring more roundness with time. The aged versions, where oxidation has taken place, are more like tawny ports: rich and nutty, with dried fruit, spice, coffee and caramel flavours. Considered *les genoux de l'abeille* (the bee's knees) with chocolate puddings.

Where next? Rivesaltes and Maury are similar (*see* **Languedoc-Roussillon, Vin Doux Naturel**). Or grab a bottle of tawny **Port**.

France's very own "port", produced near to Port Vendres

Barbaresco

No longer understudy to Barolo
Region Piedmont
Grape varieties Nebbiolo
Style Plums, damsons, chocolate, tobacco, herbs and tar
Quality/Price *----⟩*****/£££----⟩£££££

RECOMMENDED PRODUCERS
Castello di Neive
Ceretto
Cigliuti
Gaja
Bruno Giacosa
I Paglieri
Marchesi di Gresy
Fiorenzo Nada
Paitin
Pio Cesare
Produttori del Barbaresco
Bruno Rocca
La Spinetta

Barbaresco is Barolo's other half, a DOCG wine from the Langhe hills of Piedmont, to the northeast of Alba. Made from the same grape, Nebbiolo, it shares Barolo's image of quality, but the style is slightly less aggressive, gentler and easier to get to grips with – but only slightly, mind you. Barbaresco is considered the more feminine of the two, but some are as delicate as a steroid-pumping women's Olympic shot-putting team. Indeed, it is often difficult to tell the two wines apart, so whatever hormones Barolo is taking, Barbaresco is obviously getting an armful of the same. Nevertheless, in order to derive the full benefit from Barolo, it is probably best to approach it via Barbaresco.

If Barbaresco is well known today, it is due largely to the efforts of Angelo Gaja, who has shown with modern winemaking skills and no small amount of new oak that Barbaresco can be made in a style that is approachable when young. Since he took over from his father in the 1960s,

The classic rolling hills of northwest Italy, with the Alps towering in the background

his single-vineyard wines – and their prices – have stunned the world. Try his Barolo Sperss, from a plot he acquired in 1988, alongside his Barbaresco San Lorenzo and see what you think.

The Barbaresco taste Thanks to the Nebbiolo grape, Barbaresco is tannic and long-lived, but the lighter, chalkier soils around the villages of Neive, Barbaresco and Treiso tend to give it less "oomph" than Barolo. The flavour spectrum overlaps with Barolo. Plums and damsons are enveloped in the richness of chocolate, and barrel-ageing throws in whiffs of prunes and liquorice; tobacco, herbs and tar are not unusual. It is a bit gentler, less rasping, more approachable, and a bit less long-lived than Barolo. But it is still dramatic.

Where next? To enjoy the wines of **Piedmont** to the full, begin with a **Nebbiolo** delle Langhe, progress to Barbaresco, then take on **Barolo**. Or try and track down a Californian or Australian Nebbiolo.

Barbera

Italy's answer to Merlot
Style Plums and damsons, with refreshing acidity
Grown in Italy, especially Piedmont; Argentina, California

Barbera is Italy's second most widely planted grape variety, and also one of the world's most common vines. It is a high-yielding, adaptable variety that is able to thrive where many others cannot. High acidity makes it welcome in the sunnier growing regions where it disappears into anonymous blends, but it reaches a remarkable peak of achievement in Piedmont, the north western region of Italy. It is usually consigned to the lesser vineyards sites, while the great Nebbiolo gets the best sites. Its role with Barbera d'Asti and the richer Barbera d'Alba has traditionally been to provide good, basic, everyday wine.

However, plant Barbera in a good site, nurture it, vinify it carefully and age it in new oak and it emerges in splendid fashion, far more approachable than the demanding Nebbiolo, and not far away in overall quality. Blend the two varieties together and the results are equally fine. A few producers have even made Barbera/Cabernet blends, again to good effect.

Barbera also grows in other Italian regions, but the further it gets from Piedmont, the less impressive it becomes. In Lombardy, it appears as a varietal and in blends in Oltrepò Pavese, in Emilia-Romagna, Gutturnio dei Colli Piacentini is a Barbera-dominated blend, while further south, in Campania, a proportion of Barbera can be used in Taurasi.

It appears in many cheaper Argentinian wines, although so far it has never gone beyond the simply fruity. Likewise in California, where it is the fifth most widely planted red variety. Look out for Renwood, Ca' del Solo and Robert Mondavi. Perhaps the strangest place Barbera is found is in Virginia, where the Barboursville winery grows and vinifies some.

The Barbera taste Barbera has more backbone and aggression than Dolcetto, but it is more approachable than Nebbiolo-based wines. It can make anything from light, slightly tart, everyday wines, to beautiful oak-aged reds of great charm and finesse with plum-pudding flavours. High acidity, moderate tannin and good fruit give it the potential to age.

Where next? Down in intensity to **Dolcetto**, up to **Nebbiolo**.

Barolo

King of the hills
Region Piedmont
Grape varieties Nebbiolo
Style Plummy, black-cherry fruit with hints of tar, roses, truffles and violets
Quality/Price **⋯⟩*****/£££⋯⟩£££££

Nebbiolo is the power behind Barolo and Barbaresco, two of Italy's sturdiest wines. Both are made south of Turin in the Langhe hills that surround the truffle town of Alba. Barolo

RECOMMENDED PRODUCERS
Elio Altare
Azelia
Batasiolo
Brovia
Michele Chiarlo
Domenico Clerico
Aldo Conterno
Giacomo Conterno
Conterno Fantino
Corino
Gaja
Bruno Giacosa

RECOMMENDED PRODUCERS CONTINUED

Matteo Correggia
Alfredo Prunotto
Albino Rocca
Bruno Rocca
Paolo Scavino

spreads to the southwest, Barbaresco to the northeast. At its best, Barolo is among the most sublime drinking on offer anywhere in Italy. And fortunately the region is blessed with many excellent producers, so there should be no need to drink any of the awful Barolo that has tarnished the image of this potentially great wine. Too often, though, Barolo can be dull, flat, oxidised, harsh and fruitless.

What has gone wrong? Probably a logical misconception that, as good Barolo is undrinkably tannic when young, any young Barolo that is undrinkably tannic must eventually come good. Unfortunately, many simply oxidise and grow old, never becoming the delights they should. Barolo poses the same dilemma as Brunello di Montalcino. Should it be made in this traditional fashion, unapproachable and impenetrable for ages, in the hope that enough good wines will turn up often enough to justify the whole business? Or should gentler extraction, stainless steel, temperature control, maturation in small oak barriques, exclusion of air and ageing in bottle – in short, modern winemaking – be allowed to modify the Barolo style?

Barolo has changed its style before; in the last century it was fizzy, and in the early part of this century it was less tannic than many are today. Thus, there is no venerable tradition to be followed slavishly. Many winemakers are now producing Barolo that doesn't require a lifetime to soften nor a lifetime's practice to appreciate.

Even so, Barolo is not a wine for beginners, not a soft, easy wine that you can just open on the spur of the moment and drink with pleasure.

The vineyards of Barolo produce some of the world's most full-bodied reds

It is best approached in the manner of a Piemontese meal, via a Nebbiolo delle Langhe, and before that maybe a Barbera or a Dolcetto. It is a wine to decant, sip and contemplate. Good Barolo can be expensive, too, but the reward for money, patience and self-denial is a subtle and complex wine, the like of which is produced nowhere else.

The Barolo taste Barolo is big because it has a lot of alcohol (13 per cent minimum) and more tannin than a gallon of trucker's tea. It is long-lived – the tannin and acidity of Nebbiolo see to that. At its fruitiest, it should smell and taste of plums and black cherries; when mature, it should evoke woodsmoke and liquorice. If you can also get tea, tar, roses, truffles, chestnuts and violets out of it, you are obviously drinking a classic bottle. These are not the primary smells and flavours of the Nebbiolo grape, but those derived from long ageing.

Then the vineyard location contributes its particular twist: those in Serralunga d'Alba and Monforte d'Alba produce more tannic and long-lasting wines, while those of La Morra and Barolo itself are lighter and ready for drinking sooner. Some feel that the differences call for a blend in order to ensure some continuity of style; others wish to emphasise them in order to produce a more individual wine.

Where next? **Barbaresco** is the other **Nebbiolo** heavyweight. Tuscan **Sangiovese** is also a classic Italian red style, so contrast Barolo with **Brunello di Montalcino**, **Chianti** Classico Riserva and the Super-Tuscans. **Barolo** can be as subtly perfumed as red **Burgundy**, although rather more tannic.

Barossa

Little and large
Best-known wines Penfolds Grange, Jacob's Creek
Grape varieties Shiraz, Grenache, Mourvèdre,
Cabernet Sauvignon, Pinot Noir
Style Thumping rich, ripe, berry Shiraz
Quality/Price **⋯⟩*****/£⋯⟩£££££

RECOMMENDED PRODUCERS

Basedow
Wolf Blass
Grant Burge
Elderton
Henschke
Peter Lehmann
Magpie Estate
Charles Melton
Orlando
Penfolds
RBJ
Rockford
St Hallett
Torbreck
Veritas
Willows
Yalumba

A large chunk of South Australia's winemaking is carried out in this wide and gently sloping valley northeast of Adelaide. Barossa is home to large-scale wineries that process fruit from all over the state and beyond. More than 75 per cent of the wine made here originates outside Barossa, and often the wines are blends from various regions.

It can be difficult putting your finger on a Barossa style. However, since the mid-1980s, a number of small producers have been making the most of the haggard old vines grown in the valley, resulting in spectacularly rich and concentrated wines, usually Shiraz with smaller amounts of Grenache. The larger companies, which in times past would lose this old-vine fruit in one of their many blends, have also begun to produce special *cuvées* from these special grapes. While Shiraz is the dominant Barossa variety, Cabernet also thrives here, and would no doubt be producing some spectacular wines if there were 100-year-old vines.

The cooler Eden Valley also comes under the Barossa umbrella, and is mainly thought of as white wine country. However, it is home to one of Australia's greatest Shiraz vineyards, Henschke's Hill of Grace. Eden Valley Pinot Noir can also be good.

The Barossa taste Old-vine Shiraz is substantial, yet because of the ripe tannins, always approachable. Rich in texture and with plummy, berry flavour, it develops beautifully in bottle to leathery maturity. The sparkling versions are sensational. Those from the Eden Valley are rather more elegant though still powerful. Grenache can be rather top-heavy and alcoholic, but the best have spicy liquorice and mulberry flavours to balance. Cabernet is in the soft, generous, blackcurranty style, and again doesn't mind bottle age.

The attractive Barossa Valley is at the heart of Australia's winemaking industry

Where next? Clare Valley and McLaren Vale also specialise in generously flavoured reds. Try some **Shiraz** against wines from **Victoria** to see the diversity **Australia** achieves with the variety.

Beaujolais

RECOMMENDED PRODUCERS

Noël Aucoeur
Ghislaine Belicard
Berrod
Paul Boutinot
Nicole Chanrion
F Charvet
Fernand Coudert
Joseph Drouhin
Georges Duboeuf
Marc Dudet
Un Eventail des Vignerons
Château des Jacques
Jacky Janodet
André Large
Château du Moulin-à-Vent
Louis Tête
Thivin
Des Tours

Glug, glug, glug
Region Southern Burgundy
Grape varieties Gamay
Style Zippy raspberry and violet tones
Quality/Price *·····›****/£·····›££££

The trouble with wine is that it can get terribly complicated. There are nuances here, subtleties there – not to mention vintage charts and other intricacies to master and have at your fingertips on those occasions when you need to wrestle with a wine waiter. Why can't it all just be simple and straightforward? With Beaujolais it can be. One grape variety, Gamay; one region, lying between Mâcon and Lyon on the granite hills between the Saône and the Loire; one name, Beaujolais. And in most cases, a pretty straightforward taste, too.

Most people's introduction to Beaujolais is through the annual Nouveau jamboree which takes place on the third Thursday in November. As a little piece of secular ritual (at one time it would have been religious, too) it is a wonderful, if now not very fashionable, way to give thanks for the harvest safely gathered in. This is the really gluggable stuff, lots of vibrant colour, no harsh tannin, yet enough acidity to make your mouth water – and a gardenful of fruit. Serious? No, with knobs on. Chuck out the wine glasses and get in the pint pots.

What gives Beaujolais Nouveau (or Primeur as it is sometimes known) its particular character is the method by which it is fermented: carbonic maceration. Instead of crushing the grapes to break the skins and let the yeasts and sugars get at each other, the grapes are carefully handled so that they remain whole, with the skins unbroken. Bunches of whole grapes are placed in a vat; the grapes at the bottom are crushed by the weight of those on top and begin to ferment in the normal way, but the rest ferment individually, berry by berry. Because this fermentation takes place within the grape, the colour and flavour are extracted from under the skin, but much of the tannin on the outside – which tastes hard and astringent in young wine, but which acts as a preservative for long-lived wines – is excluded. The result is a soft wine, ideal for drinking young. But the method is not entirely foolproof; some wines can taste of jam, pear-drops, or even bubblegum.

About half the Beaujolais crop is made into Nouveau. Ideally it should be drunk well before the next lot comes along, but anybody who buys a case in November will be able to dip into whatever is left throughout the winter and on into spring and early summer. In any case, whatever the producers do not sell as Nouveau can be re-labelled as straight Beaujolais, so you could be drinking it under a different name after Christmas.

A striking and elegant château in the Brouilly AC of Beaujolais

Nouveau and ordinary Beaujolais generally come from the southern half of the region, but better wines are made in the north. Growers in 39 specified villages can produce the fuller, richer Beaujolais-Villages. Wines produced by a grower in one of the villages will have more individual character than a merchant's blend from several.

There are ten villages, often called *crus*, which produce wine of sufficient quality and distinctiveness to merit their own ACs. These are Brouilly, Chénas, Chiroubles, Côte de Brouilly, Fleurie, Juliénas, Morgon, Moulin-à-Vent, Régnié and St-Amour. The wines vary mainly in terms of size, richness and weight, with the lighter ones being little different from Beaujolais-Villages, while the more powerful wines from good vintages can be kept for ten years or more. Many are even matured in oak.

The Beaujolais taste The Beaujolais taste is the taste of pure Gamay: the light, but vivid purple wine oozes with soft, juicy fruit, from raspberries to strawberries to plums. A hint of pepper, sometimes a banana or two – it obstinately refuses to sit around waiting for old age and woodsmoke from barrels to creep in. Its pleasure, its charm, its fun, is all immediate. Beaujolais wears Tee-shirts, not suits, and they read "Swig-me-quick".

Beaujolais-Villages is rather fuller wine, with a taste reminiscent of morello cherries, but it's still not wine to meditate over. Some of the *crus*, however, can be more serious, although they still wear a smile. Brouilly, the largest and southernmost *cru*, is light, fruity and slightly earthy. Chénas is the smallest *cru*, making handsome, square-jawed Beaujolais that can, with a bit of ageing (and it needs ageing for best results), begin to resemble Pinot Noir. Chiroubles makes light wines for easy, early drinking, with a pronounced and attractive perfume; Côte de Brouilly, from the sunnier slopes, is fuller, riper and more powerful and vivid than straight Brouilly.

Fleurie seduces with its name and its round, supple, cherryish style; Juliénas has body and structure, with hints of spice and chocolate, and doesn't object to four years or more in bottle. Neither does the opulent Morgon with its pleasantly chewy, cherry-plummy fruit and sturdy constitution; Moulin-à-Vent is the weightiest *cru*, strong, well-structured and Burgundian in style, and definitely needing time to reach its peak. Régnié can be pleasantly fruity but is perhaps the weakest of the *crus*; and St-Amour, the most northerly, produces complete and balanced wines, which can be relatively expensive, especially around Valentine's Day.

Where next? They try in the **Loire**, but nowhere else makes **Gamay** like they do in Beaujolais. Other fruity quaffers include lighter Loire **Cabernet Francs** such as St-Nicolas-de-Bourgueil and several northern Italian reds such as **Dolcetto**, **Valpolicella** and Marzemino (*see* **Trentino-Alto Adige**).

Beaune

The heart of Burgundy

Region Burgundy

Grape varieties Pinot Noir

Style Fragrant and quite muscly, with cherry and raspberry fruit

Quality/Price ***---->****/£££---->£££££

If Burgundy has a capital, it is Beaune. This is where many of the major wine companies, such as Bouchard, Drouhin, Jadot and Latour, have their headquarters. There are smart shops and restaurants, and this is the home of the Hospices de Beaune with its famous chequered roof. Thanks to kindly benefactors, the Hospices has extensive vineyards throughout Burgundy, and on the third Sunday of November each year, the wines from the estate are auctioned barrel by barrel to a fanfare of publicity.

Perhaps because there is so much going on in Beaune, the wines produced in the locality aren't as well known as they should be. The result is that they can be very good value (in Burgundian terms). There are no Beaune *grands crus*, but several *premiers crus*. Nearby Chorey-lès-Beaune has no *premiers crus*, but again the wines are sensibly priced. Savigny-lès-Beaune is better known and has some very good producers, but yet again, its wines aren't too expensive. Are you sure this is Burgundy?

The Beaune taste Beaune sits somewhere between Pommard and Volnay, having the power of the former and the fragrance of the latter, although never quite matching the quality achieved in those two communes. But if you like your burgundy with forward raspberry and cherry fruit, Beaune can be excellent. Savigny is in a similar vein, but never rises to the same heights, while Chorey is charming and fruity, and a good introduction to the Beaune style.

Where next? Turn to the **Côte de Beaune** section for more recommendations for nearby areas. Alternatively, have a look at what the Oregonians are doing with **Pinot Noir**.

The Hospices de Beaune, in the historic town of Beaune

RECOMMENDED PRODUCERS

Champarel
Constant
Costes
Court-lès-Mûts
De Gouyat
Haut-Pécharmant
La Jaubertie
Le Raz
Richard
Tiregand
Tour des Gendres/Luc Conti

Bergerac

Apprentice claret
Region Southwest France
Grape varieties Merlot, Cabernet Sauvignon, Cabernet Franc, Malbec
Style Light, earthy blackcurrant flavours
Quality/Price **→***/£→££££

Bergerac, some 48 km (30 miles) up the Dordogne from Bordeaux, begins more or less where St-Emilion leaves off. Merlot still dominates, so the wines are country cousins of St-Emilion and Pomerol: simple, soft, light and less distinguished – but less expensive, too. Wherever circumstances call for a modest, even a humble claret – a light lunch, a Sunday picnic – Bergerac can supply the goods. Côtes de Bergerac is distinguished by one degree more alcohol. The best wines of the district come from the small appellation of Pécharmant, close to the town of Bergerac itself.

The Bergerac taste Bergerac is light, earthy and refreshing, with freshly squeezed blackcurrant flavour. Pécharmant takes this a step further, and is slightly fuller and fruitier, with a grassy edge that plain Bergerac often lacks. Although drinkable young, it will improve over 2 to 5 years.

Where next? **Côtes de Duras** is another wine from the southwest-based on the same grapes. Better still, head westwards to see what **Bordeaux** can offer at similar prices.

RECOMMENDED PRODUCERS

Grattamacco
Le Macchiole
Michele Satta
Tenuta Belvedere (Guado al Tasso)
Tenuta dell'Ornellaia
Tenuta San Guido (Sassicaia)

Bolgheri

Oh, I do like to be beside the seaside...
Region Tuscany
Grape varieties Cabernet Sauvignon, Merlot, Sangiovese, Syrah
Style Stylish Cabernets and Merlots which could pass for Bordeaux
Quality/Price ***→*****/££→£££££

Until recently, Bolgheri was a rather so-so DOC on the coast, west of Siena, making a bit of white and a bit of pink (rosé). However, lying within its boundaries were some of Italy's greatest wines, which had to be content with being *vini da tavola*. Among these was Sassicaia, the Cabernet

Sauvignon-based wine which was one of the original, and is still for many the best of the Super-Tuscans. In order to bring such wines within the DOC fold, the rules for Bolgheri have now been changed, and Sassicaia even has its own sub-appellation. It's still not DOCG; that is reserved for the very finest Italian wines such as Vermentino di Gallura and Albana di Romagna. The number of wines being made here at present is small, but a few Chianti producers are buying vineyards in the region so there could be several more in the future.

On the same coastline surrounding Bolgheri are other regions which one day could be just as successful. To the south lies Val di Cornia, and the Sangiovese-based wines made by Gualdo del Re and Tua Rita in Suvereto are excellent. To the north lies Montescudaio, where Tenuta del Terriccio is also making great progress.

The Bolgheri taste It's easy to mistake some Bolgheri reds for Bordeaux – not, of course, the Sangiovese-based wines which are full of savoury bitter-cherry fruit. However, Ornellaia's Masseto (100 per cent Merlot) is as silky, sexy and plummy as anything from Pomerol. When Cabernet Sauvignon dominates, there's deep, piercing blackcurrant fruit and hints of cigar box, and the wines could easily pass for St-Julien or Pauillac.

Where next? Tuscany has several wines with similar ambitions based on the same varieties.

Bordeaux

Simply the best
Best-known wines Pauillac, Margaux, St-Emilion, Pomerol
Grape varieties Cabernet Sauvignon, Cabernet Franc, Merlot, Petit Verdot, Malbec
Style Blackcurrant, currant, plum, cigar-box and more
Quality/Price **⋯⟩*****/£⋯⟩£££££

For many people, red wine means Cabernet Sauvignon. And the wine which virtually all Cabernets take as their inspiration is red Bordeaux. Those who want to expand their horizons might also include Merlot in their tasting schedule; again, Bordeaux provides the reference point. A few countries, such as Italy, Australia and the US have succeeded in making first-rate Cabernets and Merlots, but none can claim the track record or the large number of

RECOMMENDED PRODUCERS
Annereaux
De Belcier
Bonnet
Bousquet
Bréthous
Brulesécaille
Carsin
Charmes-Godard
La Claverie
Decourteillac
Haut-Bertinerie
Haut-Chatain
Les Jonqueyres
du Lyonnat
Méaume
De Parenchère
Puyguéraud

impressive wines that this region of southwest France can. Burgundy might seek to challenge Bordeaux as the world's finest red wine region, and it is true that, in some vintages, a larger number of great red burgundies than clarets are produced. However, production of most of these wines is minuscule – the St-Emilion appellation alone makes more red wine than the whole of Burgundy. And when it comes to greatness, the smallest of the Médoc first growths, Château Latour, is roughly the same size as five of Burgundy's finest *grand cru* vineyards put together.

Latour is one of a small number of châteaux at the top of the Bordeaux pyramid. It was one of around 60 châteaux designated as classed growths – *crus classés* – in a classification produced for the Paris Exhibition in 1855. All but one of these châteaux (Haut-Brion in Graves) were in the Médoc region on the "left bank" of the Gironde estuary. However, the five-tiered classification, which was based purely on the price each could command in the marketplace, was of *all* Bordeaux wines. Nothing from the "right bank", home of St-Emilion and Pomerol, was included because nothing was deemed to be of sufficient quality.

If a classification based on price were to be done today, the situation would be very different, as the 1855 first growths are currently outpriced by a number of right-bank properties. Does this mean that they are no longer as good? Far from it. It's just a consequence of the law of supply and demand. Château Latour has 60 hectares (148 acres) of vineyards and in a good year might make 20,000 cases of wine. By contrast, Château Pétrus in Pomerol has 11ha of vines, which will yield 4,500 cases of wine, and some properties measure their production in hundreds of cases rather than thousands. If a tiny property in St-Emilion making 700 cases of something special attracts the attention of media commentators, especially that of the American Robert Parker, it can virtually name its price.

However, Bordeaux of such a standard forms only the tip of a very large iceberg. Fortunately, not all of it is so expensive. Unfortunately, not all of it is so good. The best Bordeaux wines are the best because they are in the finest sites and can afford to invest in maintaining the quality of the vineyards and the winemaking. At the base level, it is debatable whether some of the producers really should still be making wine, since other parts of the world are capable of making Cabernet Sauvignon and Merlot to a far higher and more consistent standard.

There are still plenty of people who think that the words "Bordeaux" or "claret" on a bottle of wine are a guarantee of quality, but anyone with more than one taste bud will know that this is simply not true. Higher up the scale a wine labelled "St-Emilion" or "Médoc" may be good, or it may be lousy and overpriced. There's simply no way of working out what is good and what is bad without knowing who made the wine.

While Cabernet Sauvignon and Merlot are the main grapes of Bordeaux, virtually all the wines are blends, with Cabernet Franc, Malbec and Petit Verdot also playing their parts. Cabernet Sauvignon is the staple of the Médoc, the tongue of land stretching north of the city of Bordeaux where the villages of Margaux, St-Julien, Pauillac and St-Estèphe lie. It is also the main force in the Graves region, from around Bordeaux and moving south.

Northeast across the River Garonne, the Entre-Deux-Mers is traditionally a white wine region, but red wines are becoming more prominent under the Premières Côtes de Bordeaux, Ste-Foy-Bordeaux or simply Bordeaux appellations. As in the whole of the Bordeaux region, wines which have half a degree more alcohol than basic Bordeaux can call themselves Bordeaux Supérieur, and for once, they are for the most part actually *supérieur*. On this side of the Garonne, Merlot is dominant, with Cabernet Sauvignon in a secondary role after Cabernet Franc.

Merlot's dominance continues if you head north into the Libournais region. Here, Pomerol and St-Emilion are the best and most famous wines, but nearby districts such as Montagne-St-Emilion, Lalande de Pomerol, Côtes de Francs, Fronsac, Canon-Fronsac and Côtes de Castillon can provide a taste of the real thing at a fraction of the cost and are some of the best value in the whole of Bordeaux. To the northwest, Bourg and Blaye face the châteaux of the Médoc across the Gironde estuary, and while the wines never rise to the same heights, they, too, can be excellent value.

The Bordeaux taste

Good Bordeaux Rouge is crisp and refreshing, slightly green and herbal, with cedary, currant and blackcurrant flavours, but sadly many examples are just unripe and dilute. Move up from here and the flavours depend on the region and the winemaking. Long macerations and ageing in new oak are the norm for many modern châteaux. Where the fruit is up to such treatment, the results are excellent, but where it is not, the unripe flavours are only magnified.

Where Cabernet Sauvignon dominates, the result is blackcurrant-flavoured wines with moderate acidity and good tannin. They can be firm yet delicious and often need some time to mature – all the more so if they have been aged in oak, as most of the top wines have. They reward with complex,

spicy, cedary flavours for which wine buffs are sometimes prepared to wait half a lifetime. The plummier-tasting wines that Merlot makes are usually softer, more immediately attractive, and ready for drinking sooner than those of the Médoc, although the top wines show no lack of concentration and can safely slumber in the cellar for a decade or three.

Other varieties add to the complexity, including the softening Malbec (now mostly confined to Bourg and Blaye), the stiffening Petit Verdot and particularly Cabernet Franc. It is vigorous, slightly green, grassy Cabernet Franc, rather than Cabernet Sauvignon, which combines with Merlot in St-Emilion and Pomerol to give these wines their definition and structure, without piling on the ripe and lush fruit even further. In the Médoc, Cabernet Franc brings a whiff of perfume and good fruit flavour to the wines without the harsh tannin of Cabernet Sauvignon.

Where next? This is the style that everywhere copies to varying degrees of success. Just look for **Cabernet Sauvignon** or **Merlot** or the less widespread **Cabernet Franc** on the labels and you'll be on the right track. Close to home, **Southwest France** has several Bordeaux wannabes, mostly at the cheaper end of the range, while the Cabernet Franc wines of the **Loire** can evoke memories of the region. See also specific entries for **Fronsac/Canon-Fronsac, Graves, Margaux, Médoc, Pauillac, Pessac-Léognan, Pomerol, St-Emilion, St-Estèphe** and **St-Julien**.

Bourgueil and Chinon

To be perfectly Franc

Region Loire
Grape varieties Cabernet Franc
Style Blackcurrant-leaf flavours, with earthy herbal hints
Quality/Price **⋯⟩****/££⋯⟩££££

Bourgueil, St-Nicolas-de-Bourgueil and Chinon are three appellations within a few miles of each other in the Loire. Bourgueil comes from the north bank between Saumur and Tours, and St-Nicolas-de-Bourgueil is an enclave of some 500 hectares (1,230 acres) within it. Chinon lies across the river to the south.

What they have in common is Cabernet Franc, which is without doubt the Loire's best red wine grape, producing a wonderful style of wine. Or rather, *two* wonderful styles. There is the drink-me-quick-and-cool style made from vines on rich, alluvial soils, and the more serious cellarable type produced from chalk and clay soil hillside sites. Think of them as Beaujolais and claret if you will. Both are delicious.

The Bourgueil and Chinon taste The attraction of these Cabernet Franc wines is their distinctive, peppery, grassy, raspberry fruit and their dusty, earthy quality; sometimes a small amount of Cabernet Sauvignon helps to shift them towards more blackcurrant flavours. The lighter ones are refreshing, with lightly herby flavours. The gutsier wines, often made with old vines, are more polished and riper, also with that herbal undercurrent. While the first style should be drunk as soon as possible, the heftier wines will age impressively for between five and ten years – some well beyond that – softening as they go.

The rustic, traditional Bourgueil region in the Loire Valley

Where next? Saumur-Champigny is the best of the **Cabernet Francs** of **Anjou-Saumur**. Italy's **Friuli-Venezia Giulia**, **Trentino-Alto Adige** and the **Veneto** use the grape to similar effect. For the more muscly wines, have a look at **St-Emilion** to see the influence Cabernet Franc has there.

Brunello di Montalcino

The power and the glory
Region Tuscany
Grape varieties Brunello (Sangiovese)
Style Nuts, roses, tobacco, mulberry and blackcurrant flavours, with plenty of tannin
Quality/Price **·····⟩*****/£££·····⟩£££££

Brunello is a clone of Sangiovese, the main grape used in Chianti, and Montalcino is a hilltop town in Tuscany 40 km (25 miles) south of Siena. So Brunello di Montalcino is a sort of Chianti without the distraction of other grape varieties – but a rather expensive sort.

The growers in Montalcino consider their clone to be the best Sangiovese in Tuscany, and since production of Brunello is relatively small compared to Chianti, prices are high. However, the wines haven't always been the best, and

RECOMMENDED PRODUCERS

Altesino
Argiano
Banfi
Fattoria dei Barbi
Biondi-Santi
Caparzo
Casanova di Neri
Case Basse
Castelgiocondo
Ciacci Piccolomini
Col d'Orcia
Costanti
Maurizio Lambardi
Lisini
Mastrojanni
Pieve di Santa Restituta
Poggio Antico
Il Poggione
Talenti
Val di Suga

Sangiovese grapes ripen to make the long-ageing wines of Brunello

here's why. Traditional wisdom in Italy is that big wines need plenty of time in cask before bottling to shrug off their forbidding tannins, and the DOCG law in Montalcino used to be that the wine had to spend three and a half years in oak. For all but the richest of wines in the best of vintages, this was clearly far too long, and the rules have now been changed (from the 1995 vintage onwards) to allow wines to spend just two years in barrel. Straight Brunello must still be at least four years old on release, while *riserva* wines must be aged a year longer.

Even so, the two years in cask is still too much for many wines of the area, especially those from younger vines. In this case, producers make Rosso di Montalcino, which has no cask-ageing requirements. Very good these can be, too, rather like the "second wines" of Bordeaux. If Cabernet Sauvignon and other varieties have made their way into the blend, the wines may now go under the DOC of Sant' Antimo, although most Super-Tuscans go under an IGT designation (*see* **Italy**).

The Brunello di Montalcino taste Brunello's main attraction is the array of complex smells it develops. There are walnuts and Brazil nuts, roses, tea leaves, curls of woodsmoke and whiffs of tobacco. At times it is like a walk around the farmyard and into the woods, with autumnal smells abounding. These associations carry through into the taste, but what you notice most is the power, the structure, the tannin. In youth it can seem like hitting a wall of oak or biting on a black peppercorn, though this quality disappears by the time it is ready to drink. Some are rich, opulent, velvety and packed with dense, mulberry and blackcurrant fruit even in less good years. Others are wonderfully elegant and age beautifully. They fill the mouth but retain a delicacy and balance, like good burgundy.

Rosso di Montalcino gives a foretaste of the real thing. These are hearty wines, full of lively young fruit and demanding food and a healthy appetite rather than the quiet meditation that suits Brunello. And, of course, they are less expensive.

Where next? Chianti Classico, Vino Nobile di Montepulciano and the Sangiovese-based Super-Tuscans are the direct competition. **Barolo** and **Barbaresco** are other noble Italian wines with similar traditions. Try top **Châteauneuf-du-Pape**, **Australian Shiraz** and **California Zinfandel**.

Burgundy

The Agony and The Ecstasy
Best-known wines Chambertin, Musigny, Nuits-St-Georges,
Volnay, Corton, Beaujolais
Grape varieties Pinot Noir, Gamay
Style Silky, heady and alluring Pinot Noir; vibrant, bubbly Gamay
Quality/Price **····⟩*****/££····⟩£££££

The best burgundies are among the finest wines in the world. Europe's most northerly red wine region has been turning out wine fit for emperors, kings, even mere dukes, since Roman times. Greater Burgundy is a long sausage than runs from the Côte d'Or near Dijon down to Beaujolais near Lyon, with a little chipolata up around Chablis.

Pinot Noir is the grape of the great red Côte d'Or burgundies; Gamay makes Beaujolais; and the two grapes meet somewhere in the middle of the sausage around Mâconnais and the Côte Chalonnaise. The real fireworks, though, are in the Côte de Nuits and the Côte de Beaune, which together make up the Côte d'Or, or "golden slope", a thin strip of hillside planted with some 8,500 hectares (21,000 acres) of vines – less than one per cent of France's total vineyard area. The location is what makes it great.

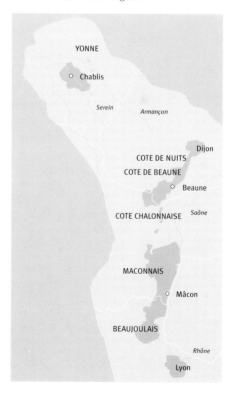

The rich marl soils on which the region's main red grape, Pinot Noir, thrives do not, on the face of it, sound very promising: usually the richer the soil, the poorer the wine. But the slopes provide good drainage to compensate. Ripening is slower at the top of Burgundian slopes than in the middle, particularly in the Côte de Nuits where the angle is quite steep. Since ripeness – especially this far north – is crucial, the tops of the hills generally remain wooded, with the *grand* and *premier cru* vineyards (*see* page 32) occupying the middle of the slope. On the flatter land by the N74, the wines are less good.

However, there's more to the location of the best vineyards than simply how far up the slope they are. The Burgundians have had hundreds of years in which to work out the minutiae of each plot of land, hence the reason why one vineyard will be a *grand cru* and the adjacent one will be a simple village wine. *Terroir* is the word the French use for the whole concept of gradient, aspect, soil, subsoil and climate, and it is this which lies behind the hierarchy of the vineyards.

Hang on a bit, you say. Why do these two wines, both from the same vineyard, taste so different? It's because the vineyard determines the potential quality, but the person in charge of it determines the actual quality. This is, of course, true all over the world, but especially so with Pinot Noir in Burgundy. The *terroir* only begins to talk when a producer tends his vines with TLC. Ask a vine to produce too much fruit, and not only will the flavours in the grapes be less concentrated, but the grapes will struggle to ripen. Use excessive fertiliser and other chemicals and the vine will rely on these rather than on the nutrients in the soil. Many of Burgundy's best domaines are now run organically, in order to let the *terroir* have more of a say in the wines.

Chaptalisation is a subject that the Burgundians get very heated about. This is the addition of sugar to a fermenting wine in order to increase its alcoholic content. But the domaines that have reduced their yields often find that their grapes have sufficient sugar, thank you very much, even in vintages which aren't so great. Some still chaptalise in order to keep their fermentations going for longer, as they feel this helps to extract better flavours. The good guys also find that their riper grapes give them wines with deeper colours. The "traditional" burgundy which many people grew

THE BURGUNDY PYRAMID

Burgundy's appellations fall into four tiers of quality. If a wine from a particular level is not as good as the producer would like, it can be downgraded to a lower status. From highest to lowest, they are:

• **Grand Cru** The finest vineyards, such as Clos de Tart in the village of Morey-St-Denis or Le Musigny in Chambolle-Musigny. Each has its own appellation independently of the village.

• **Premier Cru** The next-best vineyards – for example Malconsorts and Suchots in the village of Vosne-Romanée, or Champans and Santenots in Volnay. Wines from a single vineyard will be labelled with both village and vineyard name – Vosne-Romanée Premier Cru Les Malconsorts,

for example – while blends from two or more *premier cru* vineyards will simply be labelled with the name of the village plus Premier Cru: Vosne-Romanée Premier Cru.

• **Village** Wines coming from within the village boundary are able to use the village appellation, such as Gevrey-Chambertin or Pommard. A specific vineyard, a *lieu-dit*, may still be mentioned on the label.

• **Generic** Other vineyards will have a more general appellation such as Bourgogne, Hautes-Côtes de Beaune or Bourgogne Grand Ordinaire. These less specific ACs cover a wider area, obscuring fine differences but making less expensive wines.

up with often used to receive its colour and flavour courtesy of more southerly climes such as Algeria. But real Pinot Noir doesn't have a high level of pigmentation in its skins, so the wines will never be as dark as Cabernet Sauvignon or Syrah. Even so, there are many modern burgundies which are so pale as to need a doctor, and which shout high yields. They're to be avoided – regardless of how lofty the appellation.

Yes, picking your producer is usually the best first step to great burgundy. Unfortunately, you might find yourself part of a long and growing queue. Burgundy's red wine production in an average year is around 19 million bottles, comparable to that of St-Emilion in Bordeaux. Even if all of it were of tip-top quality, there still wouldn't be enough to go around. This means that the best wines from the best producers are both hard to find and expensive. However, other wines from the same producers aren't expensive. A typical Burgundian grower will have vineyards in everything from generic level up to *grand cru*. The *grand cru* will (hopefully) be the best wine, but if the producer is worth his salt, he will have taken almost as much care with his lesser wines. A well-made, Bourgogne Rouge can, on occasion, be as good as some *premier cru* wines, and much cheaper.

The reason growers have such a diversity of vineyard holdings is due to the Burgundian inheritance laws, whereby an estate is divided among various siblings. Monsieur Duval's 30 rows of vines in Clos Vougeot are divided so his three children get ten rows each. These children then marry into other Burgundian families, acquiring additional vineyards in the process, and their portfolio becomes shallower but more diverse. Having only enough vines to make one barrel of Le Chambertin *grand cru* is fine, as such a wine can command a high price. Having only enough vines to make one barrel of Bourgogne Rouge is rather different.

This is where Burgundy's many merchants come in. They buy that Bourgogne Rouge, or that Nuits-St-Georges, blend it with wine bought from other growers in the same appellation and sell it under their own name. The merchants have often come in for some stick for the way in which they have erased the personality of different appellations through slapdash blending. But today, they often have their own extensive vineyard holdings, are careful to separate their finest *cuvées*, and as a result regularly make some of the finest wines in Burgundy. At the same time, several growers who have small holdings in some villages have been bargaining with their neighbours in order to buy up the odd barrel or two which they can then blend with other parcels of wine. The growers are becoming merchants and vice versa, and all Burgundy benefits from this.

If you want to assess a producer, the basic appellations are a great way to start. If the wine is good, then you can move up to higher appellations. If it's bad, well you haven't wasted too much money. Bourgogne Passe-

Tout-Grains is a blend of Gamay and Pinot Noir, while Bourgogne Rouge is made from 100 per cent Pinot Noir, unless it is declassified from one of the Beaujolais *crus* – when it can be 100 per cent Gamay. An occasional Bourgogne grand ordinaire can be simple and tasty, but is usually best avoided.

Irancy, southwest of Chablis, makes simple Pinot Noir wines (with a bit of César) which, although they don't mind some time in bottle, have yet to show anything of real interest. At the other end of Burgundy, Mâcon Rouge is mostly based on Gamay. Pinot Noir here lacks the heady perfume that it achieves further north, while Gamay lacks the fruit it displays in Beaujolais.

Where next? Nowhere else makes burgundy. However, high-class **Pinot Noir** crops up in southern **France**, **Tuscany** and southern **Germany**. The New World Pinot challenge comes from **Martinborough** and Central Otago in **New Zealand**, scattered regions of **Australia**, **Carneros**, **Sonoma**, **Central Coast**, **Oregon** and Walker Bay in **South Africa**. The **Loire** has some **Gamay**, and the **Cabernet Franc** wines from here (and elsewhere) have echoes with **Beaujolais** and Mâcon Rouge. See also specific entries for **Beaujolais, Beaune, Chambolle-Musigny, Côte Chalonnaise, Côte de Beaune, Côte de Nuits, Gevrey-Chambertin, Morey-St-Denis, Nuit-St-Georges, Pommard, Volnay, Vosne-Romanée.**

Cabernet Franc

Country cousin
Style Grassy, with blackcurrant-leaf, raspberry and hints of green pepper
Grown in Loire, Bordeaux, northern Italy, Australia, California, New Zealand, South Africa, Washington State, New York State, Canada

Cabernet Franc is often seen as a poor relation of Cabernet Sauvignon. The name has something to do with it. However, more important, perhaps, is that in the region where Cabernet Sauvignon is king – the Médoc – Cabernet Franc plays not second fiddle but third even after Merlot.

Cross the river to St-Emilion and Pomerol, and Cabernet Franc is accorded rather more respect. Even so, with the notable exception of the great Cheval Blanc, where it takes up two-thirds of the vineyards, Merlot usually is the more important variety. Only in Fronsac does Cabernet Franc attain equal status. Head to the towns of Saumur, Bourgueil and Chinon in the Loire, however, and it positively shines in a cool climate that Cabernet Sauvignon just can't get to grips with.

It's the same in northern Italy, where wines referred to simply as "Cabernet" are usually Cabernet Franc. One of the most unusual versions is Quintarelli's Alzero, a superb 100 per cent Cabernet Franc made from semi-dried grapes.

In other parts of the world, it is usually grown to add perfume to a Cabernet Sauvignon-heavy blend. However, in cooler climes, such as Hawke's Bay in New Zealand, it often plays a stronger role. Pure Cabernet Franc wines aren't common, but California (Lang & Reed, Ironstone, Niebaum-Coppola), Washington State (Columbia, Château Ste-Michelle), New Zealand (Crab Farm), Canada (Château des Charmes) and Australia (Chatsfield, Heritage) have all shown how good they can be.

The Cabernet Franc taste There is less stuffing to this grape than to Cabernet Sauvignon, less tannin, lower acidity, less concentration of fruit, and a lighter, leaner, herbier style of raspberries as well as blackcurrants. Generally, Cabernet Franc wines are ready for drinking earlier than those made of Cabernet Sauvignon. Grown in warmer regions, they can acquire a slightly tar-like character, but still retains their perfume.

Where next? Dolcetto; Barbera; Marzemino (*see* **Trentino-Alto Adige**); Cabernet Sauvignon from **New Zealand** or northeast **Italy** (*see* **Trentino-Alto Adige, Friuli-Venezia Giulia**); **Beaujolais**-Villages.

Cabernet Sauvignon

Proud and peerless
Style Blackcurrants, plums, cedar and green pepper flavours
Grown in Throughout the world

The world's greatest red wine grape has proved itself time and again. At home in the Médoc and Graves it turns out not only châteaux Latour, Mouton-Rothschild and the like, but a complete range from the humble to the sublime. It does not do this entirely on its own, but calls on other grape varieties – Merlot, Cabernet Franc, Malbec and Petit Verdot – for support.

Cabernet Sauvignon's prestige also derives from its ability to travel. With its suitcase always packed and its passport ever at the ready, this grape nips smartly through the VIP lounge into a waiting limo and proceeds to make some wonderful single-varietal wines in the New World, notably in California and Australia.

What Cabernet Sauvignon wines usually have in common is dependability. It is a robust grape variety that can take a lot of knocks. Throw it about, squeeze high yields from it, subject it to extremes of temperature, and it will still produce wine of more character and distinction than we have any right to expect. The grape thrives in warm regions, needing sun and warmth to bring out the voluptuous richness of which it is capable. In cool climates it can lack both juicy ripeness and staying power, and produces quite a different taste: stalky, grassy, herbaceous and thinner-bodied, much closer to Cabernet Franc in style. Even so, it is a difficult grape to screw up, so there are very few really poor examples – a factor which contributes significantly to its popularity with both wine drinkers and wine producers. Cheap Chardonnay tastes of nothing; cheap Cabernet Sauvignon tastes of Cabernet Sauvignon and is always worth a go.

This is the grape that has made the reputation of the great châteaux of the Médoc and Graves. Yet, unlike Syrah in the Rhône Valley, which has a couple of thousand years under its belt, Cabernet Sauvignon did not assume a prominent role in Bordeaux until the 18th century, and is still outnumbered two to one by Merlot vines. Cabernet Sauvignon is not made here as a single varietal, although some wines in very warm years come close. Merlot, Cabernet Franc, Malbec and Petit Verdot among them alter the balance and soften the impact of Cabernet Sauvignon, at the same time interacting to produce more complex flavours.

The "Bordeaux blend" spreads from the region throughout France's southwestern corner into places such as Bergerac, Buzet and Côte de Duras. Other wines of the area where Cabernet is a permitted variety include Madiran, Côtes du Frontonnais and Irouléguy. Cabernet Sauvignon also appears in pockets of southern France, either on its own or with other varieties. Domaine de Trévallon in Provence blends it with Syrah to great effect, while Mas de Daumas Gassac follows more along Bordeaux lines. It also appears in the Loire, although Cabernet Franc tends to be preferred as it ripens more easily in the cool climate.

Move out of France and you'll find Cabernet Sauvignon in almost every country you look. Some places are patently too cold for the variety, but that hasn't prevented it from being planted in a few vineyards in England and Germany. However, most places can offer you a wine of at least good quality. Bulgaria leads the charge from Eastern Europe, with Romania not far behind, each capable of producing very tasty wines at low prices, while occasional glimpses of greatness can be seen from Moldova, where some cellars still have stocks of splendid old claret-like wines from the 1960s. To the south, Château Carras is Greece's finest Cabernet-based wine.

In Spain, Marqués de Riscal in Rioja and Vega Sicilia in Ribera del Duero have had Cabernet Sauvignon since the 19th century, but in the last three decades, it has begun to creep into other regions as well. It's not a permitted variety for Rioja, although producers are allowed to have some for "experimental purposes" or if, as with Riscal, they have a history of growing it. In Catalonia, Miguel Torres' Mas La Plana (Black Label) shows how successful Cabernet can be here on its own, while in Priorato, the blends with Garnacha are some of Spain's finest wines. Some of Navarra's most interesting wines are Cabernet Sauvignon with Tempranillo. Portugal has not embraced Cabernet with quite so much enthusiasm, although Quinta da Bacalhôa shows the potential.

Northeast Italy produces a lot of Cabernet, but few producers have bothered to distinguish between Sauvignon and Franc. The resulting style is overwhelmingly light and grassy, reminiscent of the Loire. However, some DOCs, such as Trentino, Collio, Friuli-Aquilea and Lison-Pramaggiore, are now making the distinction between the two varieties. Bordeaux blends are also becoming more fashionable.

The finest Italian wines which incorporate Cabernet Sauvignon come from Tuscany. Until recently, many of these had to go under the *vino da tavola* designation as Cabernet was not a permitted variety in the majority of the DOCs. Some of these Super-Tuscans were 100 per cent Cabernets; some followed Bordeaux blends, while others included varying proportions of the local Sangiovese to impressive effect. With a change in the laws, most now go under an IGT name (*see* **Italy**), although some regulations, such as those of Bolgheri, have been altered to bring some wines under the DOC umbrella. Umbria, Piedmont and Lombardy also have their own Cabernet-based "Super-Wines".

The New World's best source of fine Cabernet Sauvignon is California. While most of this comes from the Napa Valley, parts of Sonoma and Santa Cruz (*see* **Monterey and San Francisco Bay Areas**) are just as capable of making great wines. Further north, Washington State is already showing that California does not have the monopoly on great American Cabernet. Further south, Chile has taken over from Bulgaria the role of providing yummy, cheap Cabernet. Several producers are also capable of much finer wines, and the same is true in neighbouring Argentina.

Few Australian Cabernets reach the heights of the best Californian versions, but the average standard is at least equal and possibly higher, and the wines are certainly cheaper. Coonawarra is the place most associated with fine Cabernet Sauvignon, but other regions in South Australia have produced great wines, as have parts of Victoria, New South Wales and Western Australia. The blends with Shiraz are falling out of favour – which is a pity, as they can be thoroughly splendid.

New Zealand has struggled with Cabernet, with many vines being planted in places that were just too cool for the variety to ripen properly.

However, parts of the country, such as Hawke's Bay and various pockets around Auckland, have persevered and are now making some of the most elegant Cabernet Sauvignon wines from outside Europe.

South Africa is also making strides. Many of the country's Cabernet vineyards have been badly affected by viruses, with the grapes struggling to ripen. With new "clean" clones and better winemaking, the quality is rising with every successive vintage. Stellenbosch is the source of many of the best wines, but Paarl and Constantia also have their share of stars.

The Cabernet Sauvignon taste "Blackcurrants" is the universal knee-jerk response to Cabernet Sauvignon's smell and taste, and in some of the cheaper wines that is about it. But it often seems to contain other summer and autumn fruits or berries, too: from redcurrants to elderberries.

Cabernet Sauvignon is not one-dimensional, and that is a large part of its attraction. It is rarely weak and apologetic, more often dark in colour and richly aromatic. Taste it, especially in the form of young claret, and it is like a cross between printer's ink and lemon juice: often high in acidity, immensely concentrated, with powerful raw tannin that all but takes the skin off the roof of your mouth. This is because the grapes have big pips and thick skins, both of which are sources of tannin; the skins are responsible for the deep colour and for giving body to the wine.

With so much flavour, Cabernet is a natural for ageing in small oak barrels, usually with a capacity of 225 litres. If the barrel is new, it will add flavours and tannins to the wine. However, just as important is the time the wine spends "breathing" through the sides of the barrel, as this smoothes out some of the gawky edges the final product might have. French oak is the favoured type of wood in Bordeaux and most other quality-minded regions, but some of the finest wines of Australia and California prefer to use American oak.

Many Cabernet Sauvignons are made to be drunk within three or four years from vintage. However, the high extract and tannin levels of the more ambitious wines mean that they need rather longer to peak. Bordeaux takes this to the extreme – some of the vintages of the late 1800s were deemed drinkable only after the original purchasers were dead – but it does not have the monopoly on longevity. Any classy Cabernet will be fighting fit on its tenth birthday, with the best lasting for a further ten, 20 years or more. As Cabernet Sauvignon ages, the blackcurrants soften to plummier characteristics, yet the cedar, cigar box and other perfumes never let go.

Where next? Try other aristocratic grape varieties such as **Syrah**, **Pinot Noir**, **Nebbiolo** and **Sangiovese**.

Cahors

They're tough, mighty tough in the (south)west
Region Southwest France
Grape varieties Malbec, Merlot, Tannat
Style Plums, violets and tobacco, with plenty of tannin
Quality/Price *····}***/£····}£££

The wines of Cahors, tucked away in southwest France, are based on the Malbec grape (or Auxerrois), which must make up at least 70 per cent of the blend. The problem with Malbec is that it can have ferocious tannins, and producers need to find a way around this. Being able to add up to 30 per cent Merlot is one way out, while carbonic maceration (*see* **Beaujolais**) is another. However, the best solution is to find ways to extract the fruit without too much of the tannin. Wines made in this fashion will always need time to come around, but they can be very good, although some producers are rather heavy-handed with their oak.

The Cahors taste Lighter Cahors is simple and fruity, made for early consumption. The best wines develop with time into serious, plummy, violet-scented, tobacco-flavoured, spicy beauties, but remain tannic.

Where next? Argentina is the world's best source of **Malbec**. Local rivals **Côtes du Frontonnais** and **Madiran** are made from less common varieties.

California

State of flux
Best-known wines Napa Cabernet
Quality/Price **····}*****/£····}£££££

If you were a grape, the Golden State is probably one of the places in which you would most like to be planted, live and finally be crushed. It's no surprise that the finest Californian wines can hold their own against the best in the world. In the 200 years since the first vines were planted, the industry has had its ups and downs – Prohibition all but wiped it out during the 1930s – and by the 1960s only a handful of wineries remained. But the early 1970s saw a new surge of interest in Californian winemaking. In the ensuing decade, the acreage of vineyards in the state doubled, and the Californian wine industry has continued to develop at an astonishing rate ever since. California is still at the mercy of the varietal wine, although the palette of such wines is now much more colourful than it once was. Cabernet Sauvignon is still head honcho, while Zinfandel remains the quirky and occasionally infuriating delight it has always been. Merlot and Pinot Noir achieve quality and prices higher than all but the finest French versions – and attract a following of dreary wannabes. However, newcomers such as Syrah (thanks to a bunch of producers known as the Rhône Rangers), Sangiovese and Nebbiolo (hats off to the Cal-Ital brigade) are now becoming parts of many wineries' repertoire. The popularity of such grapes has caused a resurgence in interest in the ancient plantings of Mourvèdre (aka Mataro), Grenache, Carignan and Barbera which still exist in the state.

While varietals remain popular, there's a growing interest in blends, be they inspired by Bordeaux, the Rhône – or in a few cases, it seems, by the planet Zog. The number of vineyard-designated wines increases daily as the Californians discover that there is a grain of truth behind this *terroir* business – and that they sell like a dream. A band of winemaking consultants headed by Helen Turley is in demand with *nouveau riche* winery owners anxious to produce precisely 574 cases (and 42 double magnums) of Robert Parker-friendly wine which can then command first growth prices at auction. No, the top end of California is in fine fettle. Shame, then, that at the value-for-money end of the market, the state continues to underperform, with residual sweetness often being an attempt to disguise dilute flavours.

Napa Valley is the best-known region and source of most of the best Cabernets and Merlots, but Sonoma and the regions south of San Francisco Bay also offer great Cabernets. Most of Napa is too hot for Pinot Noir however, but the grape performs well in Carneros and parts of Sonoma and the Central Coast. The Dry Creek district of Sonoma is the source of some of California's finest Zinfandel, while many other spicy varieties thrive in the warmer Contra Costa County east of San Francisco. North of Napa and Sonoma lie Mendocino and Lake counties, which, like their southern neighbours, both provide a diversity of *terroirs* suitable for everything from Pinot Noir to Zinfandel.

Head east from any of these regions and you'll find yourself in the huge Central Valley, source of three out of every four bottles of Californian wine. Most of it is banal and forgettable, but an occasional old-vine Zinfandel can excite. Carry on eastwards and you're in the Sierra Foothills which are rather more promising; sub-regions include Fiddletown and Shenandoah Valley. Again, Zinfandel is the best variety, but other spicy grapes also thrive here.

The California taste

Today's California Cabernets are characterised by ripe, sweet fruit, often more inclined to blackberry and plum than blackcurrant, with occasional hints of olives, mint and eucalyptus. They are big wines, with supple tannins coming from skins and oak and are usually more approachable than both their Bordeaux counterparts and their forerunners from the 1970s, although they will age.

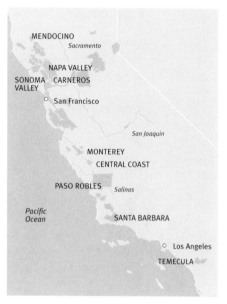

Merlot's popularity means that it is often overcropped, yielding a jammy, dilute and occasionally herbaceous wine. However, top versions can have the deep, plummy flavour of great Pomerol. Merlot's role in Bordeaux-style blends is increasing, but so, too, is that of Cabernet Franc, which can make a fine wine in its own right.

Zinfandel is being appreciated far more than it was in the 1980s. Drinkers who begin with the barbecue-friendly, brambly gluggers can graduate to densely-flavoured wines with alcohol levels of 17 per cent and more – which are impenetrable without a few years in the bottle and a large hunk of cow on the side.

The minute quantities and extortionate prices of California Pinot Noir can out-burgundy Burgundy on occasions. The best wines have clear cherry and raspberry fruit, together with some feral wildness and a heady violet perfume; the oak and alcohol are usually high.

Sangiovese is the most widespread of the Italian varieties, and is often blended with Cabernet. So far, the wines have been upfront and ripe but have lacked the bitter intensity of good Chianti. Rhône varietals have been more successful, and their recent growth in popularity has been a joy to behold. Several wineries now produce top-class Syrah, often adding a dab of Viognier with the fragrance of the northern Rhône and flavours of sweet, ripe fruit. The merits of old-vine Grenache, Mourvèdre/Mataro and Carignan from such places as Contra Costa County are now being realised, and the number of Châteauneuf-du-Pape look-alikes is on the up.

Where next?

Follow the grape variety to its origin – meaning, **Bordeaux**, **Burgundy**, the **Rhône** and **Tuscany**. Look at the **Zinfandel** entry to see who else has some. Otherwise, **Australia** is the closest competitor. See also specific entries for **Carneros**, **Central Coast**, **Monterey and San Francisco Bay Areas**, **Napa Valley** and **Sonoma**.

Carignan

A bloke of a grape
Style Spicy with high acidity; plum and cherry fruit in the best wines
Grown in Southern France, Spain, California, Sardinia

France's most widely planted red grape is usually dismissed as a less than noble variety. The kindest thing you can say about most of the wine it produces in the Languedoc is that it has a reasonable colour. However, vinify old-vine Carignan using carbonic maceration, and the wines can be very good, as Clos Centeilles in Minervois and Vaquer in Roussillon eloquently demonstrate.

Carignan originated in Spain, where it is known as Cariñena or Mazuelo. It is planted widely in Catalonia, even though it never amounts to much of interest. It is a permitted variety in the DO of Cariñena, although the producers have mostly abandoned it in favour of Tempranillo. The same is true in Rioja.

Some of the best Carignan comes from Sardinia, where Carignano del Sulcis can be excellent and age-worthy. As Carignane in California, it is usually consigned to the jug-wine role, but as in France, old-vine wines can be surprisingly good.

The Carignan taste Much of it is simple and vaguely spicy, high in acidity, low in finesse. However, old-vine *cuvées* can be full-bodied and rich, with cherry, plum and chocolate flavours and no shortage of acidity and tannin.

Where next? Mourvèdre is what Carignan would like to be.

RECOMMENDED PRODUCERS
Acacia
Carneros Creek
Domaine Carneros
Gloria Ferrer
Kent Rasmussen
Saintsbury

Carneros

The elegant end of Napa Valley
Best-known wines Saintsbury Reserve Pinot Noir
Grape varieties Pinot Noir, Merlot, Cabernet Sauvignon
Style Full-flavoured yet refined Pinot Noir
Quality/Price ***⋯⟩*****/£££⋯⟩£££££

The Napa Valley-ites started off planting Pinot Noir throughout their region in the same vineyards in which Cabernet Sauvignon thrived. The results were undeniably big and powerful, but they were far too clumsy to be great Pinot. Slowly, the realisation dawned that much of the valley was simply too warm for this temperamental variety. However, down at the cooler southern end of the valley, away from the Sunset Strip of wineries between Yountville and Calistoga, Pinot Noir did give some promising results. This was Carneros, a district which also spread over into the Sonoma region.

Today, while Carneros has few wineries, vines have now displaced virtually all the sheep and cattle which used to graze here, and the fruit is in demand from producers throughout the state. Cabernet Sauvignon grows very happily in some of the warmer vineyards, while even Pinot Noir struggles to ripen in cooler spots. Merlot can also be good, but Pinot is the main event. Just as in Burgundy, certain vineyards within the region are proving better than others for Pinot, and trials to determine which are the best clones and rootstocks to plant should result in higher standards.

The vines of Domaine Carneros give elegant red wines

The Carneros taste Even though Carneros is the source of some of California's best Pinot Noir grapes, not every winery uses them to their full potential. Some make a wine which is simply pretty and fruity, often with a rather obvious layer of oak. Top producers such as Saintsbury manage to coax lush texture and expansive feral flavours of strawberry, truffle, raspberry, cherry, earth and more out of their Pinot.

Where Next? Parts of **Sonoma** and the **Central Coast** vie with Carneros as sources for the finest **California Pinot Noir**.

Catalonia

What to drink on the Costa Brava
Best-known wines Torres' Mas La Plana, Priorato
Grape varieties Garnacha, Cariñena, Cabernet Sauvignon, Merlot, Tempranillo, Monastrell, Pinot Noir
Style Huge, spicy Priorato, and varietals with a Spanish twist
Quality/Price *┈┈⟩*****/£┈┈⟩£££££

RECOMMENDED PRODUCERS

Albet i Noya
Can Feixes
Concavins
Jean León
Masía Bach
Puig y Roca
Raïmat
Torres

For many, Catalonia is Penedès, and Penedès is Torres – perhaps this was true in the 1970s, but today it is very different. Jean León has been showing for several years that he, too, can make good Cabernet in Penedès, as has Raïmat

in Costers del Segre. Some of Spain's best-value wines come out of Conca de Barberà, and Priorato has recently emerged as one of Spain's most exciting DOs. Torres remains the leader in the region, but there is far more competition than was once the case.

The Catalonia taste A huge variation in winemaking standards is evident, and only in Priorato (*qv*) are there enough competent producers to begin to talk of a regional style. Cabernet Sauvignon veers from the

The intense landscape of Conca de Barberà in Catalonia

simple and fruity in Conca de Barberà to Torres' splendid, supple, oaky Mas La Plana. Tempranillo/Cabernet blends such as Can Feixes' Negre Selecció and Torres' Gran Coronas can be very good, like Rioja meets Napa Cabernet. With the spicier varieties such as Garnacha and Cariñena, the best wines are Spanish Châteauneufs, although there are several far less exciting, nay far more dreadful than that.

Where next? For **Cabernet Sauvignon**, try **Navarra**; for **Tempranillo**, try **Rioja**, **Ribera del Duero** or **Navarra**. For **Pinot Noir**, try **Somontano**. For Garnacha (**Grenache**) wines try Navarra, although don't expect anything as concentrated as **Priorato**. For that, head for **South Australia** or the southern **Rhône**. See also specific entry for Priorato.

RECOMMENDED PRODUCERS
Alban
Au Bon Climat
Babcock
Byron
Eberle
Edna Valley Vineyard
Firestone
Foxen
Justin
Il Podere dell' Olivos
Qupé
Sanford
Talley
Lane Tanner
Wild Horse
Zaca Mesa

Central Coast

As good as anywhere in California but without the luxury price tags
Best-known wines Bien Nacido Syrah, Sanford & Benedict Pinot Noir
Grape varieties Pinot Noir, Syrah, Mourvèdre, Cabernet Sauvignon, Nebbiolo, Barbera
Style Powerful yet perfumed Syrah; Burgundian Pinot Noir
Quality/Price ***⋯⟩*****/£££⋯⟩£££££

If you're one of that growing number of people looking for vinous life in California beyond Cabernet Sauvignon and Merlot, this is the place to come. Not that the Central Coast can't provide decent Bordeaux-style reds. The Paso Robles district of San Luis Obispo County in the north of the region provides fine Cabernet, as well as Zinfandel and Syrah. Head south, and Syrah finds itself more and more at home. Edna Valley has some fine wines from the Alban vineyard, as well as some good Pinot Noir. Further south still in Santa Barbara Country, Syrah and Pinot again grow very well in the Santa Ynez Valley, but perhaps the best-known Pinot is that from the Sanford & Benedict vineyard in the Santa Maria Valley. Thanks to Jim Clendenen of Au Bon Climat, Italian varieties such as Barbera, Nebbiolo and Friuli's Refosco are also grown, with the wines appearing under the Il Podere dell' Olivos label.

The Central Coast taste Paso Robles Cabernet is warm and generous with spicy, inky, olive, currant, blackcurrant and plum flavours, and a slight violet-like perfume. Syrah is complex and fragrant, big in spicy, tar-like flavours with berry and blackcurrant fruit and a velvety texture.

Pinot Noirs range from light, forward and fruity to wines which are tight in their youth but then open up with age to reveal their core of supple, earthy raspberry and cherry fruit.

Where next? Staying in **California**, go to **Carneros** and **Sonoma** for **Pinot Noir**, **Napa Valley** for **Cabernet Sauvignon** and **Mendocino** and the **Sierra Foothills** for **Syrah**.

Dramatic morning fogs feature across areas of the Central Coast

RECOMMENDED PRODUCERS

Amiot-Servelle
Barthod-Noëllat
Jacques-Frédéric Mugnier
Georges Roumier
Bernard Serveau
Georges de Vogüé

Chambolle-Musigny

The charm, the fragrance

Region Burgundy

Grape varieties Pinot Noir

Style Beautifully balanced and fragrant, raspberry turning to truffles

Quality/Price ***·····}*****/£££·····}£££££

Chambolle-Musigny seems to fall between two stools. Its *grand cru* vineyards overlap with those of its neighbours. Bonnes Mares is shared with Morey-St-Denis (though unevenly, Chambolle claiming 90 per cent of it) and Le Musigny, one of Burgundy's very finest vineyards, is next to Clos de Vougeot. But there is nothing middling about its wines, especially the *grands crus* and the prettily-named *premiers crus* Les Charmes and Les Amoureuses. Or there shouldn't be. Some Chambolle can be rather dilute and disappointing, perhaps because only 30 per cent of the wines are made by those actually living in the village.

The Chambolle-Musigny taste People who drink wine without smelling it will miss much of the enjoyment of burgundy in general and Chambolle-Musigny in particular. It has a scented floral character that haunts you long after the bottle is empty, and makes you want to open another.

Add to that a considerable depth of flavour, and you can have a wonderful experience, with a Musigny from de Vogüé or (Meursault-based) Jacques Prieur capable of making a rugby prop-forward's knees tremble.

Where next? Nuits-St-Georges and **Vosne-Romanée** to the south, **Morey-St-Denis** and **Gevrey-Chambertin** to the north.

Never-ending rows of vines dominate Burgundy's Chambolle Musigny AC

Châteauneuf-du-Pape

A draught of the warm south

Region Southern Rhône

Grape varieties Grenache, Syrah, Mourvèdre, plus ten others

Style Black cherry, blackberry and plum, with southern herbs

Quality/Price **⋯⟩*****/£££⋯⟩£££££

RECOMMENDED PRODUCERS
De Beaucastel
De Beaurenard
Henri Bonneau
Bosquet des Papes
Brunel (Les Cailloux)
Clos des Papes
Clos du Mont Olivet
Jean-Luc Colombo
Font de Michelle
Du Fortia
Grand Tinel
De la Janasse
Mont-Redon
La Nerthe
Du Pégau
Rayas
Tardieu Laurent
Du Vieux Télégraphe

The French appellation Châteauneuf-du-Pape owes its name to the great papal schism of the early 14th century, when Pope Clément established a rival to the papacy of Rome at Avignon, building a papal palace there. The Church always needed wine, for ritual and for economic independence. This is the prime spot in southern Rhône, a region vastly different from its northern counterpart.

The best Châteauneuf-du-Papes are rich and satisfying, but sadly, style and quality vary widely, and few qualify as being the best. Winemaking is crucial and the mix of grape varieties is important. With 13 varieties in Châteauneuf (and only eight of them red) grown in different vineyards and vinified in different ways, we are heading for the most general of generalisations.

Grenache is the dominant grape, producing wines with lots of alcohol but not much acidity. It is a high-yielding variety; colour and tannin tend to be low, and it can oxidise easily. Hmm... doesn't sound too promising, does it? That is why Grenache is not given sole responsibility for making Châteauneuf, except at Château Rayas where low yields from old vines result in a wine of massive concentration which can age for decades.

Grenache positively needs other varieties to compensate for its shortcomings. Syrah provides class, fruit and acidity, Mourvèdre acts as an antioxidant and provides more acidity, while the less noble Cinsault is also popular for bringing yet more acidity. Few producers bother with all 13 varieties, Château de Beaucastel being a notable exception.

The Châteauneuf-du-Pape taste In general, Châteauneuf is a big, warming, thumpingly fruity, peppery and cinnamon-spicy wine. It often reaches 13 to 14 per cent alcohol with no problem, but the super-ripe grapes also produce plenty of fat, rich, juicy, black-cherry, blackberry and plum flavours to balance. Despite this, top wines do acquire elegance with age.

Where next? Gigondas, Vacqueyras and top **Côtes du Rhône**-Villages are comparable. **California** and **Australia** can offer hefty **Grenaches**, as well as similarly beefy wines from **Zinfandel** (former) and **Shiraz** (latter).

Chianti

The Good, The Bad and The Ugly

Region Tuscany

Grape varieties Sangiovese and a large supporting cast

Style From frivolous to serious, all with herby, cherryish, plummy fruit

Quality/Price *⸺⟩*****/£⸺⟩£££££

Italy's best-known red wine has not settled easily into the late 20th century. Some Tuscan families have been making something akin to Chianti without a break since the 13th century. There have been many fine wines, but a greater number of dreadful ones, and although overall quality has soared in the last two decades, consistency is still not reliable.

In 1967, when it gained its own DOC, Chianti was a dull but invariably cheap staple of *trattorie*, sold in the straw-covered – and appropriately named – *fiasco* bottles. Laws restricted the proportion of the region's greatest grape, Sangiovese, to 70 per cent, while permitting up to 30 per cent of inferior white varieties. In the 1970s, this led to quality-minded producers simply bypassing the DOC and producing the Super-Tuscan *vini da tavola* (*see* **Tuscany**).

Chianti became DOCG in 1984, but while the authorities raised the maximum proportion of Sangiovese to 90 per cent, and for the first time allowed the inclusion of foreign varieties, at least five per cent of white grapes were still required. Many flouted this law, but others simply chose to carry on along the *vini da tavola* route.

It took until 1996 for 100 per cent Sangiovese wines to be allowed to be called Chianti, and then only in the Classico district, which now has its own separate DOCG. These new regulations also permitted the inclusion of up to 15 per cent of any other variety, reduced the minimum ageing time for *riserva* wines from three years to two, and instituted a mandatory period of bottle-age before release. However, many producers still eschew the right to label their wines as Chianti Classico, preferring to retain their Super-Tuscan monickers until the reputation of Chianti has distanced itself still further from the image of the *fiasco*.

Chianti Classico refers to the central and most ancient region of production, which extends from just south of Florence to just north of Siena. Most of the best Chianti comes from here, many of the wines having the body and structure that demand ageing in bottle to show at their best. Some sport a neck label with the black cockerel of the Chianti Classico

consorzio, a voluntary grouping of producers that has done much to improve the quality of Chianti. Chianti production was extended in 1933 to the hills surrounding the central region. Of the six subdivisions, Chianti Rufina to the northeast of Florence is generally rated highest, making well-structured wines designed for long keeping. The other five – Colli Aretini, Colli Fiorentini, Colli Senesi, Colli Pisane and Montalbano – make lighter wines meant for earlier drinking. Anything just called plain Chianti is likely to hail from one of these surrounding areas.

The Chianti taste Chianti is one of the more difficult tastes to pin down. It can be full of fresh, fizzy, cor blimey, purple fruit; it can look and taste like a bowl of cherries; or it can be brick-brown, mature and stately. It rarely washes over you, often having a bite which keeps it lively, and sometimes a heady, herby perfume as well, and often the all-pervading Tuscan whiff of tobacco. There are any number of reasons for this diversity.

Take the grapes. Sangiovese is the backbone, but any old grape variety can find its way in there somewhere. Given all the possible permutations, the taste ranges from very light and banal, if the maximum percentage of white grapes is used, to very stylish yet proudly Tuscan when yields of Sangiovese are kept low. Another explanation for Chianti's diversity of taste lies in the long-standing attempts to soften the wine, which, owing to Sangiovese's high tannin and acidity, has tended to be rather rasping. Four solutions were developed to counteract this problem. One solution was to use the *governo* system, whereby dried grapes (or sweet must) are added to the wine to restart fermentation, which produces a fresh prickle on the tongue and adds a sweet-sour note to its rustic simplicity, yielding slightly more alcohol and body. Another was to incorporate some white grapes in the blend, a practice still surprisingly required by the DOCG (although not for Classico). The third solution was to add soft *mosto meridionale* from the south, which is now disallowed, although some producers persist in the practice. Finally, long ageing in old oak was successful in softening the tannins – and also in destroying the fruit.

To complicate matters, not all producers want to make Chianti for drinking tomorrow with a pizza. Some are engaged on a much more serious mission, to make Chianti that will stand the test of time, hold its head up on the international stage, and not get sawdust kicked in its face by *cru classé* claret or Australian Shiraz (Syrah). They mature their wines in Bordeaux *barriques* and expect us not to uncork them for five or ten years.

As a result of all this, we are stuck with a variety of ways of making Chianti – some traditional, some innovative – all of which have an effect on the taste, but none of which operates in a simple, direct manner. This may annoy the socks off you, or it may add to the fascination. Whatever else, Chianti is no longer boring.

Where next? Tuscany has several **Sangioveses** from simple level up to the great **Brunello** di Montalcino and the Super-Tuscans.

RECOMMENDED PRODUCERS

Tim Adams
Jim Barry
Eldredge
Galah
Grosset
Knappstein
Leasingham
Mitchell
Pike's
Sevenhill
Wendouree

Clare

Iron fist in an iron glove

Best-known wines The Armagh Shiraz
Grape varieties Shiraz, Grenache, Cabernet Sauvignon, Mourvèdre, Malbec
Style Powerful, full-throttle Grenache and Shiraz
Quality/Price ***⋯⟩*****/££⋯⟩£££££

If wine quality were measured purely by concentration of flavour, then Clare would rank as one of the world's very finest regions. As it is, it's the source of some of Australia's finest Shiraz and Grenache, and can also boast impressive Cabernet Sauvignon. Much of Clare is warm and dry, and many of the vineyards are old and unirrigated. Yields are tiny, fruit is ultra-ripe, and the wines can be explosively rich and long-lasting. There are cooler districts producing more subdued Cabernet Sauvignons and Cabernet Francs which could almost be described as elegant. Try them before the 16 per cent alcohol Grenache.

The Clare taste In its youth, the Grenache can seem just too big for its bottle, brimming with liquorice, pepper, chocolate and damson flavours and packing a powerful alcoholic punch. Give it time and it calms down, relaxes, becomes – if not genteel – certainly more presentable. Clare Shiraz is similarly proportioned but better balanced with peppery mulberry-and-plum fruit and a violet-like perfume. Both varieties come chock-full of tannin, but the fruit is so ripe that you tend not to notice it. After ten years in bottle, they're splendid.

Cabernet comes in the same boisterous format, breathing spicy blackcurrant fumes wherever it goes, but some of the wines from cooler parts of Clare are more refined. Where it is blended, Malbec rather than Merlot is often the favoured partner.

Where next? **Barossa** and **McLaren Vale** are other sources of generous red wines. Alternatively, try some beefy **California Zinfandel**, old-style Spanish **Priorato** or **Châteauneuf-du-Pape**.

Coonawarra

The red centre
Best-known wines Wynns John Riddoch Cabernet
Grape varieties Cabernet Sauvignon, Shiraz, Merlot
Style Refined yet full-flavoured Cabernet; spicy, peppery Shiraz
Quality/Price ***····⟩*****/£££····⟩£££££

RECOMMENDED PRODUCERS

Bowen
Katnook Estate
Leconfield
Lindemans
Mildara
Orlando
Parker Estate
Penfolds
Penley
Petaluma
Wynns

The Australians aren't supposed to believe in *terroir*, but they can't deny the fact that many of their greatest red wines come from a patch of *terra rossa* soil in the southern reaches of South Australia. Most of Australia is red, but this particular bit stretching 12 km (8 miles) north to south, and no more than 3 km (2 miles) at the widest, is redder than usual.

Being so southerly, Coonawarra also benefits from a particularly mild climate and a long, slow ripening season which intensifies the fruit flavours. The soil also has a lot to do with it. However, it's a mistake to think that the red soil is what gives the quality. It is the limestone subsoil with its high water table which is the important factor, and many feel that the best Coonawarra vineyards are those where the *terra rossa* is actually at its most shallow. Other vineyards just off the *terra rossa* strip have shown that their wines can be every bit as good. With the Coonawarra name on a bottle, selling a wine becomes a lot easier. Cabernet Sauvignon is the king here, while Shiraz is also excellent, and these varieties are slowly squeezing white grapes out of the region. Malbec, Cabernet Franc and even Petit

The bright-red *terra rossa* soil is recognised as part of Australia's own *terroir*

Verdot appear in certain vineyards, but Merlot is the favoured blending variety, and is also successful on its own.

The Coonawarra taste Cabernet Sauvignon oozes blackcurrant fruit and shares the juicy succulence of many Australian Cabernets but with plenty of backbone and structure, too. The best wines are concentrated, even voluptuous, unfolding at leisure into attractive, cedary, cigar-box flavours, with heady whiffs of minty eucalyptus. They remain balanced throughout their lives. Shiraz is extremely fine, too, not as full blown as in other regions, but more serious, even restrained. The rich blackberry juiciness is tempered again by good structure, and the peppery, spicy style hints at France's Rhône Valley as a model – meaning they age gently and gracefully.

Where next? Cabernet Sauvignon-based wines from the **Médoc**, **Napa Valley**, **Stellenbosch**, **Hawke's Bay** and **Margaret River**. Syrah/Shiraz from **Victoria**, northern **Rhône**, **Languedoc-Roussillon** and **California**.

RECOMMENDED PRODUCERS

La Bastide
De Caraguilhes
Des Chandelles
Caves du Mont-Tauch
Fontsainte
Grand Cres
Grand Moulin
Hélène
De Lastours
les Ollieux
Vaugelas
De la Voulte-Gasparets

Corbières

Cor blimey!

Region The Languedoc
Grape varieties Syrah, Mourvèdre, Carignan, Grenache
Style Earthy and peppery, with herby black fruit
Quality/Price *⋯⟩****/£⋯⟩£££

Corbières provides ample proof of the renaissance of the Languedoc. There didn't used to be too much to the region apart from an awful lot of Carignan and a lot of awful Carignan. Now Mourvèdre, Grenache and especially Syrah are appearing in the vineyards to great effect.

It's a pretty big appellation, and many of the best wines come from hillsides in the north, where even old-vine Carignan can be made to shine with some carbonic maceration. However, those best wines tend to be Syrah backed up by Grenache, with perhaps a little Mourvèdre to add some seasoning.

The Corbières taste   Though largely dependent on the grape varieties involved and the ambitions of the producer, a typical Corbières is simple and peppery in its youth with spicy black-fruit flavours, and with a year or two in bottle can acquire hints of leather, liquorice and dried fruit. The finest Syrah-based wines are supple and full-bodied in structure, brimming with wild fruit, orange peel and herb flavours and are easily capable of lasting ten years or more.

Where next?   Languedoc-Roussillon has several wines in a similar vein, as do **Provence** and the southern **Rhône**.

Cornas

Not a wine to argue with
Region Northern Rhône
Grape varieties Syrah
Flavour Bold and tannic, with smoky damson and blackcurrant fruit
Quality/Price ***⋯⟩*****/£££⋯⟩£££££

RECOMMENDED PRODUCERS

Thierry Allemand
Guy de Barjac
August Clape
Jean-Luc Colombo
Durand
Dumien-Serrette
Paul Jaboulet-Aîné
Marcel Juge
Jean Lionnet
Robert Michel
Noël Verset
Alain Voge

Cornas is the most southerly outpost of sunburnt Syrah grapes, and has the smallest production of all northern Rhône reds. It has quietly been making big, big wines year in, year out for generations, but now finds itself in the spotlight. It's no surprise then that prices have begun to climb.

The Cornas taste   Traditional Cornas is burly and bruising, more black than red in colour, with hefty tannins and smoky damson and blackcurrant fruit. In good years and from a good producer, 10 to 15 years in bottle are needed for the wine to become enjoyable, but in most cases the tannins dominate throughout its life. A small number of producers led by Jean-Luc Colombo are showing that careful winemaking can extract all the flavour and all the colour without having so much of the killer tannin, especially if the grapes are very ripe. Pop it into a new barrel for a year or two and the results are still bold and very Cornas, but more approachable.

Where next?   **Hermitage** for a similar style; **Côte-Rôtie** for more delicacy. **Australia** has **Shiraz** of similar proportions, although few are as forbidding in their youth.

Costières de Nîmes

Languedoc meets Rhône

Region Languedoc
Grape varieties Grenache, Syrah, Cinsault, Mourvèdre, Carignan
Style Ripe and herby with mulberry and plum fruit
Quality/Price *····⟩****/£····⟩£££

Technically, Costières de Nîmes is part of the Languedoc as it lies in the Gard *département*; it was known as Costières du Gard until 1989. However, the *terroir* has rather more in common with that on the other side of the Rhône where the vineyards qualify for the Côtes du Rhône appellation. There's a diversity of wine styles ranging from simple and bland, where Cinsault and Carignan weave their sleep-inducing spells, to serious *vins de garde* where Grenache, Syrah and Mourvèdre rule.

The Costières de Nîmes taste A typical Costières de Nîmes is in the slightly peppery, slightly herby, slightly fruity, slightly banal mould. But a growing number of more adventurous and exciting wines are full of southern herbs, dense plum and mulberry fruit and smoky complexity. Where Syrah takes the dominant role, the wines can be dead ringers for something rather more pricey from the Rhône – and the northern Rhône at that.

Where next? Eastwards to the southern **Rhône** Valley, where the **Côtes du Rhône**-Villages appellation produces some lovely reds. Westwards lies the **Coteaux du Languedoc** in the value-packed **Languedoc-Roussillon** region.

Côte Chalonnaise

Suburban Burgundy

Best-known wines Mercurey
Grape varieties Pinot Noir
Style Simple burgundy with strawberry fruit to the fore
Quality/Price **····⟩****/£££····⟩££££

The Côte Chalonnaise, along with the Mâconnais, acts as a buffer between the swanky, serious Côte d'Or and the more frivolous Beaujolais. Strictly speaking it is southern Burgundy, and begins where the Côte de Beaune leaves off. Anybody looking for the Côte d'Or in miniature here will need very good eyesight. However, anybody looking for simple, tasty burgundy at a sensible price will find lots to choose from.

After the reasonably straightforward slope of the Côte d'Or, it's rather more variegated here, with the main villages scattered to the west of Chalon. Bouzeron and Montagny make white wine only, while Mercurey, Givry and Rully make red as well. These last three villages have several *premiers crus*, but few of these have yet to really stand out, and the choice of producer is still the more important factor. The basic appellation is Bourgogne Côte Chalonnaise.

The Côte Chalonnaise taste The style of Côte Chalonnaise wines is generally light strawberry to cherry, dry and medium-bodied, providing easy drinking. It is often at its best when young although some wines from the *premier cru* vineyards can mature well for five or even ten years. Mercurey provides the fullest, fruitiest style, Givry is slightly firmer and longer-lived while Rully's wines are the simplest, brightest and freshest of the trio.

Where next? First of all, head northwards into the **Côte de Beaune** and **Côte de Nuits** to see if you can pick up a Bourgogne Rouge from a good producer for the same price. **Beaujolais** to the south is made with a different grape, but can offer similar experiences. Other sources of affordable **Pinot Noir** include **Chile**, **Romania**, the **Languedoc** in France and **Somontano**.

Mercurey in the Côte Chalonnaise produces attractive and approachable red wines

Côte de Beaune

Beaune and bred

Best-known wines Pommard, Volnay, Corton, Beaune

Grape varieties Pinot Noir

Style At best, perfumed, complex and slightly earthy with raspberry and strawberry fruit

Quality/Price **·····⟩*****/££·····⟩£££££

The southern half of Burgundy's Côte d'Or stretches for about 30 km (19 miles) from Ladoix-Serrigny to Santenay, with the ancient town of Beaune at its heart. The vineyards run in a more or less continuous strip, with gentle, southeast-facing slopes. It's slightly warmer and wetter here than in the Côte de Nuits and the vineyards are more evenly divided between reds and whites. The wines peak in Aloxe-Corton, Pommard, Beaune and Volnay, but some of the lesser-known villages provide good-value drinking – yet remember that value in Burgundy may not mean quite the same as it does elsewhere.

Aloxe-Corton, at the northern end, produces wines that can be among the bigger, more powerful, structured Côte de Beaune reds. Nevertheless, they are still a shade lighter than wines from the Côte de Nuits, which begins only a short distance away. The vineyards fan out around the distinctive hill of Corton, capped with its beret of trees, mostly facing south but wheeling round from the village of Ladoix-Serrigny in the east to Pernand-Vergelesses in the west. Aloxe-Corton reds come mostly from the lower slopes. Le Corton is the red *grand cru* vineyard, the only one in the Côte de Beaune, but other names can be appended to make, for instance, *grand cru* Corton-Bressandes or Corton-Renardes.

Part of the hill of Corton lies within Pernand-Vergelesses, but because the slopes here face more or less due west, the grapes rarely achieve the rich ripeness of those facing the sun for a greater part of the day. Around the other side, Ladoix-Serrigny has also bitten off a chunk of Corton, in this case facing northeast – again, hardly the best aspect to get the most out of the grapes. Many wines are sold as Aloxe-Corton or Côte de Beaune-Villages, but the few Ladoix wines available – plain though they are – are worth trying if the price is right.

To the south is Beaune with its satellite appellations of Savigny-lès-Beaune and Chorey-lès-Beaune (*see* **Beaune**). Then come the two very fine villages of Pommard and Volnay. Both are capable of making wine every bit as good as and often much better than the typical Corton, although neither has any *grand cru* vineyards. Volnay spills over into Meursault, with some wines being labelled Volnay-Santenots if they are red, Meursault if they are white. Red Meursault does exist although the white version is deservedly far more famous. This is where white wines begin to dominate, leaving the light reds of St-Romain, Monthélie and St-Aubin rather stranded. But be grateful for the simple fact that these (and other less well-known wines such as Chorey-lès-Beaune, Ladoix and Maranges) often have to try hard for recognition, while the well-known wines rest on their laurels.

Monthélie's *premier cru* vineyards are also an extension of Volnay's, and these underrated wines can be particularly good value. Auxey-Duresses and St-Romain are rather off the beaten track behind Meursault, while St-Aubin lies behind Chassagne-Montrachet. Chassagne itself makes a fair amount of red wine, many of them very good; however the reputation of the village's whites overflows into red territory, meaning that value for money is not a strong point. Santenay produces wines in a similar style and at a cheaper price, as does Maranges, the southern point of the Côte.

Vineyards follow every contour of the Côte de Beaune

Wines from most of the major villages are also entitled to the Côte de Beaune-Villages appellation. Wines labelled simply Côte de Beaune come from particular plots within the commune of Beaune. Vineyards on the higher ground above the main villages qualify as Bourgogne Hautes-Côtes de Beaune.

The Côte de Beaune taste
Côte de Beaune reds, although also made from Pinot Noir, are generally lighter, softer and more approachable than those of the Côte de Nuits, and are often ready to drink sooner. At their best from Volnay, Pommard, Beaune and Corton, they have perfume, complexity, finesse and no lack of staying power, but a more typical wine would be fresh, with summer fruit and a slight earthyness. Chassagne-Montrachet can be peppery and plummy, oddly closer to Côte de Nuits in style, thanks to the belt of limestone they have in common, but only the best capture the burgundy silk. The lush texture of great burgundy can appear in any of the villages when a good producer and a reasonable vintage meet. The most important point to remember is to pick your producer with care.

Where next?
If Côte de Beaune prices are frightening, move further south to the **Côte Chalonnaise**, or try a mature *cru* **Beaujolais**; if your nerve (and pocket) holds, move up to fuller **Côte de Nuits**. **Pinot Noirs** from **California**, **Australia**, **Oregon** and **New Zealand** make interesting comparisons. See also specific entries for **Beaune**, **Pommard** and **Volnay**.

Côte de Nuits

Pinot Noir heaven
Best-known wines Chambertin, Clos de Vougeot,
Romanée-Conti, Nuits-St-Georges, Musigny
Grape varieties Pinot Noir
Style Thrilling, complex, sensuous and sensual
red wine – sometimes
Quality/Price **⋯⟩*****/£££⋯⟩£££££

Great burgundy is, in some ways, like an orgasm. If you're not sure whether you've had one, then you haven't. And if you have had one, you want another as soon as possible. The place you're most likely to find the required stimulation is in the Côte de Nuits, an east-facing slope running from just south of Dijon to just north of Beaune, which is home to some of the best-known, greatest and most expensive wines in the world.

All but one of Burgundy's red *grands crus* are in the Côte de Nuits, and Pinot Noir dominates. There are a few patches of Chardonnay dotted around, but good – very good – as they can be, the place is very much dedicated to red, red wine. Start at the northern end of the Côte and you might find it hard to believe the pleasures which are to come. The first two appellations you encounter are Marsannay, long famous for its rosé, and Fixin, both of them competent, occasionally more than that but seldom the stuff of dreams. Then the fun begins.

The villages from here to the foot of the Côte – Gevrey-Chambertin, Morey-St-Denis, Chambolle-Musigny, Vougeot, Vosne-Romanée and Nuits-St-Georges – are all capable of delivering magnificent wines, especially from the *grand cru* vineyards such as those which have managed to become part of the village names: Le Chambertin in Gevrey, Le Musigny in Chambolle and so on. Sadly, they don't always deliver, even at *grand cru* level, although the prices would make you think otherwise. Vougeot, the only one of those from the list above without a separate entry in this book, illustrates the dilemma. Three-quarters of this appellation, which neatly encapsulates the unpredictability of burgundy, is taken up by the *grand cru* Clos de Vougeot.

Cistercian monks enclosed the 50 hectares (125 acres) of vineyard six centuries ago, making of it a neat, manageable unit. Then came the Revolution, and the vineyard was split up into smaller holdings; families passed on a few rows of vines to each child, who in turn passed on a few plants to their children. There are now more than 80 owners, few with enough grapes to rub together to make a living. What we have today, therefore, is very close to chaos. It wouldn't be so bad if they all had a patch of similar quality, or were all equally conscientious in their winemaking. But the upper slopes generally make better wine than the lower slopes, even though the entire vineyard is *grand cru*; and growers differ in their ability to get the best from their vines. The chances of landing on the right spot and walking out with a good bottle of wine are extremely slim.

Similar happenings unfold in all of the other major villages, too. Buying a case of wine for the sort of money which not so long ago you'd have paid for a car is a risky business, so proceed with caution. Fortunately, virtually all of the domaines with holdings in *grands crus* also have plots in other lesser vineyards. If you find Monsieur Dupont's Bourgogne Rouge or Fixin to your liking, chances are that the hefty wad you blow on a few bottles of his Clos de la Roche won't be wasted.

Two more general appellations bring a taste of the Côte de Nuits within reach of more people. The top and tail ends – around Fixin and south of Nuits-St-Georges, where quality begins to shade off – make their wines into Côtes de Nuits-Villages, while up in the hills to the west, the wines of the Hautes-Côtes de Nuits perform a similar function.

The Côte de Nuits taste Côte de Nuits wines are bigger, richer, firmer and weightier than those of the Côte de Beaune, with more stuffing, more "oomph" and more staying power – in burgundian terms, that is. Pinot Noir never reaches the deep colours and thick, heavy styles of which Cabernet Sauvignon or Syrah are capable. Or almost never: anyone who can find – and afford – the wines of Domaine Leroy will find them almost black and virtually impenetrable for the first few years of their lives. However, they are atypical.

Spraying is a common viticultural practice in Burgundy

The majority of wines give off their gamy scents – and flavours that seem to fill your whole head, not just your mouth, within a framework that seems oddly lightweight by comparison with other great wines. That apparent contradiction is part of their fascination. Also fascinating but frustrating is how they taste so wonderful when they're young, but then go into a sulky phase whose length depends on the quality of the wine – the better the wine, the longer the strop. They eventually emerge in glorious fashion, having shed some of the boisterous cherry and raspberry of their youth and gained richer, deeper, earthier, more feral notes.

With regard to the specific villages, Gevrey-Chambertin, Morey-St-Denis, Chambolle-Musigny, Vosne-Romanée and Nuits-St-Georges are dealt with in detail elsewhere in this book. Vougeot can be soft, rich, meaty and ripe, with that plummy fruit and velvety texture that keeps us coming back to burgundy time and again. But they can equally be something else entirely. Fixin and Marsannay are reasonably full-bodied, sturdy and meaty, with cherry fruit to the fore. Bourgogne Hautes-Côtes de Nuits and Côtes de Nuits-Villages are both fairly light, again cherryish, and can develop well over five or even ten years. If they are not mainstream burgundy, if they lack the richness and complexity of the better-known wines, at least they are usually well-endowed with fruit and provide a tantalising glimpse of burgundy at an affordable price.

Where next? The Côte de Nuits is almost a cul-de-sac – precious few places are capable of producing wine that tastes like it. **Côte de Beaune** comes closest, as do the finest **Pinot Noirs** from **Carneros, Central Coast,** and occasionally **Australia** and **New Zealand.** Why not go off on a slight tangent and taste other powerful, perfumed wines: **Barolo, Barbaresco, Côte-Rôtie** and **Hermitage**? See also **Chambolle-Musigny, Gevrey-Chambertin, Morey-St-Denis, Nuits-St-Georges** and **Vosne-Romanée.**

RECOMMENDED PRODUCERS

Gilles Barge
Pierre Barge
Burgaud
Champet
Chapoutier
Clusel-Roch
Delas Frères
Gentaz-Dervieux
Gerin
Guigal

Côte-Rôtie

Rich, rare and roasted
Region Northern Rhône
Grape varieties Syrah, Viognier
Style Rich fragrant and alluring, with smoky berry fruit
Quality/Price ***⟶***** / ££££⟶£££££

This area known as the "roasted", or sun-baked, slope is France's northernmost Rhône appellation. As for Cornas, St-Joseph, Hermitage and Crozes-Hermitage, Syrah is the wine's principal grape. But Côte-Rôtie has something else, too, something that makes it one of France's most intriguing red wines. Like Hermitage, a proportion of white grapes – up to 20 per cent in theory, five per cent or less in practice – can be incorporated into the blend. But the grape is neither the Marsanne nor Roussanne of Hermitage; it is Viognier, the exotic variety which in neighbouring vineyards makes minuscule quantities of white Condrieu and Château Grillet.

Viognier gives the weighty Syrah a tremendous lift and perfume that makes it more delicate and refined than any straight Syrah wine. It is a spectacular partnership. Where Hermitage is bigger and gutsier, Côte-Rôtie is more complex; for those who think in terms of Bordeaux, Côte-Rôtie is more Margaux than Pauillac, and within Pauillac it is more Lafite than Latour. The only other thing to beware of is the price. Since the influential American wine critic Robert Parker discovered the Rhône, and in particular the single-vineyard Côte-Rôties from Guigal, interest has soared, and prices with it. But among the three-figure price tags, there are still many wines at a more reasonable level. The question is: for how long?

The Côte-Rôtie taste Côte-Rôtie has the weight and style of other Syrah-based wines, the same basketful of spiced blackcurrants, elderberries and damsons that turns tarry with age. However, the Viognier brings an ethereal, perfumed, flowery air that is utterly charming. You can drink the wines young, but to do so means you miss out on much of the pleasure. Leave lesser vintages for at least five years,and good years for much longer.

Where next? There is nothing else quite like Côte-Rôtie. **Hermitage** is on a par for quality, but weightier, **Cornas** is weightier still. **Syrah/Shiraz** from the **Languedoc**, **Australia** and **California** are always interesting to compare.

Coteaux du Languedoc

Big and beautiful
Region Languedoc
Grape varieties Syrah, Grenache, Mourvèdre, Carignan, Cinsault
Style Huge variation, but the best are rich, fruity, herby and complex
Quality/Price *---⟩****/£---⟩£££££

The Coteaux du Languedoc AC sprawls disjointedly between Narbonne and Nîmes, producing some of the brightest and liveliest reds of the Midi. Since 1992, the

RECOMMENDED PRODUCERS

Alquier
D'Aupilhac
Mas Bruguière
Cazal-Viel
Cazeneuve
De la Coste
Estanilles
L'Euzière
Flaugergues
Fonsalade
De Font Caude
De Granoupiac

Carignan and Cinsault which used to dominate the region have only been permitted to make up 40 per cent in total of a wine, while the higher quality Mourvèdre, Syrah, Grenache and Lladoner Pelut (a close relative of Grenache) must among them contribute a minimum of 40 per cent. As a result of this measure, wine quality has soared, and the light wines of yesteryear are giving way to serious, full-bodied reds of real class.

The adoption of innovative techniques here means that this is an appellation to enjoy now while the wines are good value, and also one to watch for further exciting developments. The best results generally come from the 11 villages which can add their names to the basic AC (Pinet makes a 12th, although for white wine only). La Clape, Montpeyroux and Pic-St-Loup are the best of these, and may one day become appellations in their own right (as St-Chinian and Faugères, which lie within the confines of the Coteaux du Languedoc, have already done). Some producers in St-Georges-d'Orques, Cabrières, St Drézéry and St-Saturnin have shown that they, too, are capable of making some lovely wines.

The Coteaux du Languedoc taste The bulk of the wines are simple, peppery, fruity, spicy quaffers. But a few pennies more buys you a spicy and herby style, with ripe fruit of any of blackberry, black-cherry, blackcurrant, mulberry, plum, damson and many more, depending on which grape varieties have been used. Although few have track records to see how they will last, many are built for the long run, and anyone with reasonable storage space should consider filling it with these wines before prices go up.

Where next? There's also lots of excitement in other parts of Languedoc-Roussillon, either under *vin de pays* labels or in recognised appellations. The southern **Rhône** is a good bet, too.

Côtes du Frontonnais

RECOMMENDED PRODUCERS

Baudare
Bellevue-la-Forêt
Ferran
Flotis
Côtes de Fronton Co-op
Montauriol
Le Roc

The silky southwest

Region Southwest France
Grape varieties Négrette, Fer, Syrah, Cabernet Sauvignon, Cabernet Franc
Style Gentle, plummy and silky, with a hint of fennel
Quality/Price **⋯⟩***/£⋯⟩£££

Côtes du Frontonnais is an AC just north of Toulouse in southwestern France. Négrette, a variety found practically nowhere else, is the main grape here, making up 50 to 70 per cent of the wines. Possible additions to

Frontonnais wines include Cabernet Sauvignon, Cabernet Franc and Malbec from Bordeaux, Cinsault from the Midi, Syrah from the Rhône Valley, and Gamay from Beaujolais. Such a mixed bag reflects the region's "where-am-I?" location, but this is just the sort of "find" you hope to stumble across as you are idly motoring through France, taking pot-luck in local restaurants.

The Côtes du Frontonnais taste The wines are gentle and plummy, soft-textured and juicy, with a herby, fennel-like signature and sometimes the tell-tale smoky, toasty whiff of an oak barrel. They are best drunk within about two to three years of the vintage, but will not suddenly die if left for a year or two longer, and they can be extremely good value.

Where next? Other wines from the **Southwest France** made from less than famous grapes include **Madiran**, Irouléguy (Tannat), Marcillac (Fer) and **Cahors** (Malbec).

Côtes du Rhône

Côte of many colours

Region Rhône
Grape varieties Grenache, Syrah, Mourvèdre, Cinsault, Carignan and several more
Style From light and chillable to mini-Châteauneuf
Quality/Price *·····⟩****/£·····⟩£££££

The Côtes du Rhône appellation accounts for four out of every five bottles produced in the entire Rhône Valley; it covers some 59,000 hectares (146,000 acres), making on average ten times as much wine as the Médoc in Bordeaux, about 60 times as much wine as Gigondas in the southern Rhône, and 450 times as much wine as Hermitage in the northern Rhône. So, it is not surprising that Côtes du Rhône wines are extraordinarily variable in style and quality.

Most of the appellation is in the southern Rhône, but there are a few small pockets in the north. The co-operatives impose some consistency on output by virtue of controlling more than 60 per cent of it, but few wines have much pretension beyond that of daily drinkability. Grenache, Carignan and Cinsault form the reliable, if not especially distinguished, base material. There is not, frankly, a lot to

RECOMMENDED PRODUCERS

Daniel & Denis Alary
Ameillaud
De Beaucastel (du Coudoulet)
De Cabasse
Cave de Cairanne
Clape
JL Colombo
De Fonsalette
JM Gerin
Gramenon
Grande Bellane
Du Grand Moulas
Guigal
Lombard
De l'Oratoire St Martin
Pascal Frères
Rabasse-Charavin
Cave de Rasteau
Marcel Richaud
Rocher
Ste Anne
St Estève
De la Soumade
Tardieu Laurent
Des Tours
Du Trignon

get excited about in the Côtes du Rhône, although these wines make convivial and relatively inexpensive winter drinking. Nevertheless, the southern Rhône has just about kept pace with developments. Over the last 50 years it has edged slowly towards better quality. Syrah and Mourvèdre contribute more spice and character to the blends; stainless steel and carbonic maceration have brought freshness and a new vigour to the wines, making them richer, juicier, fruitier and much more appetising. Some of the beefier wines are long-lived as well; to taste them, you would not imagine they were from the same AC as the older style.

The other wines worth looking out for are those from the top producers in appellations such as Châteauneuf-du-Pape and Gigondas who, for whatever reason, (young vines, vineyards in just the wrong spot) have produced a Côtes du Rhône rather than something loftier. As with, say, Beaujolais-Villages, the better villages – 16 in this case, all in the southern Rhône – have gone to the trouble of reminding us that they are a cut above the rest, and these appear as Côtes du Rhône-Villages. Lower yields and a greater proportion of Syrah, Mourvèdre and Cinsault help enormously.

If no specific village name is attached, a wine will be a blend from several of them. A village can append its name to the label, provided the wine comes entirely from there, and these are generally a better bet. The best villages include Cairanne, Rasteau, Sablet, Séguret and Valréas, although all the others are capable of producing the odd stunner or two. Brézème is not one of the 16 villages but is a separate appellation just south of the northern Rhône vineyards. Here Jean-Marie Lombard makes excellent 100 per cent Syrah wines, labelled Brézème Côtes du Rhône-Villages, which are definitely worth seeking out.

The Côtes du Rhône taste Simple Côtes du Rhône wines are fresh and fruity, softish, rounded and gently warming. The lighter ones can even be chilled slightly before serving. The wines coming from some of the Châteauneuf-du-Pape producers and from the Côtes du Rhône-Villages are rather more powerful and complex. The raspberry and blackcurrant fruit can really come through in these characterful wines, as can the herbs of the *garrigue*. Five years is a reasonable age to drink them, but many will happily wait for ten.

Where next? To see the main competitors, move further south in **France** into **Languedoc-Roussillon** and **Provence**. And, for more class, move to **Gigondas** and then on to **Châteauneuf-du-Pape**.

Côtes du Roussillon

Needs to catch up with the Languedoc

Region Roussillon

Grape varieties Syrah, Mourvèdre, Carignan, Cinsault, Grenache

Style Juicy, fresh and herby, ageing to a leathery, raisiny maturity

Quality/Price *⋯⟩****/£⋯⟩£££

This is the main appellation in the Roussillon part of Languedoc-Roussillon, and, sadly, is generally not as inspiring as its Languedoc relatives. Côtes du Roussillon patrols the eastern end of France's border with Spain, and along with Collioure, is the most southerly *appellation contrôlée* in the country.

The wines are a blend in which Carignan used to predominate, with Grenache and Cinsault in support, but recent changes (1996) in the AC law are encouraging growers to use more Syrah and Mourvèdre. Compared with the Coteaux du Languedoc, there are far fewer "star" producers at present, but the new regulations may change that. The Côte du Roussillon-Villages appellation covers the 25 best villages in the north of the region along the border with Corbières, and quality here is higher.

Three villages – Caramany, Latour de France and Lesquerde – can append their names on the label, but none of them at present makes anything startlingly better than in the regular appellation. Fernand Vaquer is a rather stubborn producer who feels that he deserves the villages appellation, but his vineyards lie just the wrong side of the boundary line. In protest, he labels his wines, among the finest in the region, as simple *vin de pays*.

The Côtes du Roussillon taste At base level, Côtes du Roussillon is a typical southern French glugger: simple, fruity, everyday stuff with a spicy ring to it. Above there, the wines divide into ancient and modern, with the newer style being full of plummy, cherry fruit, often with oak in obvious attendance, while the more traditional wines are – when well made – full of rich raisin, prune and leather flavours.

Where next? First of all, look at the wines of Collioure (*see* **Banyuls**) to see what more producers should be doing. Then head anywhere in the south of **France**, beginning with **Corbières**, **Minervois** and the **Coteaux du Languedoc**.

Crozes-Hermitage

Learn to pick your Crozes

Region Northern Rhône

Grape varieties Syrah

Style Ripe, friendly, blackberry and damson fruit with hints of violet

Quality/Price **⋯⟩****/££⋯⟩££££

This is the younger brother of Hermitage, made on the lower, gentler slopes above Tain in France's northern Rhône. It is juicier, less tannic, less serious and more straightforward than Hermitage and consequently matures more quickly. Its great advantage is that it is more readily available than Hermitage (since there is more than ten times as much of it) and, therefore, less expensive. It can give a rough idea of the Hermitage style for a lot less money.

The Crozes-Hermitage taste There's a wide variety of *terroirs* here, so there's a correspondingly wide variation in style. Lighter wines from the flatter alluvial soil are simple, lightly perfumed Syrah, with berry flavours but not a great deal of backbone. The bigger wines, usually from vines on the hillside next to Hermitage itself, are full of juicy, chunky, blackberry and damson fruit, together with a more delicate perfume of violets and orange peel. They're never as firm and tannic as Hermitage so they can be drunk almost from the word go, but they're at their best from 5 to 10 years old.

Where next? Apart from other northern **Rhône** reds – **St-Joseph** is closest in weight but not as fine – seek out some of the **Syrah**-based wines being made in the south, **Coteaux du Languedoc**, **Costières de Nîmes**.

Curicó

The curiosities of Curicó

Grape varieties Cabernet Sauvignon, Merlot, Malbec, Cabernet Franc, Pinot Noir

Style Sweet, fleshy, blackcurranty Cabernets

Quality/Price *⋯⟩****/£⋯⟩£££££

Curicó forms the middle part of Chile's Central Valley and, although the daytime temperatures are much the same as in Santiago, 200 km (124 miles) to the north, the nighttime is much cooler, so the fruit ripens more slowly.

It was this which attracted Miguel Torres to the region in the 1970s to cultivate white grapes, but much of the noise being made today concerns the red wines. While most of the producers based here also source fruit from other Chilean areas, Cabernet Sauvignon and Merlot are already showing that they can perform well here, and Cabernet Franc, Malbec and Pinot Noir are also being used to good effect.

The Curicó taste It's still the producers who dictate the style of the wines. Cabernet Sauvignon tends to be sweet, fleshy and blackcurranty; Cabernet Franc (from Valdivieso) is similar but more perfumed; Merlot has an exotic hint of pepper on top of the plummy fruit; Malbec varies from simple and dusty to dense and powerful, all the time having spicy, perfumed, black-fruit flavours; Pinot Noir is simple and ripe, although occasionally over-oaked.

Where next? Nip over the Andes to **Argentina** to see what's happening there with **Cabernet Sauvignon** and **Malbec**, then have a look at the better varietal *vins de pays* of southern **France**.

Dão

Signs of promise
Region Central Portugal
Grape varieties Alfrocheiro Preto, Bastardo, Jaen, Tinta Pinheira, Tinta Roriz, Touriga Nacional
Style Often dry and hard, but can have juicy fig, bramble and berry flavours
Quality/Price *····⟩****/£····⟩££££

RECOMMENDED PRODUCERS

Caves Aliança
Caves São João
Fonte do Ouro
Quinta das Maias
Quinta da Pellada
(Quinta de Saes)
Quinta dos Roques
Sogrape

First of all, let's get the pronunciation right. Say "Dow". Say "Dung". Say something halfway between. Now you've got it. South of the Douro, and inland from Bairrada, Dão vineyards scramble over granite hills in between tracts of pine forest. Although considerably larger than Bairrada, Dão produces barely half the volume. To the extent that wines reflect the nature of the soil, Dão possesses something of the obduracy of granite.

It is meant to be Portugal's best, classic, flagship, dry red wine, and it probably could be if it would loosen up a little, relax and let the fruit have its say. Its principal grape is Touriga Nacional, a high-quality grape which only now is beginning to be fully appreciated, and even then not by all the producers. It can make solid, sturdy, age-worthy wines, providing it is carefully handled – which sadly, it usually isn't.

The Dão taste Dry, sinewy, hard – that is the general verdict. With a few years in bottle and just as long in old oak, the result can be brown and dull, an object lesson in how not to make wine. But, with TLC and perhaps a new barrel or two, the change is extraordinary, and those gloriously fruity, tarry, tobacco notes which you imagined were there in the old-style wines suddenly spring to the fore. Suddenly there are figs, brambles, berries, sandalwood and vanilla where once was a mouthful of dirt. Do we want more of this style of Dão? Yes, please.

Where next? **Alentejo**, **Bairrada** and the **Douro** in **Portugal**; the wines of southern **Italy** and **Greece** also have echoes here.

Dolcetto

The little sweet one
Region Piedmont
Style Lively, scented, berry fruit

Although it may sound like a sweet white wine, or possibly an Italian ice-cream, Dolcetto – the little sweet one – is a red grape that makes dry red wine. Its home is Piedmont in northwest Italy, where no fewer than seven DOCs scrabble for attention: Dolcetto d'Alba, di Diano d'Alba, delle Langhe Monregalesi, d'Asti, di Dogliani, d'Acqui and di Ovada. Alba, Dogliani and Ovada are considered the best sources. Apart from odd spots in California (Il Podere dell' Olivos and a few others) and Australia (Best's, Brown Brothers), Dolcetto doesn't grow anywhere else.

It's mostly a third-class citizen in Piedmont, bowing to Barbera which in turn bows to Nebbiolo. It is picked early, typically a couple of weeks before Barbera and a month before Nebbiolo, and its fermentation is usually complete by the time Nebbiolo arrives to use the same, recently-vacated vat. The better Dolcettos are hard to beat for simple, no-nonsense drinking.

Generally, the most recent vintage is the best choice, though there are very few producers who give their wines more structure by allowing them to age for a couple of years or more. The few blends with Nebbiolo, most notably that of Cascina Drago, can be very good.

The Dolcetto taste A young Dolcetto wine is easy to recognise before you even take a sniff of it. At its most dramatic, it is a glorious, deep, day-glo, electric, beetroot purple. Wines made from Dolcetto are rich and usually stuffed full of velvety, soft, scrunchy, plummy fruit – much like a perky Merlot.

There can be hints of liquorice, scented truffles, tobacco, spicy meatballs, exotic teas, and sweet-smelling hazelnuts, which still linger after the light chilling which renders Dolcetto even more refreshing.

Where next? The fresh, juicy gulpability of **Dolcetto** puts it in the same league as **Beaujolais** or any **Gamay**-based wine for light drinking, although it often has more stuffing than ordinary Beaujolais wines. Its softness is reminiscent of **Merlot**, with which it makes an interesting comparison.

Douro

Unfortified port
Region Northern Portugal
Grape varieties Touriga Nacional,Tinto Roriz, Touriga Francesa, Tinta Barroca, Tinta Cão
Style Spicy tobacco and dark-berry flavours
Quality/Price **⋯⟩****/££⋯⟩£££££

RECOMMENDED PRODUCERS
Ferreira (Barca Velha)
Niepoort
Quinta do Côtto
Quinta do Crasto
Quinta de Gaivosa
Quinta de la Rosa
Quinta do Vale de Raposa
Ramos Pinto

Had modern winemaking techniques and means of transportation been available in the 17th century, perhaps port would not have been invented. The producers in Portugal's Douro Valley found that the best way to make their red wines survive the lengthy journey down the river and then to various foreign parts was to fortify them with spirit. The sweetness and high alcohol of the new drink appealed particularly in the colder climes of northern Europe.

Steeply terraced vines in the Douro are positioned for maximum exposure to sunlight

So port was born, and Douro table wine was more or less ignored. With today's well-equipped wineries, dry red Douro wine is at last receiving the attention it deserves. The grapes that are the driving forces behind the best wines are Touriga Nacional and, to a lesser extent, Tinto Roriz (Tempranillo). One or two producers use Cabernet Sauvignon as well, in which case the wines are labelled Tràs-os-Montes. Barca Velha, for a long time considered Portugal's finest table wine, now has several serious competitors.

The Douro taste The wines are rich, dry, medium- to full-bodied, often deep-coloured, with scents of tobacco and leather supported on a solid base of glorious fruit. In the lighter styles of wine, this is gutsy, red-berry flavours, with more than a little in common with Zinfandel. At the weightier end, it's plums, blackberries and mulberries, often with hints of vanilla as a result of its ageing in new oak.

Where next? Dão, Bairrada and Alentejo first, then head upstream and over the border to see what the Spaniards do in **Ribera del Duero.**

Fitou

RECOMMENDED PRODUCERS
Les Fenals
Caves du Mont-Tauch
Des Nouvelles
Cave Pilote de Villeneuve
Roudene

Dozing while those around are waking up
Region Languedoc-Roussillon
Grape varieties Carignan, Grenache, Lladoner Pelut
Flavour Sturdy with spicy, berry-fruit flavours
Quality/Price *---⟩***/£---⟩£££

In 1948, Fitou became the first appellation of the Languedoc, and it was also one of the brightest southern appellations of the 1980s. Since then, however, the place has rather stood still while those around it such as neighbouring Corbières have made great progress. While Carignan's contribution is being decreased elsewhere, the variety is still important here. When the yields are low, the vines old, and the wine well-made, the results can be good. But such instances, outside a handful of admirable co-operative cellars, are rare. Other appellations can boast mavericks who are pushing their region's reputation forward and making exciting wines. These individuals are notably absent from Fitou. (But as is the way with southern France, having committed these words to print, just watch for half a dozen super-Fitous to appear...)

The Fitou taste Good Fitou is a dark, beefy, tannic and substantial wine with spicy berry fruit that benefits from five years' bottle age. There are better versions where the Syrah influence has been increased to the legal limit – not that the French would ever dream of going beyond it – and these are slightly more elegant.

Where next? See what they do with **Carignan** in the **Minervois** region and **Italy's Sardinia.**

Friuli-Venezia Giulia

Friuli Madly Deeply

Best-known wines Collio, Colli Orientali del Friuli, Isonzo

Grape varieties Cabernet Sauvignon, Cabernet Franc, Merlot, Refosco, Schioppettino, Pinot Nero

Style Light, refreshing and fruity, and sometimes rather better

Quality/Price *······}****/££······}£££££

Apart from the occasional Pinot Noir, the main grapes here are the Bordeaux varieties – Cabernet Sauvignon and Franc and Merlot, but, there are also the native Refosco and Schioppettino varieties. Top-class wines are rare, but those in search of interesting lighter reds will find much to their liking, with more than a few pleasant surprises. The region's DOCs include Colli Orientali del Friuli, Collio, Friuli Aquileia, Grave del Friuli, Isonzo and Latisana.

The Friuli-Venezia Giulia taste The best wines are based on the Bordeaux varieties, with both blends and varietal versions, especially Merlot, being very good. Spicy berry fruit is a character of many. The local Refosco makes soft, gutsy, damsony wines, while Schioppettino is lightly fragrant.

Where next? Head to **New Zealand** next for the international varieties, where you'll find the same fresh, grassy quality but with a little more fruit impact. For the native grape varieties, either head north to **Trentino-Alto Adige** or south to **Veneto**.

Workers in the vineyards of the Collio zone, in Fruili-Venezia Giulia

RECOMMENDED PRODUCERS

Canon
Canon de Brem
Canon Moueix
Croix Canon
(formerly Charlemagne)
De la Dauphine
Fontenil
Mazeris
Moulin-Pey-Labrie
La Vieille Cure

Fronsac and Canon Fronsac

Grab it while you can

Region Bordeaux

Grape varieties Merlot, Cabernet Franc, Cabernet Sauvignon

Style Full-bodied, chunky, spicy claret

Quality/Price **⋯⟩****/£££⋯⟩££££

Now here's an interesting pair of wines sitting cheek-by-jowl. Canon Fronsac, less than half the size of Fronsac, may have the edge in terms of quality, but the gap is marginal and the styles are similar. These wines are not well known; indeed, they would test the geography of a knowledgeable wine buff. They lie just west of Pomerol on the right bank of the Dordogne and share the relatively large Merlot component, although the proportion of Cabernet Franc used here is higher, and Cabernet Sauvignon and Malbec also make their presence felt. The really good news is, despite their famous neighbour, they're still good value (in Bordeaux terms). But it will only take a couple of enthusiastic write-ups from Robert Parker to change that.

The Fronsac and Canon Fronsac taste These are full-bodied, stylish, rich, lively, colourful, strong and cheerful wines, with a spicy, cedary edge that confirms their seriousness. They are usually drinkable within five years, but may take twice that to open up properly.

Where next? Other sources of good value in **Bordeaux** include Côtes de Castillon, the St-Emilion satellites, Lalande-de-Pomerol (*see* **Pomerol**), *cru bourgeois* **Médoc** and **Graves**.

Gamay

The juicy one

Style Refreshing raspberries, strawberries and pepper

Grown in Beaujolais, the Loire

Given the success of Beaujolais, and especially of Nouveau, it's surprising that Gamay hasn't been taken up with more enthusiasm in other parts of the world. It appears just to the north of Beaujolais in Burgundy, where Mâcon Rouge is usually 100 per cent Gamay. Bourgogne Passe-Tout-Grains, made with up to two-thirds of the grape plus Pinot Noir, can be made anywhere in the Burgundy region.

In the Loire, where one in six of France's Gamay vines are planted, Gamay de Touraine can be a match for young Beaujolais, but is a bit more reserved. Gamay is also a part of other Loire reds, including Coteaux d'Ancenis and Coteaux du Giennois. Elsewhere in France, Gamay appears in isolated pockets in Haut-Poitou which follows the Loire style, in the Coteaux du Lyonnais and Côtes d'Auvergne, and particularly in the Coteaux de l'Ardèche, with good Beaujolais-like *vins de pays*. The environs of Lyons are especially Gamay friendly, among them Côtes du Forez and Côte Roannaise.

Outside France, the Swiss of the Valais region grow Gamay alongside Pinot Noir, and blend the two varieties to create a light wine known as Dôle (*see* **Switzerland**). Turkey's Villa Doluca is Gamay-based, while in Canada, in British Columbia and Ontario, some Gamay is made. California has a number of wines labelled Gamay which are made from different grapes, and the number of true Gamays is very small.

The Gamay taste Gamay really is the taste of Beaujolais, but much depends on the method of production. Made by carbonic maceration, the results are simple, direct, innocent, deliciously fresh and enormously fruity with aromas of raspberries, strawberries and pepper. High acidity gives it a fresh, mouthwatering gulpability and low tannin. Fermented in the conventional way, it has more tannin and structure, and if left long enough, can develop something of the plumminess and gaminess of mature Pinot Noir. However, these are only made by some Beaujolais *crus*.

Where next? If you like Gamay, try also the juicy fruit of **Dolcetto**, **Cabernet Franc** and lighter **Pinot Noir**.

Gevrey-Chambertin

Gevrey-Chambertin is NOT unwell
Region Burgundy
Grape varieties Pinot Noir
Style Plums, cherries, damsons, undergrowth
Quality/Price **⋯⟩*****/£££⋯⟩£££££

Gevrey-Chambertin has an awesome reputation for producing some of the biggest and finest wines of the Côte de Nuits. The juxtaposition of differing qualities – lightness and strength, power and fragrance – is a large part of the attraction. Chambertin and Chambertin Clos de Bèze are the best of the eight *grand cru* vineyards, the other

RECOMMENDED PRODUCERS
Bachelet
Alain Burguet
Charlopin-Parizot
Pierre Damoy
Claude Dugat
Dugat-Py
Frédéric Esmonin
Faiveley
Denis Mortet
Joseph Roty
Armand Rousseau
Serafin
Louis Trapet
Vallet Frères/Pierre Bourrée

The perfect match: wine, bread and cheese in a cool, Burgundian cellar

six include Charmes-Chambertin, Latricières-Chambertin, Chapelle-Chambertin, Griotte-Chambertin, Ruchottes-Chambertin and Mazis-Chambertin. These, along with the finer *premiers crus* such as Clos St-Jacques, Varoilles, Estournelles and Cazetières, can produce magnificent wines in a good year and from a savvy producer.

Such producers used to be thin on the ground, but many of those who used to be in charge have now passed on control to their rather more enthusiastic offspring. The result is that the appellation is one of the most exciting in the Côte d'Or. It's also one of the largest, with a good allocation of *grand* and *premier cru* land, so it should be possible to find good Gevrey-Chambertin with minimum effort.

The Gevrey-Chambertin taste The wines have a rich, satisfying character of ripe plums, damsons, cherries and woodsmoke, with wafts of truffles and violets. They are full-bodied, but never ungainly, and drink well from around six years old for the village wines to ten years or more for the *grands crus*. The best can mellow for another decade into the sort of wines that almost persuade you no price is too much to pay for good burgundy.

Where next? Try wines from other **Côte de Nuits** villages, along with top **Côte de Beaune** reds from **Volnay**, **Pommard**, Corton and **Beaune**.

Gigondas

The pauper's Châteauneuf
Region Southern Rhône
Grape varieties Grenache, Syrah, Mourvèdre and others
Style Warm, hearty, bramble, blackcurrant and herb
Quality/Price **·····>****/££·····>££££

This upwardly mobile village, formerly part of Côtes du Rhône-Villages, was elevated to its own AC in 1971. It's made with the typical southern Rhône mixed-bag of grapes, with Grenache to the fore supported by Mourvèdre, Syrah, Cinsault, Carignan and several others. It's a handy halfway house between Côtes du Rhône-Villages and Châteauneuf-du-Pape, both in terms of style and price. It is generally reliable in quality and rarely suffers the excesses of jamminess and raw alcohol that afflict many southern Rhône wines. Like neighbouring Vacqueyras, this is a good point from which to get a feel for the southern Rhône without spending *un bras et une jambe.*

The Gigondas taste It is a big, deep-coloured, plummy red with extrovert, broad-shouldered, yeoman-like flavours of brambles, berries, blackcurrants and herbs. Its solid, sturdy character, usually bolstered by 12 months in oak, means that five years' bottle age (sometimes more) will not come amiss.

Where next? Lirac, Vacqueyras, the better **Côtes du Rhône**-Villages and several **Languedoc** wines can challenge **Gigondas** on quality. The upwardly mobile should go for **Châteauneuf-du-Pape**.

Graves

True grit

Region Bordeaux
Grape varieties Cabernet Sauvignon, Cabernet Franc, Merlot, Malbec, Petit Verdot
Style Soft, juicy, blackcurranty, sometimes with a stony edge
Quality/Price **······>*****/££······>£££££

RECOMMENDED PRODUCERS

D'Archambeau
La Grave
De Landiras
Rahoul
Roquetaillade-La-Grange
Du Seuil
Vieux Château Gaubert

The Graves region of Bordeaux begins where the Médoc leaves off. It runs in a wide band, south of the River Garonne and Entre-Deux-Mers, from Bordeaux to Langon. The Langon end is where the great sweet white wines of Bordeaux are produced. The finest reds are made closer to Bordeaux in Pessac-Léognan, an area that acquired its appellation in 1987 – and an area the Italians might call the *classico* region of Graves.

Graves red wines offer good value and consistent quality

But what is still called Graves is still worth investigating for the large number of medium-priced wines of very sound and consistent quality. Graves is a variation on the theme of Bordeaux Cabernet Sauvignon, generally with less Cabernet Sauvignon and more Merlot than in the Médoc, but usually less Merlot than in St-Emilion or Pomerol. There are exceptions, of course, but the rule of thumb may help to explain why its wines are somewhere between the two in style. They are less appreciated than they might be, and can thus be particularly good value.

The Graves taste These wines do not have the toughness or ageing capacity of many wines of the Médoc. But they do have something of the silky, plummy softness of Pomerol, allied to the blackcurrant fruit of the Médoc in a juicy and beguiling combination.

Where next? Graves is one of several good places to begin tasting the reds of **Bordeaux**. If the easy-drinking softness appeals, then **St-Emilion** and **Pomerol** are the next logical steps. For something firmer, with more backbone, try the **Médoc**.

Hawke's Bay

New Zealand at its ruddiest and best
Best-known wines Te Mata Coleraine
Grape varieties Cabernet Sauvignon, Cabernet Franc,
Merlot, Syrah
Style Plum and blackcurrant fruit with a leafy, earthy edge
Quality/Price **⸳⸱⸳****/££⸳⸱⸳£££££

RECOMMENDED PRODUCERS
Babich
Brookfields
Church Road
Clearview Estate
Crab Farm
Esk Valley
Morton Estate
Ngatarawa
Stonecroft
Te Awa Farm
Te Mata
Trinity Hill
Unison
Vidal
Villa Maria
Waimarama

Hawke's Bay has a long history of winemaking. It boasts both the oldest winery still under the same management – Mission Vineyards, founded in 1851 – and the oldest winery still operating in the shape of Te Mata which dates back to the 1870s. In terms of vineyard plantings, the region is second to Marlborough, but when it comes to red wines, Hawke's Bay is top dog.

It comes as no surprise to hear that in a region that enjoys similar sunshine hours and temperatures to Bordeaux, the best wines are those made from Cabernet Sauvignon, Merlot and Cabernet Franc. The tendency in recent years has been to move from wines dominated by Cabernet Sauvignon to blends in which Cabernet Franc and Merlot have the upper hand. The current quest is to seek vineyards away from the alluvial plains on better drained and less fertile hillside sites and, as this happens, the wines will become even better. Already, the Gimblett Road district is making a name for itself. Look out, too, for the few examples of Syrah, which shows real promise here.

The Hawke's Bay taste The green flavours which speak of hyperactive vines and less than fully ripe fruit are still present in many wines, but the best producers have learned to prune accordingly or grow their vines in better vineyards. Typical Bordeaux-style wines today are dense and deep in colour with plum and blackcurrant fruit, a leafy, earthy edge and a ripe tannic structure which will help them age. Over-enthusiastic maceration of slightly underripe fruit can be a problem – but then the same is true in Bordeaux. Syrah has the wonderful fresh-pepper and berry aromas of the Rhône, and gets better and better with each vintage.

Where next? The districts around **Auckland**, especially Waiheke Island, are sources of other fine Kiwi **Cabernets**. See also what the Italians do in **Friuli-Venezia Giulia**.

Hermitage

King of the hill
Region Northern Rhône
Grape varieties Syrah
Style Raspberry, blackcurrant, plum, herbs, tar and woodsmoke
Quality/Price ***⋯⟩*****/££££⋯⟩£££££

RECOMMENDED PRODUCERS
Cave de Tain l'Hermitage
Chapoutier
Chave
Delas Frères
Bernard Faurie
Ferraton
Grippat
Guigal
Paul Jaboulet-Aîné
Jean-Michel Sorrel
Marc Sorrel
De Vallouit

During the 19th century, Hermitage was given the back-handed compliment of being allowed into claret to provide backbone, stuffing and, simply, taste. Then it sank back into oblivion. Fortunately for wine-lovers, but unfortunately for their wallets, this Syrah-based wine from the northern Rhône has now been rediscovered. On this steep, sun-baked, south-facing hill above the town of Tain, Syrah achieves a delicious power and, in the best of mature bottles, a glorious complexity that is hard to beat.

The appellation laws actually allow a small proportion of the white grapes Roussanne and Marsanne to be blended in, but few bother. Any blending that goes on in Hermitage occurs when a producer has holdings on different parts of the hill, some of which bring perfume, others structure and so on. Only those with extensive vineyard holdings have the luxury of being able to put together the perfect wine, but when they do and the vintage is a good one, the results rank among the very greatest red wines in the world.

The Hermitage taste It runs up and down the scales of flavour from raspberry to blackcurrant to plum, through herbs, briar, spice and pepper, from youthful inky intensity to mature tar, woodsmoke and leather, composing wonderful music along the way. Its concentrated fruit and high tannin make it a candidate for oak ageing. The structure built into Hermitage means that there is no point in opening a bottle much before it is ten years old; in riper vintages, consider 20 years the norm but be prepared to wait for 30.

Where next? Côte-Rôtie is the other star of the northern **Rhône**, although a few producers in **Cornas** might dispute that. Australian **Shiraz** can match the depth of flavour, but only the finest can offer the same complexity. Some Californian examples from the **Central Coast** and **Napa Valley** also come close. There is a similarity, too, between the size and tarry smokiness of mature Hermitage and that of some Italian wines such as **Brunello** di Montalcino and **Barolo**. Mature wines can resemble first-growth claret, and have been known to confuse some very sophisticated palates.

Hunter Valley

RECOMMENDED PRODUCERS

Brokenwood
Lake's Folly
McWilliam's
Rosemount
Rothbury
Tyrrell's

For saddle sniffers

Grape varieties Shiraz, Cabernet Sauvignon
Style Muscly, slightly rustic Shiraz and minty, earthy Cabernets
Quality/Price **⋯⟩****/££⋯⟩££££

Hunter Valley may be one of Australia's best-known wine regions, but today it's far from the hot-bed of activity it once was. The Shiraz and Cabernet from the Lower Hunter can still excite, but the hot, humid conditions are not ideal for consistent quality grape growing. The few who persist with Pinot Noir are to be admired more for their perseverance than their good sense. The climate is slightly more favourable in the Upper Hunter, but the writing is on the wall when the region's most important producer, Rosemount, sources red grapes for practically all its most impressive wines from other parts of Australia.

The Hunter Valley taste Traditional Hunter Shiraz is big, bold and brassy: dark, chocolate-rich, alcoholic and not exactly very fruity. Even if you are not in the habit of smelling "sweaty saddles" you can see why people use this description. That was the old style, and there are still a lot of them about. But a lot of drinkers prefer something more modern, cleaner and still packed with flavour as long as it's the fresh, peppery, fruity kind. This style is now in the ascendancy, and wines vary from simply fruity, ready-to-drink styles, to inky, spicy, liquorice-rich ones made for longer keeping. Many Hunter Shiraz wines will keep, and improve, for a decade or more.

Cabernet Sauvignon doesn't always have the succulent flavour of blackcurrants that we might expect of, say, Coonawarra Cabernets, but there are some surprisingly elegant wines. They may be more minty and can have a hint of tobacco with a bit of age. The best Pinot Noirs are the simple wines where the strawberry fruit is everything. More ambitious oaked versions just tend to be too muddy.

Where next? Apart from other Australian Shiraz and **Cabernet**, try Californian **Zinfandel**, **Douro** reds, **Priorato** and southern Italian wines.

Languedoc-Roussillon

France's New World
Best-known wines Corbières, Minervois, Fitou
Grape varieties Carignan, Grenache, Mourvèdre, Syrah, Cinsault, Cabernet Sauvignon, Merlot, Pinot Noir
Style As diverse as the area is large
Quality/Price *·····>****/£·····>£££££

RECOMMENDED PRODUCERS
Mas Baruel
De La Baume
Chemins de Bassac
Clovallon
Mas de Daumas Gassac
Galet
Grange des Pères
Jougla
Louis Latour
Patrick Lesec Selections
Limbardie
Lurton
De La Marfée
Quatre Sous
Val d'Orbieu
Virginie

It's official. The Languedoc-Roussillon has finally arrived as a quality wine region. The proof is that Bordeaux's famous Mouton-Rothschild has bought a 100-hectare (250-acre) estate near Limoux and is aiming to release a high-class wine made from Cabernet Sauvignon, Cabernet Franc and Merlot within a few years. Of course, those outside France realised that this large region in the warm south had the potential for greatness several years ago.

The famous Mas de Daumas Gassac made its first wine in 1978, since when dozens of other quality-minded estates have sprung up. Bordeaux's Cabernet Sauvignon was/is the driving force behind the Daumas Gassac red, but others have chosen to follow a slightly more orthodox path, using the traditional grapes of the south. Usually, the blends have been tweaked so that the inferior Carignan and Cinsault take a back seat to the superior Syrah, Mourvèdre and Grenache (although old-vine Carignan can be surprisingly good). Some producers choose to blend the local grapes with the newcomers. For example, the superb red wine from Daumas Gassac's neighbour, Domaine de la Grange des Pères, is Syrah, Mourvèdre and Cabernet Sauvignon.

While some of the wines conform to local AOC regulations, many do not, and have to be labelled as *vins de pays*. Few are finding this a hardship, especially as any reputation the region's appellations have is generally not favourable. But that is changing, albeit slowly. Coteaux du Languedoc (especially the Pic St-Loup district), Costières de Nîmes, Collioure, Faugères and Corbières all have more than a handful of quality-minded producers who are making better and better wines with each vintage. Such producers usually work on a small scale with production measured in thousands of cases. Think of them as the châteaux of the Médoc, Pomerol and St-Emilion.

So what is there at Bordeaux Rouge level? There's still far too much cruddy wine under both AOC and *vin de pays* labels, but there's far less than there was. New winemaking equipment has meant that a typical cheap wine may not have a great deal of flavour and character, but it is clean and fresh and – unlike Bordeaux Rouge – is usually made with ripe fruit. For not very much more money you can buy a varietal *vin de pays* made from Syrah, Cabernet Sauvignon, Merlot or other decent varieties. If this sounds rather like the Riverland, Murray River and Riverina regions of Australia, it will come as no surprise that Aussie winemakers work extensively in Languedoc-Roussillon, with BRL Hardy having its own winery there, Domaine de la Baume.

Whether you prefer Old World finesse and complexity or New World depth of flavour, this is an excellent place to find interesting and occasionally exceptional wines. Quality is still erratic, and many would-be superstars still equate higher quality wines with new oak and a fancy label. But there are few regions anywhere else in the world which can match the value for money offered by Languedoc-Roussillon.

The Languedoc-Roussillon taste
If you consider the scale of the Languedoc-Roussillon region, the diversity of grapes used there and the varying ambitions of the producers, there is no such thing as a single Languedoc-Roussillon style.

The wines vary from cheap and cheerful to huge, beefy reds which can make a Hermitage from the Rhône slightly worried. The range is exhaustive, from elegant Pinot Noirs (such as Clovallon's) to wines which could be mistaken for classed-growth clarets; from pale and thin to rich, syrupy, sweet and fortified.

Where next?
For similar wines, try those from the southern **Rhône** and **Provence**. Other regions which have come a long way in a short time and have the potential to get better still include **Portugal**, southern **Italy**, especially **Apulia**, and **Argentina**. See also the specific entries for **Banyuls**, **Corbières**, **Costières de Nîmes**, **Coteaux du Languedoc**, **Côtes du Roussillon**, **Fitou**, **Minervois** and **Vin Doux Naturel**.

Loire

Underrated, underpriced

Best-known wines Chinon, Bourgueil, Saumur

Grape varieties Cabernet Franc, Pinot Noir, Gamay, Cabernet Sauvignon

Style Earthy, blackcurranty Cabernet Franc; light and fruity Pinot Noir

Quality/Price *·····›****/£·····›££££

The Loire is known more for whites and rosés than for reds. Along its length (more than 1,000 km/621 miles) it takes in a variety of styles from dry to sweet to sparkling, made from umpteen different grape varieties. Three red varieties figure prominently: the Pinot Noir of Sancerre, the Cabernet Franc of Anjou, Saumur, Bourgueil and Chinon, and the Gamay that crops up wherever there is not much else going on.

While grape varieties are the principal determinants of style, what all the wines here have in common, at least in the middle and lower reaches of the river, is the cool northern climate. The overall effect is to produce light, fresh wines, rather than the big, warming, concentrated wines found further south – in the Rhône Valley for example. Red wines made from Cabernet Franc are one of the great delights of the Loire, and unique to the

One of the many beautiful châteaux found along the length of the river Loire

six appellations of Anjou, Saumur, Saumur-Champigny, Chinon, Bourgueil and St-Nicolas-de-Bourgueil that lie on either side of the river between Angers and Tours (*see* **Anjou-Saumur**, **Bourgueil and Chinon**). Further upstream, the Burgundian emigré Pinot Noir is used for red Sancerre, Reuilly and Menetou-Salon, and in the same region, Pinot is blended with Gamay for Coteaux du Giennois reds.

Loire Gamay seldom measures up to Beaujolais. What is needed above all in such a gulping wine is fruit, and the Loire can sometimes be a bit mean in this respect, although the odd Gamay d'Anjou can be pleasantly light and quaffable.

The Loire taste The Cabernet Franc wines are covered in the Anjou-Saumur and Bourgueil and Chinon entries. Loire Gamay is seldom as succulently fruity as Beaujolais, although it can be sappily refreshing with raspberry flavours to the fore. Pinot Noir seldom ripens sufficiently to give wines of Burgundian depth, but wines such as Sancerre can be refreshing, bright and fruity, wearing their cherry and raspberry fruit with a smile, and not objecting to spending half an hour in the 'fridge before they are served.

Where next? As an alternative to the **Cabernet Franc**-based wines, try a light **Cabernet Sauvignon** from **Friuli-Venezia Giulia** or **Trentino-Alto Adige** (or one of that region's Schiava or Marzemino wines). For **Pinot Noir** alternatives, try **Alsace**, **Germany** or **Burgundy's** Passe-Tout-Grains (*see* **Gamay**). See also specific entries for **Anjou-Saumur** and **Bourgueil and Chinon**.

Lombardy

RECOMMENDED PRODUCERS

Bellavista
Ca' del Bosco
Fay
Le Fracce
Gatti
Guarischi
Monte Rossa
Nino Negri
Aldo Rainoldi
Conte Sertoli Salis
Triacca
Uberti
Vercesi del Castellazzo
Villa

For the fashionable set

Best-known wines Valtellina
Grape varieties Nebbiolo, Barbera, Bonarda, Cabernet Sauvignon, Merlot, Pinot Noir
Style Can be dilute but, at their best, Lombardy's Bordeaux blends are quite sumptuous, while Valtellina Superiore is rich and herby
Quality/Price *⋯⟩****/££⋯⟩£££££

Italy's wealthiest province isn't quite so wealthy where wine is concerned, although there are some decent reds to be found. Oltrepò Pavese is what the Milanese drink in large quantities, and in its red form, this is made from Pinot Noir,

Barbera or Bonarda. Valtellina, made mostly from Nebbiolo, is perhaps the best-known wine. In its basic form, it's not much to shout about, but Valtellina Superiore, especially that from Sasella (one of four sub-districts) is far better. Some producers make wines labelled *sforzato* using semi-dried grapes, rather like Veneto's *amarone*, and these can be very good. Franciacorta is now only used for sparkling wines. Reds from the region which used to come under this DOC (as it then was) are now labelled Terre di Franciacorta. Cabernet Franc and Cabernet Sauvignon are the main grapes here, with Barbera, Nebbiolo and Merlot also being permitted.

Traditional baskets used by grape pickers in Italy's Lombardy region

The Lombardy taste Many of the modern wines are characterised by the chosen grape variety and its treatment by an ambitious producer. The *terroir* influence may be there but it will only become apparent when several adjacent properties begin to make similar wines.

Oltrepò Pavese Bonarda is dark and plummy with a bitter edge, made in an attractive, rustic style. Basic Valtellina is simple and light, but *superiore* wines are rich yet elegant with deep, herby plum and cherry fruit. The *sforzato* versions are even more intense.

Where next? Follow the varietal path throughout the northern half of Italy. For **Nebbiolo** and **Barbera**, head for **Piedmont**. For the **Bordeaux** grapes and **Pinot Noir**, **Tuscany** offers many fine examples.

Madiran

As tough as they come
Region Southwest France
Grape varieties Tannat, Cabernet Franc, Cabernet Sauvignon, Fer
Style Tough, dense and meaty with savoury black fruit
Quality/Price *┈⟩****/££┈⟩££££

RECOMMENDED PRODUCERS
Boucassé
Capmartin
Lafitte-Teston
Montus
Peyros
Plaimont Co-op

Madiran is one of Southwest France's more curious survivors. It is made largely from the Tannat grape with back-up provided by Cabernet Sauvignon, Cabernet Franc and Fer. Tannat's skin is pretty thick, and winemakers struggle to tame the inherently high level of tannin. Where they fail, the wines are rather like those of Cahors, showing us an ankle, which is obviously attached to a leg, but always reluctant to expose the whole limb. Where they succeed, however, the wines can be very good, like chunky claret with a southwest accent. They still need time in bottle to soften, but not the decade or two that once was necessary.

The Madiran taste Once the finest Madiran has shrugged off its tannic shroud, fruit appears – rich berry and blackcurrant fruit with a hint of violets. Add a robe of spicy new oak and the wines can be excellent and very good value.

Where next? Cahors and Côtes du Frontonnais in the same region. Alternatively, try Uruguayan Tannat and Argentinian Malbec.

Maipo

RECOMMENDED PRODUCERS

Aquitania/Paul Bruno
Cánepa/Mapocho
Carmen
Concha y Toro
Cousiño Macul
Portal del Alto
Santa Carolina
Santa Inés
Santa Rita
Viña Tarapacá
Undurraga

Capital stuff

Best-known wines Cousiño Macul Antiguas Reserva
Grape varieties Cabernet Sauvignon, Merlot
Style At best, intense and spicy with lush, blackcurrant fruit
Quality/Price *····⟩****/£····⟩£££££

Chile's best-known red wine region is bang on the doorstep of the capital, Santiago. The two are closely connected, indeed rather too closely in some cases, with the suburbs spilling over into what was once prime vineyard land. Maipo was the first place to be fully exploited for wine production, and the producers have had rather longer than those in other parts of the country to work out which vineyards give the best fruit. Combine this with vines which, on average, are older than those in most other Chilean vineyards and it's no surprise to discover that this is where many of the country's finest reds come from. That the Bordeaux duo of Paul Pontallier (Margaux) and Bruno Prats (ex-Cos d'Estournel) chose Maipo as the place to plant their vines suggests that the region's reputation is based on more than having Santiago so close by.

The Maipo taste Although Cabernet Sauvignon dominates the vineyards, the wines vary markedly in style. Rich soil and excessive irrigation leads to simple, fruity flavours – blackcurrant pastilles in a glass but not much else. From better plots, which tend to be in the east of the region on the foothills of the Andes, the blackcurrant flavour becomes fuller and creamier, and spicy mint and tobacco flavours make their presence felt. Where other varieties appear, be they Merlot/Carmenère (*see* **Chile**), Syrah, even Nebbiolo and Sangiovese, they have proved very successful.

Where next? Other parts of **Chile**'s Central Valley and Aconcagua offer fine **Cabernet**s, albeit in smaller quantities. Hop, or rather pole-vault, over the Andes to **Argentina** to see what's happening in Mendoza.

Malbec

The chunky monkey
Style Berries, plums, violets and lots of rustic tannin
Grown in Bordeaux, Southwest France, Argentina, Chile, Australia, northeast Italy

Think of Malbec (or Cot, or Auxerrois, or Pressac, depending on where you are) as an honest, well-meaning grape, but one which will never quite make it into the major league. Its home is in Southwest France where it plays a minor role in the wines of Bordeaux, Bergerac, Côtes du Frontonnais and others, and a more prominent one in Cahors.

In Australia's Clare Valley, the winemakers blend it with Cabernet Sauvignon to good effect, but in common with most New World countries, it hardly ever appears as a pure varietal. South America is different. Malbec is Chile's third most widely planted variety where it makes juicy, chunky wines – apprentice Merlot, if you like. However, the variety seems to have found its true home in Argentina. This is the only place where Malbec shows some real class, either on its own or in blends with other grape varieties – most commonly Cabernet Sauvignon.

The Malbec taste Malbec in Southwest France makes solid, workmanlike wines sporting plenty of earthy tannins, behind which a glimpse of blackberry flavour is just about visible. Time tempers the structure, but not by much.

The best South American wines have that tannin and the chunky berry flavour, but there's less of the former and more of the latter, along with plums, violets and vanilla. They drink well from their youth, but can also age well.

Where next? First stop: **Piedmont**. If it's Malbec's fruit you're after, try **Dolcetto** or **Barbera**; if it's the structure, try **Nebbiolo**.

Margaret River

Australia's answer to Cornwall

Grape varieties Cabernet Sauvignon, Merlot,
Cabernet Franc, Pinot Noir, Shiraz, Zinfandel

Style Elegant Cabernet Sauvignon, fruity Pinot Noir

Quality/Price ***·····\}****/£££·····\}£££££

The Margaret River is warm, dry and sunny, with sea breezes to stop it getting too hot. Grapes love it, providing they get enough water, and ripen at a leisurely pace, acquiring rich, full flavours as they do. Cabernet Sauvignon is top dog, and performs very well, whether it's on its own or blended with Cabernet Franc and Merlot. Pinot Noir has proved slightly more problematic, although the best wines are very good indeed. Shiraz is wonderful, elegant stuff, while the Cape Mentelle winery even produces an ultra-rich and tasty Zinfandel.

The Margaret River taste At best, Margaret River Cabernet could easily be mistaken for claret, although the dense plum and blackberry flavours, hints of cedar and chocolate and silky tannins often have more in common with Merlot-based wines such as St-Emilion than with the Cabernet-heavy Médoc. Some wines can display eucalyptus and mint tones, which are pleasant providing they're only incidental. Pinot Noir tends to be rather lumpen and only a few examples have the silky texture of great Pinot. Shiraz is rich, spicy and peppery, while Cape Mentelle's Zinfandel shows sufficient berry and liquorice flavour to balance the 16 per cent-plus alcohol.

Where next? Australia's **Coonawarra** and **Yarra Valley** regions give similar elegance. Also see what the South Africans are doing.

Margaux

Perfume and refinement

Region Médoc

Grape varieties Cabernet Sauvignon, Cabernet Franc, Merlot, Petit Verdot, Malbec

Style Full of smooth, silky, blackcurrant, and cedarwood flavours

Quality/Price ***·····\}*****/£££·····\}£££££

Margaux makes, or can make, the most delicately, ethereally perfumed wines of the Médoc. It is the southernmost commune separated from the other major appellations (St-Julien, Pauillac and St-Estèphe) by five or six miles of nothing in particular. It is also the largest of the big four by virtue of including the villages of Arsac, Labarde, Soussans and Cantenac. It has more *cru classé* wines than any other commune, with the first-growth Château Margaux being the crowning glory. Unfortunately, consistency is a problem at many properties, with certain classed growths performing well below their potential. The distance from the other major communes also means that the weather conditions here are slightly different than in, say, Pauillac. For example, 1982 is considered a superb year for the Médoc, but the 1983 Margaux wines are every bit as good – and considerably cheaper.

The Margaux taste Margaux wines are characterised by finesse and an elegant, subtle, soft, velvety complexity. The perfume is what gets you. Anybody who drinks wine without smelling it first will miss most of the point of Margaux. But anybody who likes to sit with a glass, sipping, sniffing and savouring contemplatively will get their money's worth. Although apparently lightweight, the wines are not lacking in substance. They are smooth and silky, and easily age for 10 to 15 years.

Where next? Pauillac, St-Julien and St-Estèphe are the other great Médoc villages.

RECOMMENDED PRODUCERS CONTINUED

Margaux
Monbrison
Palmer
Prieuré-Lichine
Rauzan-Ségla
Siran
Du Tertre
La Tour-de-Mons

A château in the world-famous Margaux appellation

Marlborough

Not red Sauvignon Blanc
Grape varieties Merlot, Pinot Noir, Cabernet Sauvignon, Cabernet Franc, Syrah, Pinotage
Style Green-tinged Cabernet Sauvignon, fruity but simple Pinot Noir
Quality/Price **---}****/££---}£££££

RECOMMENDED PRODUCERS

Corbans
Cloudy Bay
Fromm
Grove Mill
Isabel Estate
Jackson Estate
Seresin

Unless something drastic happens to the global climate, Marlborough will always be best-known for its white and sparkling wines. That doesn't mean, however, that this part of New Zealand's South Island isn't capable of producing decent reds. Marlborough got off on the wrong foot by planting lots of Cabernet Sauvignon which only ripened in the best sites, and then

only in three years out of every ten. The few producers who have persisted with Cabernet now tend to blend it with Merlot, and the wines have improved, although not drastically. Merlot on its own can be successful, and plantings are now roughly equal to those of Cabernet. Pinot Noir is the most widely planted red grape, although most of it is used for sparkling wines. However, the still red versions can be very good, with the best – Fromm – matching those of anywhere in New Zealand. Fromm also makes a startlingly good Rhône-like Syrah, while Grove Mill's Pinotage is also highly rated.

The stunning, almost endless vineyards of Marlborough's Montana Brancott Estate

The Marlborough taste Marlborough Cabernet Sauvignon has quite intense blackcurrant flavours, but there is often the impression of greenness lurking in the background, no matter how skilful the winemaking. Merlot is better – rich and chocolatey with spicy, plummy fruit. Pinot Noir is usually correct rather than exciting, with raspberry and strawberry flavours but none of the wildness of great Pinot.

Where next? Still in NZ, try **Hawke's Bay** and Waiheke Island for Bordeaux-style reds, or **Martinborough** and Central Otago for **Pinot Noir**.

RECOMMENDED PRODUCERS
Ata Rangi
Dry River
Martinborough Vineyard
Palliser Estate
Te Kairanga

Martinborough

New Zealand's answer to Burgundy
Grape varieties Pinot Noir, Cabernet Sauvignon
Style Silky, alluring and fruity Pinot Noir
Quality/Price ***⋯⟩*****/£££⋯⟩£££££

You can't fault the folks in Martinborough at the base of New Zealand's North Island for not playing to their strengths. Nearly 60 per cent of the vineyards are taken up with the Burgundian varietals Chardonnay and Pinot Noir. And for once, Pinot is more prolific than Chardonnay, due to the fact that the people behind the region's three pioneering wineries – Dry River, Ata Rangi and Martinborough Vineyard – are all Pinot nuts. Their infectious enthusiasm has spurred on their neighbours to try Pinot, and guess what. Their wines are good, too, although not (yet) in the same class as the big three. There's twice as much Pinot Noir as all the rest of the red varieties put together, but there are some impressive Bordeaux blends and even a decent Syrah or two to be found.

The Martinborough taste The best wines offer texture, perfume and the wild, hard-to-pin-down, sexy allure that keeps you coming back for another sniff and sip. The Bordeaux blends have ripe, fleshy, blackcurrant fruit, with decent structure – they're good, but can't match the Pinots.

Where next? Central Otago, also in **New Zealand**, could threaten Martinborough's **Pinot** crown. See how **Australia's Yarra Valley**, **South Africa's** Walker Bay, and **California's Carneros** and **Central Coast** match up. For the **Bordeaux**-style wines, head up the east coast to **Hawke's Bay**.

McLaren Vale

As honest as the day is long
Grape varieties Shiraz, Cabernet Sauvignon, Grenache, Mourvèdre
Style Rich, full-flavoured, ripe and very fruity
Quality/Price ***⋯⟩****/££⋯⟩£££££

Perfect for the good old Aussie barbecue – finesse gives way here to intensity of flavour, and even the cheaper wines pack a good, fruity punch. The Shiraz is rich and mouth-filling, and also blends with other Rhône varieties such as Grenache and/or Mourvèdre (aka Mataro). Old-vine Grenache has been making strides in recent years, and Cabernet Sauvignon also thrives, giving excellent value at the lower end of the market, and some refined reds at higher levels.

RECOMMENDED PRODUCERS

D' Arenberg
Burton's Vineyard
Chapel Hill
Clarendon Hills
Coriole
Tim Gramp
Hardy's
Haselgrove
Maglieri
Geoff Merrill/Mount Hurtle
Chateau Reynella
Seaview
Tatachilla
Wirra Wirra
Woodstock

The McLaren Vale taste McLaren Vale Shiraz is rich and soft with honest, full, black-fruit flavours and ripe tannins. The same is true of the region's Cabernet: again ripe and fleshy with flavours of blackcurrant, liquorice, chocolate and pepper. Grenache is bigger still, with dense, juicy, berry and liquorice fruit, white pepper and soft, ripe tannins. Opening the bottle and decanting the wine a couple of hours before serving gives it time to breathe, otherwise you'll end up wrestling with a fruity monster.

Where next? Shiraz and Grenache from Clare and Barossa; Châteauneuf-du-Pape and some of the larger California Zinfandels.

Beaumont
Belgrave
Camensac
Cantemerle
Caronne-Ste-Gemme
Chasse-Spleen
Cissac
Citran
Clarke
Fourcas-Dupré
Fourcas-Hosten
Hanteillan
La Lagune
Lamarque
Lanessan
Liversan
Maucaillou
Moulin-à-Vent
Patache d'Aux
Potensac
Poujeaux
Sociando Mallet
La Tour de By
La Tour Haut Caussan
Vieux Robin

Médoc

Home of the stars

Best-known wines Margaux, Pauillac, St-Estèphe, St-Julien

Grape varieties Cabernet Sauvignon, Cabernet Franc, Merlot, Petit Verdot, Malbec

Style Refined, with blackcurrant, cedar and spice, good acidity and relatively high tannin

Quality/Price **·····⟩*****/££·····⟩£££££

The Médoc covers the region north of Bordeaux between the Gironde estuary and the Atlantic, incorporating eight appellations. Médoc is itself one of the eight, denoting wines made in the northern part of the region, in what used to be known as the Bas-Médoc because the land there is lower than in the Haut-Médoc.

There is much to be said for beginning an exploration of the region with the simple appellation Médoc. The heavier, clay-like soils of the northern Médoc are less well-drained than those of the Haut-Médoc, and have large plantings of Merlot, so the wines can be relatively soft and attractive when young. These are light, simple but flavoursome wines that do not need long to mature, and they are affordable.

Like Médoc, the Haut-Médoc is also itself a catchment appellation for wines made in the southern part of the region that are not covered by the six smaller AOCs within its boundaries. From south to north these are Margaux, Moulis, Listrac, St-Julien, Pauillac and St-Estèphe.

Haut-Médoc wines act as a bridge between straightforward Médoc and the village appellations. Varying in quality and style right across the spectrum, some are big-flavoured, occasionally rough and ready, while others are lighter, softer and gentler. Fairly well-drained and mostly gravel soils make a difference to quality in this southern half of the region nearest to Bordeaux, and Cabernet tends to be the dominant grape. Unlike in the Médoc, there are some *crus classés* here, the best of which are La Lagune and Cantemerle, as well as an impressive array of *cru bourgeois* properties led by Sociando Mallet.

Of the six appellations within the Haut-Médoc region, Moulis and Listrac are the junior members. Neither can boast a *cru classé*, but Moulis in particular with Chasse-Spleen, Maucaillou and Poujeaux can offer wines of *cru classé* quality. At the top of the Médoc tree are four of the world's most famous wine names. Margaux is wonderfully perfumed with great finesse, St-Julien is elegant and balanced, Pauillac can be stern and

Vines are not
the only things
to thrive in
the rich land
of the Médoc

forbidding when young but ages to cedary perfection, while St-Estèphe is robust and full-bodied. Wine-lovers the world over are familiar with châteaux such as Lafite, Latour, Cos d'Estournel, Margaux, Léoville-Las-Cases and Mouton-Rothschild, and demand for such wines is high. Fortunately, (and unlike France's other great wine region) Burgundy production is not limited to half a dozen barrels of each, and there is usually little problem getting hold of any of the top wines – providing you can afford them.

If you can't, there are two solutions. The four villages have several properties making wine which, while not a match for the big boys, is still of very good quality and is much more reasonably priced. The other solution is to look for a château's "second wine". In an effort to ensure that their top wine is of the very highest quality, Médoc winemakers often exclude batches of wine which are not up to scratch or don't fit in with their blending regime. These "rejects" can still be of very good quality and are used to produce these second wines (some producers take the process one stage further, even making third wines).

Some second wines regularly outclass – and outprice – *cru classé* châteaux. The best of the Médoc second wines are Clos du Marquis (from Léoville-Las-Cases), Les Forts de Latour (Latour), Carruades de Lafite-Rothschild (Lafite-Rothschild) and Pavillon Rouge du Château Margaux (Margaux). Not far behind are Haut-Bages-Averous (Lynch-Bages), Lady Langoa (Léoville and Langoa-Barton), Réserve de la Comtesse (Pichon-Lalande), Réserve du Général (Palmer) and Sarget de Gruaud-Larose (Gruaud-Larose). The rule of thumb is that if the first wine is good, the second wine is worth a punt.

The Médoc taste The thick-skinned Cabernet Sauvignon grape dominates in the Médoc, making glorious, blackcurranty wines with good acidity and relatively high tannin. But the softer Merlot and other varieties, including Cabernet Franc, Malbec and Petit Verdot, bring an element of complexity to the wines that Cabernet Sauvignon rarely achieves by itself. They combine with the gravelly soil to make a lot of highly drinkable wines and quite a number of excellent wines. The best are utterly sublime and inimitable.

Haut-Médoc and the better Médoc wines have good structure and good blackcurrant fruit, while oak-ageing gives them more than a hint of the attractive, cedary spice of classic Bordeaux. Listrac tends to be rather tannic and solid, like a lesser St-Estèphe, and can take a decade to unwind. Moulis is a bit softer, more balanced and more approachable. Many are ready at five years old but will then last a decade or more.

Where next? After sampling the delights of **Margaux, Pauillac, St-Julien** and **St-Estèphe**, try the wines of the **Graves** (also based on Cabernet Sauvignon). Rivals from other parts of the world come from **Tuscany, Napa Valley, Sonoma, Coonawarra, Margaret River, Stellenbosch, Maipo** and Mendoza in **Argentina**.

Merlot

Soft and sellable
Style Soft and sweet with an easy, plummy, berry-fruit texture
Grown in Bordeaux, northern Italy, eastern Europe, California, New Zealand, Australia and South Africa

Easy to grow, easy to sell, easy to pronounce and easy to drink. No wonder Merlot is the current darling of wine marketing men everywhere. Americans in particular can't get enough of this plump, plummy grape, and the magic "M" word on a bottle of wine means that it won't hang around on the shelves for long, almost regardless of where it comes from.

But this hasn't always been the case. Merlot used to be the bridesmaid, shuffling up the aisle behind Cabernet Sauvignon. It was the weak twin with a shorter life expectancy, the "where-would-I-be-without-strong-tall-dark-handsome-Cabernet Sauvignon" grape. Never mind that in the stronghold of Cabernet, Bordeaux, it was Merlot that was more widely planted by a factor of two; Merlot was still the second-class citizen.

So what happened? Put it down to the two P's: Pomerol and Parker. Of the Bordeaux appellations, Pomerol is the one where Merlot performs at its best and where it frequently forms the largest proportion of the blend, usually with Cabernet Franc in support. The most famous Pomerol, Pétrus, is over 90 per cent Merlot. Throughout the 1980s, Pétrus and a growing number of other châteaux made a succession of impressive wines which attracted the attention of American wine critic Robert Parker. Parker's high marks sent "buy" signals to thousands of American wine-lovers. But with some châteaux measuring their output in hundreds of cases, rather than in tens of thousands as is often the case in the Médoc, demand vastly exceeded supply and prices soared.

Word got out that Merlot was behind Bordeaux's most sought after wines and demand rose to the extent that Merlot is now the red equivalent of Chardonnay, with many people buying varietal versions regardless of their origin. The soft, quite sweetish, fruity wines for early consumption which Merlot most wants to make provide an ideal introduction to novice red wine drinkers.

It is used in the Bordeaux blend to bring softness, sweetness and an easy-drinking nature to the harder, greener Cabernet Sauvignon. But even in the traditional Merlot strongholds of Pomerol and St-Emilion, Cabernets Franc and Sauvignon play a major part in the final wine, bringing the tannin and acidity which Merlot lacks. The rare wines that are more than 90 per cent Merlot crop up only where exceptional *terroir* is combined with great attention to detail in the vineyard and winery.

Left to its own devices, Merlot runs riot in many vineyards, producing high yields of rather flavourless grapes which, because of the heavy crop on the vines, can struggle to ripen fully if conditions aren't favourable. The resulting wine may be pleasant, perhaps with a slightly herbal edge, but nothing to crow about. In these situations, the long macerations often used with Merlot to extract as much tannin and flavour from the grapeskins as possible only succeed in extracting more of the underripe flavour.

So which places are succeeding with Merlot? Let's start with Bordeaux. Only in the Médoc and Graves is Merlot not the most important variety, and then it's the second most important. Apart from Pomerol, St-Emilion and their satellites, other "right bank" appellations such as Fronsac, Canon Fronsac, Côtes de Castillon and Côtes de Francs use Merlot to good effect, although always in a blend. Basic Bordeaux Rouge is generally Merlot-heavy and usually rather less appealing, although there are several notable exceptions.

Merlot also plays its part in other wines of Southwest France such as Bergerac, Pécharmant, Côtes de Duras, Buzet and Cahors – although rarely as a single varietal. Languedoc-Roussillon, however, offers blends and stand-alone versions, the latter varying from insipid to deep and rich. In Eastern Europe, wines from Bulgaria, Romania and

Hungary also vary widely in quality, with the best, such as those from Bulgaria's Haskovo region, being among the finest Merlot value available.

Merlot came to Italy with Napoleon, and is produced as a varietal in more than a dozen of the country's northeastern DOCs (*see* **Friuli-Venezia Giulia, Veneto**), as well as over the border in Switzerland's Ticino region. While many of the wines are pale and not very interesting, a growing number of more ambitious winemakers are turning out very good versions. Throughout the country, Merlot is appearing in the vineyards and being used either on its own or in Bordeaux-style blends, again with rapidly increasing success. Spain hasn't taken to Merlot with the same enthusiasm, though the grape does appear in Ribera del Duero, Navarra and a number of other regions.

The New World region that has embraced Merlot with the greatest success is Washington State. The wine quality is uniformly high, with some real superstars such as Andrew Will, but even so, many producers feel that Cabernet Sauvignon will eventually provide the better wines. Northern neighbour British Columbia has some reasonable Merlots from the Okanagan Valley, with the best demonstrating real potential. Further south in California, there's a huge range of quality, with the simple, sweetish Merlots of the Central Valley having little in common with the high-alcohol, ultra-ripe wines of Howell Mountain in Napa Valley.

Chile produces some of the world's best value Merlot – only most of it isn't Merlot, but Carmenère (*see* **Chile**). Where producers have managed to separate the two varieties successfully, true Merlot often seems to miss that extra-spicy bite of Carmenère, although this may change as the vines age.

Australia hasn't embraced Merlot with great fervour. It's used mostly in blends, although much of the Cabernet is ripe and soft enough not to need it. Shiraz is often preferred as a partner. The few stand-alone varietal versions have been good – sometimes very good.

New Zealanders are more enthusiastic about Merlot, since Cabernet can struggle to ripen in some of their vineyards. Hawke's Bay is the main outpost, although even here, blends are usually the order of the day. Marlborough has switched allegiance from Cabernet to Merlot, and the small number of varietal versions get better with each vintage. In South African vineyards, there is less than half as much Merlot planted as there is Cabernet Sauvignon, but its influence is spreading, both for blending and for varietal wines.

The Merlot taste Crop it too high and Merlot is simply pleasant and fruity and instantly forgettable. However, top-class Merlot is sweetly fruity, full-flavoured, plummy, juicy, forward, supple, soft, rich, smooth, velvety and silky. It scores as much for texture as for taste. Thinner-skinned than

Cabernet, it produces less tannin and its wines are therefore softer and ready to drink sooner. The sweetness is deceptive, however. The wine is dry, but because its acidity may be low (especially in mature wines) the fruit can appear broad and languorous. This may also be accentuated by the grape's typically high alcohol levels. It takes well to oak, the spiciness giving it a lift of flavour, just as a handful of fresh mint improves a blackcurrant pie.

Where next? Other grapes that produce particularly soft wines include the Italian Montepulciano and **Dolcetto**, although the latter always has perky acidity to freshen it up. Wines made by carbonic maceration, such as **Beaujolais**, can also be quite soft. And many wines that begin life aggressively will soften with age, so try a mature wine made from some of the major grape varieties.

Minervois

Spicy southern value
Region Languedoc
Grape varieties Carignan, Syrah, Mourvèdre, Grenache, Lladoner Pelut
Style Warm, spicy and resiny, with plum, blackcurrant and berry fruit
Quality/Price *····⟩****/£····⟩£££

RECOMMENDED PRODUCERS

Clos Centeilles/Domergue
Coupe Roses
Fabas
De la Fontberterie
De Gourgazaud
Maris
Les Ollieux
Piccinini
Ste-Eulalie
La Tour Boisée
Villerambert-Julien

Minervois lies to the north of Corbières and the River Aude in Languedoc. Its wines are good value, but something of a lucky dip in terms of style. Carignan is the main grape, although its influence is decreasing. From the 1999 vintage, this variety will account for no more than 40 per cent of Minervois blends. Meanwhile, Syrah, Mourvèdre and Grenache are becoming more important. So your Minervois may be a simple carbonic maceration glugger or it may be a rather more serious 100 per cent Syrah wine. How do you tell which is which? Buy some bottles and pull the corks; the wines aren't expensive.

The Minervois taste Lighter Minervois is juicy, raspberry-fruity and made for drinking now. Better versions are warm, welcoming and spicy, full of rich, sweet, smoky, blackcurrant, plum and berry flavours, often with a hint of vanilla on the finish courtesy of oak ageing.

Where next? **Côtes du Roussillon**, **Corbières**, St-Chinian, Faugères and the **Coteaux du Languedoc** are the local competition.

Monterey and San Francisco Bay Areas

Diverse and delicious

Best-known wines Ridge Monte Bello

Grape varieties Cabernet Sauvignon, Pinot Noir, Zinfandel, Mourvèdre, Syrah

Style Earthy Santa Cruz Cabernet, violety Calera Pinots

Quality/Price ***·····⟩*****/££·····⟩£££££

This region in America might not be the first on the tip of a wine-lover's tongue. Yet, when it comes to quality, this disparate region has some of the State's finest wines, which if they came from Napa would be able to charge two or even three times the price and still sell out before you could say "hand-crafted wine".

East of San Francisco is Contra Costa County, where Zinfandel, Mourvèdre and other spicy grapes thrive. While there aren't too many wineries here, producers throughout California take advantage of the excellent quality of the old-vine fruit. The Livermore and Santa Clara valleys produce good, medium-priced wines, although encroaching suburbs and the expanding Silicon Valley enterprises threaten both.

The star region is the Santa Cruz Mountains where the altitude and sea breezes keep the temperatures down, enabling growers to produce dark, small-berried and intensely flavoured Cabernet Sauvignon grapes, used most memorably in Ridge's superb Monte Bello. The wine regions around Monterey Bay are similarly spread out. Pinot Noir vineyards are to be found perched on hills, with Mount Harlan's Calera being the best example. Cooling breezes from the bay make the northern end of the Salinas Valley ideal for Merlot, while districts further upstream are more suited for Cabernet Sauvignon. Carmel Valley lies between Salinas and the coast and so far has concentrated on Cabernet blends, although the occasional Pinot Noir can be found.

Cabernet Sauvignon vines in the Smith and Hook estate in Monterey

The Monterey and San Francisco Bay taste Santa Cruz Cabernet is earthy, with rich, baked-berry fruit and hints of moccha. Calera's Pinot Noirs have lovely summer fruit, with violets, leather and earth. Contra Costa Mourvèdre has lovely, ripe, sweet fruit and nuances of cloves and mint.

Where next? Napa Valley for **Cabernet**; **Carneros** and the **Central Coast** for **Pinot Noir** and wherever-you-can-find-it for **Mourvèdre**.

Morey-St-Denis

The forgotten one
Region Côte de Nuits
Grape varieties Pinot Noir
Style Perfumed and fruity, with the structure to age well
Quality/Price ***⋯⟩*****/£££⋯⟩£££££

RECOMMENDED PRODUCERS

Clos de Tart
Dujac
Des Lambrays
Robert Groffier
Georges Lignier
Hubert Lignier
Perrot-Minot
Ponsot
Jean Raphet

Quite why Morey-St-Denis has never elicited the same reverence as Gevrey-Chambertin to the north or Chambolle-Musigny to the south is something of a mystery. While there is no vineyard with the renown of Musigny or Chambertin, there are no fewer than five *grands crus*: Bonnes Mares (shared with Chambolle-Musigny), Clos des Lambrays, Clos de la Roche, Clos St-Denis and Clos de Tart. Clos de la Roche is considered the finest of these. But if the wines from Clos des Lambrays and Clos de Tart, both *monopoles* (having only one owner), continue to improve in the way they have done since the mid-1990s, they could challenge Clos de la Roche for top spot. There are also 25 *premiers crus*, although none really stand out, and their wines are often blended together.

Years of people saying that Morey-St-Denis is the best-value village in the Côte d'Or have meant that the wines are not as cheap as they used to be, but they are still good value – in Côte de Nuits terms.

The Morey-St-Denis taste The wines of Morey-St-Denis are generally lighter than those of Gevrey and more delicate, which seems to emphasise their perfume. But they are still up with the best wines of the Côte for quality, for mouth-filling fruitiness and staying power (15 to 20 years' ageing for the top wines). The best wines have a stylish, velvety quality about them that develops into coffee and liquorice flavours with age.

Where next? North to **Gevrey** for more power, south to **Chambolle** for more perfume.

Mourvèdre

Give me sunshine
Style White pepper, pine resin, blackcurrants, berries and dried-fruits
Grown in Southern Rhône, southern France (especially Provence),
Spain, California, South Australia

It's a shame there's not more of this characterful grape around. However, it does need a spot of heat; otherwise it doesn't ripen. As Monastrell, Mourvèdre is Spain's second most widely planted red grape after Garnacha, with much of it being found in the regions around Valencia. It's also used for Cava rosé.

The antioxidant properties of Mourvèdre are made use of throughout southern France where it brings a touch of discipline to the rather wayward and oxidation-prone Grenache in appellations such as Châteauneuf-du-Pape. It is also, along with Syrah, gaining ground in the Languedoc at the expense of the less interesting Carignan and Cinsault. Few French wines use it on its own, though Bandol is an exception being at least 50 to 100 per cent Mourvèdre.

In South Australia and California, the grape is often known as Mataro. Both regions had large plantings of the variety in the past, but ripped much of it out between the 1960s and late 1980s. However, when the Rhône varieties began to regain popularity, the demand for Mourvèdre grew, and there are even a few new plantings of the variety. It usually appears in blends with Grenache and Syrah, but varietal versions from California's Contra Costa County can be excellent. Fairview Mourvèdre is at present South Africa's one example.

The Mourvèdre taste In wines such as Châteauneuf-du-Pape, Mourvèdre is the seasoning, bringing a touch of white pepper and some tannin to Grenache. On its own in Bandol, the wines are steamy and meaty with rich, savoury fruit characters, and need plenty of time to show their true class. Californian Mourvèdre has sweet, berry and blackcurrant fruit seasoned by notes of cloves, mint, chocolate and pine resin.

Where next? Of the other southern French grapes, **Syrah** is more elegant and fruitier, **Grenache** jammier and sweeter. For a slight change of tack, try **Malbec**, which can have similar flavours, or look for the rare examples of Petit Verdot, as **Mourvèdre** is often used to provide backbone and seasoning.

Napa Valley

Bordeaux quality, Bordeaux prices
Best-known wines Opus One, Stag's Leap Wine Cellars Cask 23,
Heitz Martha's Vineyard
Grape varieties Cabernet Sauvignon, Merlot, Cabernet Franc,
Syrah, Pinot Noir, Sangiovese
Style Glossy, polished Cabernet Sauvignon; rich, earthy Merlot
Quality/Price ***⋯⟩*****/£££⋯⟩£££££

RECOMMENDED PRODUCERS

Beringer
Cain
Caymus
Chappellet
Château Montelena
Clos du Val
Corison
Diamond Creek
Dominus
Duckhorn
Dunn
Elyse
Flora Springs
Franciscan
Frog's Leap
Green & Red
Hess Collection
Jade Mountain
Pahlmeyer
Joseph Phelps
Kent Rasmussen
La Jota
Monticello
Newton
Niebaum-Coppola
Opus One
Robert Mondavi
Shafer
Silver Oak
Stag's Leap Wine Cellars
Swanson

For many people Napa Valley *is* Californian wine. Production in the Central Valley may be far greater, but it can't boast over 200 wineries – nor a wine train. Napa has been making great wines since the mid-1800s, but *phylloxera* and then Prohibition combined to almost destroy the region's wine industry. The turning point in Napa's history came when Robert Mondavi decided to establish his own winery in the valley in 1966, since when the region hasn't looked back.

Cabernet Sauvignon is Napa's main grape. However, styles have changed considerably over the last 30 years from wines which were often 100 per cent Cabernet to wines where Merlot and Cabernet Franc play a much more active part. Merlot is also very popular for varietal wines, and the small number of Cabernet Francs on the market have been very successful.

Other than the Bordeaux grapes, you'll find a few very fine Syrah wines, as well as some Sangiovese, either by itself or blended with Cabernet. Napa Zinfandel can also be very good, although Cabernet is tending to displace it from most vineyards. Pinot Noir used to be planted in the valley, but now is more common in the cooler Carneros region where it makes some of California's finest Pinot.

Napa Valley is not one homogeneous entity, as the success of Pinot in Carneros shows. As you travel north up Highway 29 away from the town of Napa, the cooling influence of San Francisco Bay diminishes so that difference in temperatures from south to north can be as much as 5 °C (41 °F); that's on the valley floor. Head up the hills either side, and again the temperature falls. Add in the wide variety of soil types, and it's easy to see that not all Napa wines will taste the same. Cabernet's traditional stronghold has been around the towns of Rutherford and Oakville, especially on the west side of the valley. However, it's also very successful in Stags Leap District, further south on the east side of the valley, and on

Clos du Val winery in the excellent Stags Leap district of Napa Valley

Mount Veeder, opposite. The two other Cabernet beauty spots, Howell Mountain and Spring Mountain, face each other across the northern end of the valley near Calistoga. Robert Louis Stevenson, who honeymooned here, described the wines as "bottled poetry". It's still true today, although some of them go for the price of first editions. Many of these come from micro-estates – Bryant Family, Grace, Screaming Eagle, Araujo, Dalla Valle and others – which make tiny quantities of wine that is virtually impossible to find apart from in the smartest restaurants. Never mind that they have little or no track record; the influential critics like them and that, sadly, for many people, is all they're interested in.

The Napa Valley taste Napa Cabernet has swung from 1970s monster through early 1980s recluse to the well-balanced individual it is today. Black olives, blackberries, blackcurrants, cherries, plums, vanilla, cedar, spice and tar are common tasting notes. The raw tannins of yesteryear have given way to a more polished structure which will make the wines just as age-worthy, but means that many can be enjoyed soon after release. Merlot can be almost as expansive, with similar flavours.

Where next? The majority of **America's** finest **Cabernet Sauvignon**s are produced here, so for valid comparisons an intercontinental journey is needed – to **Bordeaux** and **Tuscany** or to **Coonawarra** and **Margaret River** in **Australia**. If the **Carneros Pinot Noir**s appeal, see what **Oregon** has to offer before returning to the Old World classics of **Burgundy**.

Navarra

More than just Rioja in short trousers
Grape varieties Tempranillo, Cabernet Sauvignon, Garnacha, Merlot
Style Dusty, with spicy chocolate, berry and plum flavours
Quality/Price *⋯⟩****/£⋯⟩££££

Navarra has traditionally depended on the Garnacha and Tempranillo grape varieties, making wines which wanted to be Rioja but never quite managed to achieve the class. However, recent years have seen Cabernet Sauvignon and, to a lesser extent, Merlot, taking hold in the vineyards, often at the expense of Garnacha, and the wines being made today are among the best value in Spain. The Tempranillo/Cabernet blend is proving especially successful, and the newer grapes are also making some fine varietal wines. But don't write Garnacha off just yet. It still makes some lovely, easy-drinking wines, and the occasional old-vine blockbuster.

The Navarra taste There's a spicy, dusty note to many Navarra wines, whatever the variety, with chocolate, plum and berry flavours. Unoaked wines are upfront and juicy and Tempranillo/Cabernet blends are full-bodied and fleshy, not the most complex wines, but honest and full of flavour.

Where next? Rioja is the obvious first port of call, but after that see how good Garnacha is, often with a helping hand from **Cabernet**, in **Priorato**.

Chivite's Arinzano estate is an oasis in Spain's Navarra region

Nebbiolo

Tough and foggy
Style Tar, roses, truffles, prunes, violets and raspberries
Grown in Piedmont, California, Mexico, Australia

This grape variety is a sort of Italian Pinot Noir, in the sense that, like Pinot Noir in Burgundy, it shines brilliantly in one small area: the hills of Piedmont in the northwest. The light spills over into surrounding Lombardy and illuminates a corner of Valle d'Aosta but, Nebbiolo-wise, most of the rest of the world is pitch black. Nebbiolo differs from Pinot Noir in that few winemakers elsewhere in the world have been inspired to grow it in more than tiny experimental quantities. In addition, the big, long-lasting, tannic red wines that it makes are totally unlike anything from Burgundy.

Barolo and Barbaresco are the best and best-known incarnations of Nebbiolo, but it also contributes to another dozen or so wines from northwest Italy, including Nebbiolo d'Alba, Valtellina, Gattinara and Ghemme. It is a thick-skinned variety that ripens as late as October and November – several weeks after Dolcetto has been picked. During the long autumns that separate hot summers from cold winters in this predominantly continental climate, Nebbiolo's thick skin enables it to withstand any rot that might develop in the foggy Langhe hills around Alba (*nebbia* is Italian for a pea-souper).

The thick skin is also responsible for one of Nebbiolo's most marked and obvious attributes: tannin. Another characteristic is high acidity, which late ripening helps to reduce slightly, although it never drops very low. Not surprisingly, tannin and acidity combine to make wines that need long ageing before they are ready to drink. Add a little Barbera, however, and Nebbiolo calms down, keeping its flavours but having its structure fleshed out by the come-hither charms of Barbera. Wines such as this can be very good, and provide an ideal introduction to Nebbiolo.

Nebbiolo does appear outside northwest Italy, but not widely. In the Veneto, Quintarelli makes a *recioto* (*see* **Italy**) from it which has an outstanding reputation. There are also commercial versions available if you can find them from producers in South Africa (Steenberg), Mexico (LA Cetto) and Australia (Dromana Estate), while Californian Nebbiolos even manage to stretch into double figures, with Il Podere dell' Olivos and Robert Mondavi being the highest-profile producers.

The Nebbiolo taste For size, beefiness, longevity and alcohol, Nebbiolo can easily give Shiraz/Syrah a run for its money. But, it can be a tough nut to crack because its appeal usually derives from those aromas and tastes that develop with age. Many's the time you can search for violets, tar, wild herbs, raspberries, cherries, tobacco and truffles and find none of them – or find that they are still covered in an blanket of harsh, gum-puckering material, as impenetrable as a thick *nebbia*. Not a beginner's wine.

Where next? Other weighty wines like **Châteauneuf-du-Pape**, Australian **Shiraz, Hermitage, Cornas, California Zinfandel** and **Syrah**, top Argentinian **Malbec, Brunello** di Montalcino, Super-Tuscans (*see* **Tuscany**).

New South Wales

Good but not great
Grape varieties Shiraz, Cabernet Sauvignon
Style Rich, peppery Hunter Valley Shiraz; plump Mudgee Shiraz and Cabernet
Quality/Price **·····⟩****/£·····⟩£££££

RECOMMENDED PRODUCERS
Bloodwood
Botobolar
Canobolas Smith
Cassegrain
Doonkuna
Huntington Estate
Miramar
Montrose
Trentham Estate

In terms of both quality and quantity of wine produced, New South Wales is very firmly in third place, after South Australia and Victoria. Even the Hunter Valley, perhaps Australia's most famous wine region, struggles to keep up with the standards set in other parts of the country.

There is more to new South Wales than the Hunter, however. Second in the quality league comes Mudgee, which lies about 240 km (150 miles) northwest of Sydney at an elevation of 1,500 to 2,000 feet (500 to 600 m) which keeps it relatively cool. The grapes, mostly Cabernet and Shiraz, benefit from a long, slow growing season that produces balanced, ripe fruit flavours. There is a much vaunted appellation system, "Certified Mudgee Appellation Wine", which requires that the grapes come from where they say they do, ie Mudgee. If the Mudgee-ites devoted as much energy to making better wines than they give to devising such schemes, they could produce wines at least as good as those from the Lower Hunter. At present, an outsider – Rosemount – makes the region's finest wine.

Riverina, otherwise known as the Murrumbidgee Irrigation Area or MIA, is the high-volume region, the equivalent of Victoria's Murray River or South Australia's Riverland. Other pockets of vines appear at Port Macquarie, Orange, around Canberra and at Cowra, the last three all benefiting from the cooling effect of high altitude.

The New South Wales taste Mudgee Cabernet Sauvignon and Shiraz are full-flavoured and rich with moderate to high tannin levels and good acidity to keep them lively and help the ageing process. Some wines can be quite elegant, especially if they are allowed to age for five years or more. Oak-ageing develops spicy, cedary flavours. With so few wineries in the other districts, regional styles have yet to emerge, although Orange Cabernet seems to offer something of the same elegance and depth of flavour as Mudgee, while Canberra Shiraz can be crisp and peppery.

Where next? **Victoria** and **South Australia** are the main wine-producing states in **Australia**. See also the entry for **Hunter Valley**.

New York State

RECOMMENDED PRODUCERS

Bedell
Bridgehampton
Gristina
Hargrave
Lenz
Millbrook
Palmer
Paumonok
Peconic Bay
Pellegrini
Pindar
Schneider

There's more to Long Island than just Iced Tea
Grape varieties Merlot, Cabernet Sauvignon, Cabernet Franc, Pinot Noir
Style Simple, plummy Merlot; easy, blackcurranty Cabernet Sauvignon
Quality/Price *⋯⋯⋟****/££⋯⋯⋟£££££

There's still plenty of wine made in New York State from labrusca and hybrid grapes, but more and more, we're seeing vintners having success with more orthodox *vinifera* grapes, especially Merlot and Cabernet Sauvignon. Some of these come from the Finger Lakes region, but the majority come from the North Fork of Long Island, where the surrounding water tempers both winter and summer temperatures and the growing season is almost three weeks longer than in other parts of the state.

The New York State taste With only around 14 wineries in New York State's most densely populated region, many of which have few vintages under their belt, it's the winemaking doing the talking in most cases.

Merlot tends to be full-flavoured and plummy, but never matching the intensity of the finest Washington State or Californian versions. Cabernet Sauvignon tastes like well-made Cabernet Sauvignon: ripe and blackcurranty, with a slight herbal edge.

Where next? See how the **Merlot** and **Cabernet Sauvignon** compare with those of Ontario to the north or **Washington State** way over to the west.

Nuits-St-Georges

Back on form

Region Côte de Nuits
Grape varieties Pinot Noir
Style Sturdy, sweet and plummy
Quality/Price **⋯⟩*****/£££⋯⟩£££££

RECOMMENDED PRODUCERS

RECOMMENDED PRODUCERS

Bertrand Ambroise
De l'Arlot
Daniel Bocquenet
Chauvenet
Chauvenet-Chopin
Chopin-Groffier
Michel Chevillon
Robert Chevillon
Faiveley
Jean-Jacques Confuron
Henri Gouges
Machard de Gramont
Dominique Laurent
Fernand Lecheneaut
Alain Michelot
Prieure Roch
Remoriquet
Daniel Rion
Thomas-Moillard

Nuits-St-Georges has recovered from a temperamental past when much of what appeared under its name came from distant and rather warmer regions – keep going when you get to the Med, let's put it that way. Indeed, today's wines are some of the most reliable in Burgundy, and are usually fairly priced. While there are no *grands crus*, there is no shortage of *premiers crus* (27) and they cover a lot of ground. Les St-Georges, Les Vaucrains, Les Pruliers, Les Boudots, Les Porrets and Les Cailles are considered the best vineyards.

The Nuits-St-Georges taste As you move southward through the appellation, there's quite a variation in style. Wines from vineyards abutting those of Vosne-Romanée tend to be more elegant and silky than those from the southern end, where the wines are rather less refined. Typical Nuits may not have the nobility or breeding of Vosne-Romanée or Gevrey-Chambertin, but it does have Pinot Noir's flavoursome plums and sweet gaminess in a well-structured and sturdy frame.

Where next? Gevrey-Chambertin, Corton and **Pommard** are among the more muscly wines of **Burgundy**.

Oak barrels sit snuggly, maturing wine in a cellar in Nuits-St-George

Oregon

As tasty and frustrating as Burgundy
Best-known wines Willamette Valley Pinot Noir
Grape varieties Pinot Noir, Cabernet Sauvignon,
Merlot, Zinfandel
Style Full of silky, spicy, raspberry and plum flavours
Quality/Price **····}****/££····}£££££

Most of Oregon is about as suitable for viticulture as
Mongolia. The high plateaux, the Gobi Desert latitudes and
the long, cold winters are enough to frighten the pips out
of even the most half-witted grape. Oregon, though, has
the moderating Pacific lounging on its doormat. Above all
it has a long valley – the Willamette – south of Portland, cut
between two mountain ranges, where grapes are able to sit
and ripen lightly beneath an uncertain sun. It is the
uncertainty of this sunshine that has won Oregon fame, for
"marginal ripening conditions" are exactly what Pinot Noir
is supposed to want (although the Pinot Noir grown very successfully in
parts of California doesn't seem to be aware of this fact).

Oregon first showed the world that it could make Pinot Noir in 1979,
when Eyrie's 1975 Pinot Noir was runner-up to Robert Drouhin's 1959
Chambolle-Musigny in a Paris tasting. But anyone who thought this was
the start of a deluge of top-class Oregon Pinot was wrong. Occasional wines
popped up to demonstrate that Eyrie's
success wasn't a freak, but they were
accompanied by a rather dreary entourage.

It wasn't until the 1990s, when producers
began to replant their vineyards with better
clones more suited to their climate, that
Oregon began to achieve more consistency,
with the best wines being very good indeed.
Some of these come from local producers
who have been gradually getting better and
better over the years, but some are the result
of investment from outside the state. Much
of this is from California, but some comes
from further afield. Robert Drouhin's
reaction to the 1979 tasting was to establish
Domaine Drouhin Oregon, which today
makes arguably the finest Pinot in the state.

Oregon's temperamental climate is perfect for ripening Pinot Noir grapes

Most of the Pinot comes from the northern Willamette Valley, Oregon's largest wine region. As you travel south into the Umpqua, the rainfall drops, the sun appears more regularly and, while Pinot is still to be found, it's possible to grow other grapes such as Cabernet Sauvignon and Syrah. The southernmost region, the Rogue Valley, lies very close to the Californian border, and there's even some Zinfandel and Sangiovese here. But unless something changes drastically, Oregon will be known for many years to come for its Pinot Noir.

The Oregon taste Oregon's Pinot Noirs are moving slowly beyond the light, acidic and unbalanced style, becoming instead more carnally perfumed and gracefully structured, full of raspberry and blackberry fruit and peppery excitement. Now they are capable of acquiring complexity over a decade or more without ever losing liveliness, poise and pungency.

Where next? In **California**'s less erratic climate, **Pinot Noir** thrives in cooler regions such as **Carneros** and in parts of the **Monterey** Bay Area and **Central Coast**. After that, there's always a place called **Burgundy**...

Paarl

The Pearl of South Africa
Grape varieties Cabernet Sauvignon, Merlot, Cabernet Franc, Pinotage, Shiraz
Style Hugely varied
Quality/Price *⋯⟩****/£⋯⟩£££££

RECOMMENDED PRODUCERS
Backsberg
Bellingham
Boschendal
Cabrière
Claridge
Fairview
Glen Carlou
Haute Provence/Agusta
KWV/Cathedral Cellars
La Motte
Nederburg
L'Ormarins
Plaisir de Merle
R de R Fredericksburg
Simonsvlei
Veenwouden
Villiera
Welgemeend

While Paarl – meaning "pearl" – can't boast the same number of high-class wineries as neighbouring Stellenbosch in the south, tucked into its many nooks and crannies are several extremely fine producers who are making wine of excellent quality. Much of Paarl is warm and flat, but there are also higher hillside vineyards and adjoining valleys, the most famous of which is Franschhoek.

This is a region of innovation, especially in the shape of Fairview Estate, where as well as more mainstream varieties, Charles Back's range includes Mourvèdre, Carignan, Zinfandel and Gamay. It is also home to the massive KWV, which, having relinquished its role as South African wine's governing body, is now concentrating on producing some extremely fine wines under the Cathedral Cellars label, as well as improving the cheaper wines.

The Paarl taste It's generally warmer here than in regions closer to the coast, so the wines tend to be more weighty and less refined than in Stellenbosch. However, there is a world of difference between the arid, sandy soils of the valley floor and the granite slopes of Franschhoek, where Pinot Noir grows well.

The huge variety in both *terroir* and styles of winemaking means that both Cabernet Sauvignon and Merlot can vary from light and slightly rubbery to something which could be mistaken for Bordeaux.

Where next? Check out the more established wines of **Stellenbosch**.

RECOMMENDED PRODUCERS

D' Armailhac
Batailley
Clerc-Milon
Duhart-Milon-Rothschild
Grand-Puy-Ducasse
Grand-Puy-Lacoste
Haut-Bages-Averous
Haut-Bages-Libéral
Haut-Batailley
Lafite-Rothschild
Latour
Lynch-Bages
Mouton-Rothschild
Pichon-Lalande
Pichon-Longueville
Pontet-Canet
La Tour Pibran

Pauillac

Great expectations

Region Bordeaux

Grape varieties Cabernet Sauvignon, Cabernet Franc, Merlot, Petit Verdot, Malbec

Styles Cassis, cigar-box, cedar – classy stuff

Quality/Price ***>*****/£££>£££££

Some wines in Pomerol and St-Emilion may attract higher prices, but for many people, Pauillac is the very top of the Bordeaux tree – which also means for several of those people that this is the finest red wine in the world. Taste the three first-growth wines, Latour, Lafite-Rothschild and Mouton-Rothschild, and you can see their point. These are massive, compelling wines which bowl you over with their depth of aromas and flavour rather than their power – although this is not inconsiderable. Beside the big three, there's a handful of other classed-growth châteaux which are capable of wines of almost as high a standard, together with some fine *cru bourgeois* properties. This is where Cabernet Sauvignon rules; indeed, in some years where the Merlot isn't up to scratch, a few wines can be virtually all Cabernet.

The Pauillac taste These are the most intense, concentrated, deeply coloured, powerful, flavoursome, massive and compellingly rich wines of the Médoc. Pauillac is the commune to which "great" and "grand" apply most. Cigar-box sniffers, pencil-shaving collectors and cedar junkies will find their favourite smells wrapped around essence of blackcurrants, sometimes damsons. These are the most dignified, aristocratic, majestic, the most totally accomplished and fulfilling wines. They take time to

Mouton Rothschild, home of one of the world's most highly prized wines

unfold magisterially – one decade, often two, and occasionally more; they simply will not be hurried.

Where next? St-Julien has a little more elegance and can come close to **Pauillac** in quality. However, for similarly powerful, intense **Cabernet Sauvignon**, try **Tuscany** or **Napa Valley**.

Pessac-Léognan

Rising from the Graves
Region Bordeaux
Grape varieties Cabernet Sauvignon, Cabernet Franc, Merlot, Petit Verdot, Malbec
Style Smooth and spicy, with velvety blackcurrant fruit
Quality/Price ***⋯⟩*****/£££⋯⟩£££££

RECOMMENDED PRODUCERS

Carbonnieux
De Chevalier
Fieuzal
Haut-Bailly
Haut-Brion
La Louvière
Malartic-Lagravière
La Mission-Haut-Brion
Pape-Clément
De Rochemorin
Smith-Haut-Lafitte
La Tour-Haut-Brion
La Tour-Martillac

Pessac-Léognan was created in 1987 as a sort of Graves *premier cru* appellation, and takes in all the best Graves châteaux. When the 1855 classification (*see* **Bordeaux**) was done, Haut-Brion was the only wine in the region to be included (it's a *premier cru*). The rest were not graded at all until 1953, when a further dozen red wine properties were classified. These are simply *crus classés*, without any further division into a league table, and they are all now within Pessac-Léognan. Haut-Brion remains the star, and even its second wine, Bahans-Haut-Brion, puts most other wines into the shade, including the *crus classés*. As in the Médoc, Cabernet Sauvignon is the dominant grape, although the proportions of Merlot and Cabernet Franc tend to be higher here.

The Pessac-Léognan taste Soil is supposed to account for the taste – particularly the gravel that gives the Graves region its name – but try slipping someone a glass without saying what it is; I should be very surprised if they came up with "Ah, gravel".

Certainly, the wines are densely constructed, with a good concentration of fruit and, in the best examples, an appealing smooth, velvety texture. They have a rich, spicy, tobacco character and deep, dark, voluptuous, velvety fruit, with finesse rather than power.

Where next? The Médoc for more **Cabernet Sauvignon**-based wine, or **St-Emilion** for similar quality but more **Merlot**.

Piedmont

RECOMMENDED PRODUCERS

Antoniolo
Cascina La Barbatella
Antichi Vigneti di Cantalupo
Le Colline
Marco Maria Crivelli
Ferrando
Gastaldi
Malvirà
Martinetti
Scarpa
Giancarlo Travaglini

Italy's Burgundy?

Best-known wines Barolo, Barbaresco
Grape varieties Nebbiolo, Barbera, Dolcetto, Freisa, Ruché
Style Firm, long-lived and intensely perfumed
Barolo and Barbaresco
Quality/Price **····⟩*****/£····⟩£££££

Piedmont ranks with Tuscany as Italy's greatest wine region, but it would be a mistake to think that there is nothing beyond Barolo and Barbaresco. Nebbiolo is the force behind Barolo and Barbaresco, but it is also responsible for several other wines. In the north of Piedmont, where the grape can be known as Spanna or Picotener, Carema is 100 per cent Nebbiolo, Gattinara can include up to ten per cent Bonarda, while Ghemme includes both Vespolina and Bonarda in the blend. The Langhe DOC covers a large region west of Alba, including Barolo and Barbaresco. Three red varieties – Nebbiolo, Freisa and Dolcetto – are permitted for the red wines. A few producers in Barolo and Barbaresco use the Langhe DOC as a way of eliminating lesser-quality batches from their main wines, so some of those that remain can be of very high quality.

The other catch-all DOC is Monferrato, centred on the town of Asti. There's not as much Nebbiolo here as there is around Alba; instead, you'll find Dolcetto, Barbera, Cabernet Sauvignon and Pinot Nero (Pinot Noir), as well as less well-known varieties such as Freisa, Grignolino and Ruché.

A view over
Barbaresco
and the rolling
landscape of
Piedmont

The Piedmont taste   Nebbiolo, Dolcetto and Barbera are all covered seperately in this book. The delightful Freisa has hints of raspberries and pepper, and can be dry or sweet, still or sparkling, while Grignolino is light and fruity with hints of herbs and flowers.

The most exhilarating grape is the lesser-known Ruché, which manages to be aromatic and floral yet have rich, plummy fruit and the occasional Christmas-cake flavour.

Where next?   See specific entries for **Barbaresco**, **Barbera**, **Barolo**, **Dolcetto** and **Nebbiolo**.

Pinot Noir

A thrill to the senses
Style Full of raspberries, cherries, strawberries
and – hopefully – truffles and violets
Grown in Burgundy and all over the world

The main difference between Cabernet Sauvignon and Pinot Noir, arguably the world's two greatest grapes, is that Cabernet appeals to the head, while Pinot goes for the heart. Put a great Pinot Noir in front of experienced and normally rational wine tasters and the notes will say things like: "Wow... sexy... yummy... delicious... yes, Yes, YES!"

Unfortunately, like motorway service stations for the incontinent, great Pinot Noirs are few and far between. However, anyone who has ever had one will be eager to repeat the experience. But finding great Pinot Noir isn't that easy even in Burgundy, the grape's homeland. Pinot is very particular about where it grows, and the Burgundians have spent hundreds of years mapping out their region in order to show which vineyards are the most successful. But, not every wine from the top sites – the *grands crus* – will provoke the "yes, Yes, YES!" response. Pinot is also especially sensitive to how you grow and vinify it. Yields must be low, fruit must be picked at optimum ripeness and handling in the winery must be minimal, otherwise the result can be an expensive disappointment.

Burgundy used to have the monopoly on great Pinot Noir, but that is no longer the case. Pinot features in the red wines of Champagne, the Loire, Alsace, Savoie and the Jura, but the wines seldom rise above the "interesting" level. A few producers in the Languedoc have made good wines, but there's nothing approaching *premier cru* level, let alone *grand cru*.

Pinot Nero, the Italian name for the grape, sounds like one of the more obscure Roman emperors, and most of the DOC wines produced from it in northeastern Italy – Alto Adige, Collio, Colli Orientali, Grave del Friuli, Breganze and Trentino – are barely worth more than a footnote in history. However, some ambitious producers have made wines with more structure, fruit and enough elegance to remind us that it is a noble variety after all. Even so, at present, Lombardy (Ca' del Bosco) and Tuscany (Castello della Sala, Pancrazi) offer Italy's best Pinot Noirs.

Spain and Portugal aren't great Pinot havens, although Somontano and Penedès in northeast Spain have both shown that there is the potential for the variety. In Germany as Spätburgunder, the wines made are rated highly locally, but rarely develop into anything beyond merely respectable, and the same is true in Austria. Swiss versions from the Valais can be good, although certainly not great; the Pinot Noir-Gamay blend (which goes by the name of Passe-Tout-Grains in Burgundy) is known here as Dôle. Romania is the main source of Pinot Noir from Eastern Europe, and can on occasion be surprisingly delicious in a slightly jammy and very juicy way.

Oregon used to be the New World's highest hope for Pinot Noir, but the state's producers seemed to lose their way in the 1980s. At the same time, the southern neighbours in California were improving rapidly, thanks to better site selection, better clonal material and better winemaking. And the Oregonians? They do seem to be finally sorting out their act, and depth and complexity are featuring in more and more wines.

Canada has also shown that it can turn its hands to Pinot, with admirable versions from both Ontario and British Columbia. Much further south, Chile has a handful of producers making Pinot which, while not exactly complex, is certainly packed with juicy fruit flavours, and puts many a burgundy at twice the price to shame.

Much of Australia is too hot for Pinot Noir, but certain regions such as Yarra Valley, Mornington Peninsula and Geelong in Victoria and Lenswood in South Australia are enjoying great success. Not as much, however, as in New Zealand, where some of the wines are of *premier cru* burgundy level.

The Pinot Noir taste Pinot Noir is very responsive to circumstances – its taste is affected by climate and soil – and early ripening allows it to cope with cool growing regions. Yet, the grape see-saws up and down in quality so much that you get dizzy trying to follow it. In the simple, youthful wines which form the majority of Pinot Noirs, raspberries, strawberries and cherries predominate. In maturity, the flavours can develop into a glorious complexity, with a sweet and noticeably fragrant floral bouquet, sometimes with whiffs of exotic tea. Pinot Noir often turns a disturbingly mature brick-orange in a very short space of time, so colour is not always a sure guide to readiness for drinking.

Great Pinots transcend the merely fruity. The berry, plum, blackcurrant and cherry flavours are seamlessly linked with those of violets and truffles, undergrowth, minerals and earth, coffee, chocolate and exotic spices and many other things. Then there's the texture. Great Pinot Noir slithers around your mouth and down your throat, caressing as it goes. Yummy, yummy, yes, Yes, YES!

Where next? No other grape variety really comes close to Pinot Noir. But if you're keen, try **Gamay**-based wines – in particular, one of the Beaujolais *crus*. **Nebbiolo** can match Pinot for perfume, but that's all.

Pinotage

South Africa's very own – almost
Style Spicy, with plum, bramble, chocolate and banana flavours
Grown in South Africa, New Zealand

Pinotage is Pinot Noir crossed with Hermitage. Sadly, Hermitage has nothing to do with the northern Rhône; it's just what they call Cinsaut in South Africa. The idea behind the crossing was to produce a grape with the quality of Pinot Noir and the productivity of Cinsaut. Did they succeed? In the 1980s, the answer would have been "no" even in the Cape. With the exception of Stellenbosch's Kanonkop, no one seemed interested in this odd variety. But with the disappearance of apartheid, many producers took a renewed interest in Pinotage, since in a world where

Cabernet Sauvignon and Merlot abound, it was the one thing that was distinctively South African. Today's wines are a far cry from the clumsy nail-varnish-and-rusty-nails concoctions of the past, and popularity is at an all-time high, both at home and abroad. Even so, you have to ask if it is such a great grape, why haven't more countries planted it? New Zealand has some, but beyond that, it's not very apparent in the many high-class vineyards around the world.

The Pinotage taste Bananas. No, it's not an insult, just a common tasting note for a South African Pinotage. There's also spicy bramble and plum, together with hints of chocolate, earth and an occasional whiff of rubber. Then just when you think you've got a handle on the Pinotage taste, you try a version from New Zealand: the rubber and bananas aren't there. The fruit is more like a lighter Australian Cabernet-Shiraz. Confused? So are we.

Where next? If it's the **South African**-ity you like, try Cape **Cabernet Sauvignon**, **Merlot** or **Shiraz**. Other spicy, plummy grapes include Montepulciano and **Zinfandel**.

Pomerol

Bordeaux at its sexiest

Region Bordeaux
Grape varieties Cabernet Sauvignon, Cabernet Franc, Merlot, Petit Verdot, Malbec
Style Plums, blackcurrants and woodsmoke flavours
Quality/Price ***⋯⟩*****/££££⋯⟩£££££

Pauillac is great, Pomerol is great, but the two lie at opposite ends of the Bordeaux spectrum. Pauillac is austere and aristocratic, appealing to the intellect as much as anything, while Pomerol is voluptuous and glamorous, a very friendly assault on the senses.

Yet Pomerol is more than just a painted lady. This is where the Merlot grape (usually aided by 10 to 30 per cent Cabernet Franc) achieves its greatest expression – apparently against all the rules. Go to the Médoc, ask anybody if they would like to swap their gravel for clay, and they would laugh at you. But in Pomerol it is on dense, impervious clay (with a high mineral content) that the best vines grow. Merlot loves it, and manages to produce wine which, in an un-Merlot-like fashion, can last for decades.

Pomerols are also extremely attractive at a rather more tender age, and this combined with their tiny scales of production has made them especially popular in America and the Far East – that and the 90+ ratings from Robert Parker. The result is that the wines have escalated in price to such an extent that it's not just the famous Château Pétrus which out-prices the top Médoc wines. Yet, there are several Pétrus and Le Pin wannabes whose prices are still at fairly reasonable levels, as well as some interesting wines from the rather more rustic neighbour Lalande-de-Pomerol, where Annereaux, Garraud, Haut-Chatain and Tournefeuille are among the top properties.

Pomerol's rich clay soils produce some of the world's most expensive wines

The Pomerol taste Pomerol wines are soft, smooth, plummy and blackcurranty, plump, ripe and juicy, rich, concentrated and voluptuous, yet quite dry. The hint of cedar or sultry, smouldering woodsmoke comes from oak. They are not heavy, but neither are they as light as St-Emilion; just more close-textured, velvety and more intense.

Where next? Pomerol is the top of the tree for **Merlot**, although some in **California** and **Washington State** can give them a run for their money. Other types of opulent, fleshy wines include **Priorato**, South Australian **Shiraz** and **California Zinfandel**.

Pommard

Sturdy but not stolid
Region Côte de Beaune
Grape varieties Pinot Noir
Style Firm with dark, plummy fruit
Quality/Price ***⋯⟩****/£££⋯⟩£££££

RECOMMENDED PRODUCERS
Comte Armand
Jean-Marc Boillot
Coste Caumartin
De Courcel
Michel Gaunoux
Mussy
Parent
De Pommard
Royer Girardin

Pommard is famous, infamous perhaps, for its powerful, solid wines. In the past this has been used as an excuse to pass off rather thick, soupy wines of dubious origin, but today the village has some excellent growers who are doing an excellent job to revive Pommard's reputation. There are no *grands crus*, and no vineyards to match the finest sites in neighbouring Volnay, but among the fine *premiers crus* are Les Rugiens, Les Epenots and Clos des Epeneaux.

The Pommard taste Pommard sits geographically between Beaune and Volnay, but the wines tend more to the rather solid style of the former than the grace of the latter. They are firm in their youth, but still manage to display the dark, plummy fruit which stays with them throughout their long life; a decade is not at all unusual, and some will live for twice that.

Where next? Stay in the **Côte de Beaune** and head for **Volnay** for more silk, Corton for more power. From the **Côte de Nuits**, **Gevrey-Chambertin** (which has similar soil to Pommard) provides the sturdiest wines.

Port

Great and gripping

Region Douro Valley, Portugal
Grape varieties Touriga Nacional, Tinta Roriz, Touriga Francesa, Tinta Cão, Tinta Barocca, Tinta Amarella, Mourisco Tinto, Bastardo
Style From robustly fruity with blackberry and violet notes to subtle and nutty with dried-fruit flavours
Quality/Price ***·····⟩*****/£££····⟩£££££

RECOMMENDED PRODUCERS
(Recommended single-*quinta* wines in brackets)
Churchill
(Quinta da Agua Alta)
Cockburn
Croft
Delaforce
Dow (Quinta do Bomfim)
Ferreira
Fonseca Guimaraens
(Quinta do Panascal)
Gould Campbell
Graham (Quinta dos Malvedos)
Niepoort (Quinta do Passadouro)
Quinta do Crasto
Quinta do Noval
Quinta de la Rosa
Quinta do Vesuvio
Ramos-Pinto (Quinta da Ervamoira, Quinta da Urtiga)
Smith-Woodhouse
Taylor (Quinta de Vargellas)
Warre (Quinta da Cavadinha)

Port is made in the inhospitable Douro Valley in northern Portugal. It is the terrain, of course, that is inhospitable, not the people who make port. They are *very* hospitable, and like nothing better than to open a bottle ot two. The grapes, a bewildering mix of local varieties, the best-known of which are Touriga Nacional and Tinta Roriz (Spain's Tempranillo), are grown on narrow terraces that have been hewn, wrested, scavenged or blasted from the granite rock. In winter, it is freezing cold, but in summer, it is hotter than hot, baking the thick skins to produce lots of deep, juicy, purple colour and stacks of tannin. Port is anything but wimpish.

The grapes are crushed – sometimes, though rarely, by foot in an open concrete trough or *lagar* – and begin to ferment. Most is produced in a special stainless-steel tank that automatically and regularly pumps the juice over the cap of skins in order to extract maximum colour in the shortest time. After only a few days, when it reaches about six per cent alcohol and the colour and sweetness is judged to be right, the must is poured into barrels filled to one-fifth with *aguardente* – grape spirit – at 78 per cent alcohol. The spirit kills the yeasts at once and the wine stops fermenting. It is sweet because it retains unfermented grape sugar, and it has been fortified to an alcohol level of around 20 per cent. The following spring, the barrels (or more often road tankers these days) are taken from the isolated farms or *quintas* 80 km (50 miles) down to the lodges in Vila Nova da Gaia at the mouth of the River Douro, opposite Oporto.

In the less torrid conditions by the sea, this is where port has traditionally undergone the rest of its maturation, although a few producers now have air-conditioned cellars at the *quintas* for this purpose. Different styles begin to emerge. Variations in quality of the vineyards, their altitude or angle towards the sun, age of the vines and so on, all contribute to differences in grape and therefore wine quality; the job of the blenders, tasters and scientists is to send each barrel or pipe (a cask of around 600 litres) on the most appropriate course through the system. And it is quite a system, with a rather confusing array of styles.

Port lodges in Vila Nova de Gaia house port wines as they mature

Ports split into two categories: ruby and tawny. The ruby styles are bottled when young, fiery and fruity, and do any maturing that is necessary in the bottle. Basic ruby port, usually a blend from recent vintages, spends a minimum of three years in barrel, while vintage character is simply a higher-quality ruby port.

True vintage port is a wine from an exceptional year which has spent two to three years in barrel before being bottled. When first bottled, it is alarmingly easy to drink, especially with peppered steak. It is estimated that Americans, not the largest vintage-port buyers in the world, drink more than two-thirds of their vintage ports before they hit their fifth birthday (the ports, not the Americans). However, it then goes, if not exactly sulky, then certainly rather reticent for a period. During this time, you sometimes wonder whether it really is as great as you thought it was when you bought it. Then it emerges, maybe 15, maybe 20 years later, and all is forgiven. It is then capable of lasting for decades – you will decline faster than decent vintage port. Most vintage port is a blend of wines from different estates.

In years which are not good enough for making true vintage ports, some estates will release single-*quinta* ports. While not as long-lived as the top vintage wines, they offer something of the same experience at a lower price. More affordable still is Late Bottled Vintage (LBV), which spends four to six years in barrel before bottling. Crusted port is a blend of several years, bottled (unfiltered) after three or four years, that throws a distinct sediment (or crust) and so needs decanting just like vintage port. These are usually closer than LBV to the big, incisive, mouth-filling vintage port style, and can be some of the best-value ports on the market.

Tawny port – real tawny – does most of its maturing in barrel instead of bottle. It can stay there for decades, very gradually turning the colour that gives it its name. Real tawny will be sold as 10-year-old, 20-year-old, 30-year-old and over 40-year-old. The figure is an average age, not an exact number of years and not a minimum; the wines simply have to correspond to a style. A tawny which comes from a single vintage is called a *colheita*.

The wines seem to achieve a balance between youthful zip and relaxed maturity at something between ten and 20 years; if they made a 15-year-old that would be ideal. The older tawnies develop a more pronounced raisiny flavour and slight oxidation that can seem rather strange and unnecessary. It is best to begin with a 10- or 20-year-old, and to consider carefully before spending a lot of money on a 40-year-old.

A quick word about serving. Tawny ports don't need decanting, ruby styles, especially vintage port, do. However, in older wines, the sediment has often solidified to such an extent that you don't have to worry as much about standing bottles upright for a couple of days as you may have to with younger ports. Once you have opened a vintage port, it needs drinking within the next few days. Tawnies are much more forgiving and an opened bottle can safely be kept for a month or more without deterioration.

The Port taste Mature vintage port has a deep red hue, a gloriously perfumed smell, and an immensely rich, concentrated, powerful taste that includes plums and blackcurrants, perhaps with the scent of mint leaf or a swirl of black pepper. It declines ever so gently over the years, like the fading sound of a band marching away, never quite disappearing. In tawny port, the fresh berry and damson fruit gives way to dried-fruit flavours such as figs, citrus peel and raisins, and the wines develop great complexity, a splendid nuttiness, and a hauntingly long flavour that makes it one of the most delightful after-dinner drinks there is. It is not bad at any time, and it can even be chilled slightly (as the Portuguese often do) to good effect.

Where next? Australia, California and South Africa all offer port-style wines, although few are much like the real thing. **Vins Doux Naturel**s are fortified to a lesser degree, retaining a higher degree of natural sweetness. *Recioto* (*see* **Valpolicella**) is not fortified, but it is still highly alcoholic.

Priorato

Move over Rioja

Region Catalonia

Grape varieties Garnacha, Cariñena, Cabernet Sauvignon, Merlot, Syrah

Style From liquid Christmas cake to stunningly rich and plummy wine

Quality/Price **⋯⟩*****/£££⋯⟩£££££

RECOMMENDED PRODUCERS

Alvaro Palacio
René Barbier (Clos Mogador)
Costers del Siurana
Daphne Glorian (Clos Erasmus)
Masía Barril
Mas Martinet
Pasanau Germans
Scala Dei

One of Spain's most thrilling regions. The wines, based on Garnacha and Cariñena (Carignan), have traditionally been old-fashioned, alcoholic and full-bodied, like rustic Châteauneuf-du-Pape. Then from the mid-1980s, new winemakers crept into the region and turned it upside down. They've added French grapes to the old-vine Garnacha, and with the help of modern winemaking techniques, the wines are turning heads the world over.

The Priorato taste Old-style Priorato is at best full-bodied and nutty with dried-fruit flavours, like Christmas cake, but some are over oxidative. The new style, with heavy bottles and price tags, is what you imagine you'd end up with if you crossed a top Pomerol with a vintage port. There is amazing richness, extract, fruit and complexity, with spicy orange, plum, blackberry and liquorice flavours. This style has only been being made since the 1980s, so at this stage we can only say they will *probably* last for at least 30 years.

Where next? **Pomerol** is similarly flashy although not quite as sturdy. Others of equivalent weight include top **Syrah/Shiraz** from the northern **Rhône** and **Australia**, **California Zinfandel**, **Barolo** and **Brunello** *riserva*.

Provence

What Peter Mayle drinks

Best-known wines Bandol

Grape varieties Mourvèdre, Syrah, Grenache, Cinsault, Tibouren, Cabernet Sauvignon

Style From light and fruity to serious and steamy

Quality/Price **⋯⟩*****/££⋯⟩£££££

RECOMMENDED PRODUCERS

Les Bastides
De Calissanne
Commanderie de Peyrassol
De la Courtade
Du Deffends
Féraud
De Fonscolombe
Gavoty
Jas d'Esclans
Mas de la Dame
Mas de Cadenet

The wines of Provence do not have a single recognisable style. They are as varied as the region itself, which extends along the coast from the edge of the Camargue to Nice, and inland through the herby hills of the Var *département*. The standard of the reds is, on the whole, much better than that of whites and rosés, but there are still several indifferent overpriced wines aimed at wealthy visitors.

The region has some huge appellations and some tiny ones. Côtes de Provence is the largest, and the numerous grape varieties permitted mean that the wines vary widely in style. Coteaux d'Aix-en-Provence is also huge, with again a large spread of quality. Palette is an enclave in the southeast with only two producers. To the west, wines from the rocky and mineral-rich town of Les Baux de Provence now have their own appellation. However, in a rather short-sighted move, the regulations regarding permitted grape varieties have been changed to exclude the finest wine. The Cabernet-Syrah blend from Domaine de Trévallon must now be sold as a *vin de pays* – a category which has never really taken off in Provence.

Coteaux Varois was upgraded from VDQS to AC in 1993. From 2000, the wines must contain a minimum of 80 per cent Mourvèdre, Syrah and Grenache. South of here is Provence's greatest wine, Bandol (*qv*), where Mourvèdre shows its class. On the coast is Cassis and Bellet. Pretty as they are, neither of these tiny appellations offers much in the way of red wine.

The Provence taste It may just be imagination, but there are times when it is difficult not to smell the thyme-filled, fennel-heavy, pine-scented, anise-tinged air of Provence wafting up from a glass. Perhaps it is simply

The beautiful and rustic Provençal landscape features many acres of vines

wishful thinking to try and bring the Mediterranean closer than it really is, but it is surprising how often it works. Beyond that, the flavour depends largely on the grape varieties used, and as these aren't given on the label, you're going to have to do some experimenting. Notes of raspberry, strawberry, cherry and blackcurrant appear in many wines, most of which are made for early drinking. However, where Mourvèdre, Syrah and Cabernet Sauvignon, not to mention an oak barrel, make their presence felt, the wines can be kept for a few years.

Where next? Head to the **Languedoc** and then on to **California** and **Australia** for more **Mourvèdre**, **Syrah** and **Grenache**.

Rapel

RECOMMENDED PRODUCERS
Casa Lapostolle
Cono Sur
Luís Felípé Edwards
Mont Gras
Santa Emiliana
Torreón de Paredes
Viña Gracia
Viña de Larose/Las Casas del Toqui
Viña La Rosa/La Palma
Viña Porta

Already challenging Maipo
Grape varieties Cabernet Sauvignon, Merlot, Pinot Noir
Style Spicy, plummy Merlot; pure, blackcurranty Cabernet
Quality/Price **····⟩****/£····⟩££££

Rapel is part of Chile's Central Valley, lying south of Maipo and north of Curicó. There have been vineyards here for several years, but the number of wineries until recently has been few. However, the 1990s saw the establishment of new wineries and new vineyards, where impressive Merlot and Cabernet Sauvignon can now be found. This is also home to some of Chile's best Pinot Noir from Chimbarongo in the southeast of the region.

The Rapel Taste Merlot/Carmenère makes the biggest impression here. It's lush and fruity, spicy with damson and blackberry flavours and a hint of – honestly – soy sauce. Jazz it up with oak and it becomes even more classy, and doesn't mind five years bottle-age. Cabernet Sauvignon achieves something of the same intensity, with pure blackcurrant flavours shining through, but despite the intensity, it can be slightly one-dimensional. The Pinot Noir dazzled when it was first introduced with its vibrant, raspberry, strawberry and vanilla flavours. Since then, attempts to make it more serious have merely resulted in wines with more oak.

Where next? North is **Maipo**, south is **Curicó**. Also try **Languedoc Cabernets** and **Merlots**.

Rhône

RECOMMENDED PRODUCERS
Des Anges
D'Aquéria
Grangeneuve
Maby
Méjan-Taulier
De la Mordorée
De Ségriés
Val-Joanis
La Vieille Ferme
Vieux Micocoulier

The spicy side of France
Best-known wines Hermitage, Côte-Rôtie, Châteauneuf-du-Pape
Grape varieties Syrah, Grenache, Mourvèdre, Cinsault, Carignan
Style Intense and perfumed in the north, warm and welcoming in the south
Quality/Price *····⟩*****/£····⟩£££££

In winespeak, the Rhône begins at Vienne and then heads south to Avignon, after which one ceases to bother. The reegion is divided rather conveniently into two by the more or less vineless stretch from Valence to the nougat town of Montélimar. To the north are the wines of Cornas, Hermitage, St-Joseph and Côte-Rôtie. Here are warm summers and coldish winters, with vines planted in terraces on dramatically steep slopes of granite. Syrah is the only red variety grown, although some of the wines are pepped up by the addition of small proportions of white varieties: Marsanne and Roussanne in Hermitage, Crozes and St-Joseph, Viognier in Côte-Rôtie.

To the south are the wines of Châteauneuf-du-Pape, Gigondas, Vacqueyras and other villages of the Côtes du Rhône. Here are olives, herbs and a Mediterranean climate of hot summers and cool winters. The valley opens out into a broad plain, where a great volume and variety of grapes are grown. Syrah is still used, but Grenache is the base for most wines, although very few use it to the exclusion of all other varieties. The southern wines have a warm generosity of spirit (often literally, due to high alcohol levels), with lighter colours, simpler flavours, and shorter lives than those of their northern counterparts.

Châteauneuf may be the most famous southern appellation, but the most dynamic appellation at present is Côtes du Rhône-Villages, where places such as Cairanne, Sablet and Séguret are making excellent-value wines. Lirac, Gigondas and Vacqueyras sit between these two appellations in quality. The Côtes du Ventoux and Côtes du Lubéron spread southeastwards from Gigondas, making wines which are little different from Côtes du Rhône, with some of the better reds achieving similar quality levels to the villages wines. Coteaux du Tricastin lies to the north of the Côtes du Rhône-Villages appellation, and produces wines which, in general, are similar to those of the Côtes du Rhône, with some 100 per cent Syrah wines rising well above that level.

If the Rhône seems confusing, start your exploration of the region by picking a company that sells wines from several different appellations. Best among these are Cave de Tain l'Hermitage, Chapoutier, Delas Frères, Guigal (which also owns Vidal-Fleury), Paul Jaboulet-Aîné and Tardieu-Laurent.

The Rhône taste Northern Rhône wines vary from fairly elegant and perfumed in Côte-Rôtie to dense and forbidding in Cornas, all the while with the orange-peel, smoky-berry-and-plum fruit of Syrah underpinning them. When used sensitively new oak adds a sheen of vanilla. Southern wines tend to be more languid, with warm, spicy flavours, sometimes dried fruit rather than plums, and higher alcohol levels. They are not generally as long-lived as their northern counterparts, although low-yielding old-vine Grenache can be gloriously dense and age-worthy.

Where next? See Châteauneuf-du-Pape, Cornas, Côte-Rôtie, Côtes du Rhône, Crozes-Hermitage, Gigondas, Hermitage and St-Joseph.

Ribera del Duero

Spain's best wine region?

Region Northern central Spain

Grape varieties Tinto del País, Garnacha, Cabernet Sauvignon

Style Berry, cherry and plum fruit with spicy overtones

Quality/Price **⋯⟩*****/£££⋯⟩£££££

Ribera del Duero used to be easy for the wine-lover to understand. There was Vega Sicilia, producing Spain's most expensive and (in its day) greatest red wine, and not a lot else. No one took a great deal of notice when, in 1975, a new wine called Tinto Pesquera appeared, nor when a few more *bodegas* were established at the end of the 1970s. The region received its DO in 1982, and another batch of new wineries appeared. Then, in the mid-1980s Robert Parker – he of the influential nose and pen – pronounced that Pesquera was the Pétrus of Spain. Since then, this barren region high up in northern Spain has been a hot-bed of activity, to the extent that there are now over 100 *bodegas*, with more appearing each year.

As a result, land prices have soared, grape prices have soared and – of course – wine prices have soared. Some of the newcomers are most definitely bandwagon jumpers, keen to make as much money from Ribera's success, but several of the newbies are already making wines which rank among the finest, not just in the region but in the whole of Spain.

Opinion is divided as to whether the best wines are those made entirely from Tempranillo, known locally as Tinto del País or Tinto Fino, or those where up to 25 per cent of other varieties have been used. There are several wines which provide eloquent arguments for both sides of the debate. Where blending occurs, Garnacha, Cabernet Sauvignon, Malbec and Merlot are the main grapes used, but some producers prefer the white variety Albillo, which brings a touch of perfume to the wines.

As in Rioja, the wines are graded according to how long they have been aged. A *crianza* must be a minimum of two years

The castle of Peñafiel: a stunning Spanish landmark

old on release, having spent at least a year in barrel; a *reserva* must be three years old, with at least one year in barrel; and a *gran reserva* must be five years old, with at least two years in barrel.

The Ribera del Duero taste These are, or should be, full-bodied, rich wines full of damson, cherry, blackberry and raspberry fruit, with a spicy, earthy edge and the occasional hint of citrus peel.

With age, the vibrant fruit mellows to give a lusher texture, while the spicy, woody notes become more pronounced. Unfortunately, many wines have a hard and sometimes sulphury edge, a result of insufficient aeration during the winemaking process. This is especially noticeable in young wines, although age does mellow it. Opinions vary about the amount of oak ageing a wine should receive. What is certainly true is that only the best wines are up to the two years in cask required for the *gran reservas*.

Where next? For Spain's other sources of top-class reds try the wines of **Rioja** and **Priorato**.

RECOMMENDED PRODUCERS

Artadi
Barón de Ley
Berberana
Bretón
Campillo
Campo Viejo
Contino
El Coto
CVNE
Faustino Martínez
López de Heredia
Marqués de Cáceres
Marqués de Griñón
Marqués de Murrieta
Marqués de Riscal
Martínez Bujanda
Montecillo
Muga
Olarra
Palacio
Remelluri
La Rioja Alta
Bodegas Riojanas
Viña Ijalba

Rioja

Oaky-cokey

Region Northeast Spain
Grape varieties Tempranillo, Garnacha, Graciano, Mazuelo
Style Oaky, with strawberry, plum and cherry fruit
Quality/Price *⋯⟩****/£⋯⟩£££££

Spain's best-known wine is made in the north-central part of the country along the valley of the Ebro, after whose tributary, the Rio Oja, the wine is named. Rioja's origins go back a long way, but the region was set on its modern course by a disaster in France. When mildew (*oïdium*) and *phylloxera* devastated French vineyards toward the end of the 19th century, some Bordeaux *vignerons* hopped over the Pyrenees looking for unaffected vineyards with which to pursue their livelihood. With them they brought the practice of long ageing in *barriques*. While oakiness in Bordeaux diminished over the years, it persisted in Rioja.

Indeed, so much is oak ingrained into the Riojans that they grade their wine not by the quality of the fruit, but by the length of time it spends in oak. *Sin crianza* wines see no oak; *crianza* wines are aged for a minimum of two years,

The Ebro River and flat-topped hills of the famous Rioja region

with one of these in oak; *reserva* wines have three years' ageing, with at least one year in oak; and finally *gran reserva* wines have five years' ageing, with a minimum of two years in oak. It's certainly true that oak is part of the Rioja appeal. The best producers have always used oak with sensitivity, making sure that only their finest grapes are made into *gran reservas*. And the *sin crianza* wines can be vibrant and fruity, but there's nothing about them to suggest that they come from a top-class wine region. In general, the level of oaking is decreasing, but the quality of fruit behind the wines is not always as good as it could be. It's easy to understand why. Virtually all Rioja estates have to buy in a large proportion of their grapes from the region's 18,000 growers, so quality control is difficult. Fortunately, nowadays there are a small number of single-vineyard Riojas such as Remelluri, Contino and Martínez Bujanda's Finca Valpiedra.

However, like Champagne, Rioja is essentially a blended wine. The region is subdivided into three smaller regions. The highest, coolest vineyards lie in the Rioja Alta and Rioja Alavesa, and are planted mostly with Tempranillo, with other grapes – Mazuelo (France's Carignan) and the delicately aromatic, high-quality Graciano – being grown in tiny quantities. Vineyards on alluvial soils in the Rioja Baja, which edges toward hot, Mediterranean-like summers, are planted mostly with Garnacha, which makes big, alcoholic, rather coarse and jammy wines. A typical Rioja would be 60 to 70 per cent Tempranillo and 15 to 20 per cent Garnacha, with the balance split between Graciano and Mazuelo.

While not an officially sanctioned variety, some *bodegas* are allowed to include Cabernet Sauvignon in their wines, which brings the backbone that Tempranillo sometimes lacks. However, there is also a move in the region towards using Graciano in a similar bolstering role. Rioja was for several years unchallenged as Spain's premium red wine region, but the success of Ribera del Duero and Priorato in recent times has threatened that position. But Rioja is not beaten yet. There are still several splendid old-fashioned wines being made, especially by La Rioja Alta, while the more modern producers are wielding new-oak barrels with aplomb.

The Rioja taste Oak-free Rioja is simple, juicy and fresh, with strawberry flavours and not a great deal else. But to think of the higher-quality wines as being something similar with a woody vanilla sheen is a mistake. Modern wines often have cherries, plums and blackcurrants in addition to the berries, with spicy, peppery, earthy overtones. Old-fashioned wines at their best have smoky, almost savoury flavours with notes of tobacco, herbs blackberries and mulberries. The oak, though noticeable, is never the main event. Sadly though, in many wines the fruit has faded and the juiciness has gone, leaving little apart from that oak.

Where next? **Ribera del Duero** is the other outpost of high-quality oaked **Tempranillo**, with the best of **Navarra** not far behind. The better wines of **Valdepeñas** and Toro can be excellent-value alternatives.

Sangiovese

By Jove!
Style From light and thin to full-bodied and powerful, always with a hint of bitter cherry and spice
Grown in Tuscany and throughout Italy, California, Australia, Argentina

This grape variety – the "blood of Jove" – is grown all over Italy, but its origin and its most emphatic current expression is in Tuscany. Although few wines are actually labelled Sangiovese, it is the major ingredient in the region's four DOCGs – Chianti, Carmignano, Brunello di Montalcino and Vino Nobile di Montepulciano – and in many Super-Tuscans (*see* **Tuscany**) such as Cepparello, Fontalloro and Concerto, no, not the three tenors.

The Tuscans have traditionally blended Sangiovese with other grape varieties, both red and white, with Brunello di Montalcino and its sibling Rosso di Montalcino being the only wines for which 100 per cent Brunello – the local clone of Sangiovese – was obligatory. Indeed, the requirements drawn up in 1967 that Chianti should include a proportion of 10 to 30 per cent white grapes in its wines were what prompted many producers to go outside DOC regulations to produce the Super-Tuscan *vini da tavola*. Even now, Chianti Classico is the only Chianti for which 100 per cent Sangiovese wines are allowed.

Outside Tuscany, Sangiovese is the main grape in Umbria's Torgiano, and is grown in vast amounts in Emilia-Romagna, where it makes Sangiovese di Romagna. Heading southwards, it appears as a blending partner in several wines, especially in Apulia where it can be used in Castel del Monte, Copertino and Squinzano.

Elsewhere in the world, Argentina has plenty of Sangiovese, although so far there is nothing to challenge either the Tuscan versions or the local Malbec. Californian plantings are less numerous, but more than 50 wineries have a Sangiovese-based wine in their portfolios, some of which are extremely classy. The famous Antinori family of Tuscany is a partner in the Atlas Peak vineyard overlooking Napa Valley, where it makes a fine varietal as well as a Cabernet-Sangiovese blend called Consenso. Australia also boasts a handful of versions, the best of which comes from Coriole in McLaren Vale.

The Sangiovese taste Sangioveses vary considerably in style and quality from thin and undistinguished quaffing wines to some of the most exciting wines made anywhere in Italy, the ones with the funny names. This variety of styles, compounded by an elastic yield that sometimes stretches to breaking point and any number of different clones, makes it difficult to generalise about taste. The grape has good acidity, which makes it refreshing when young – there is a healthy market for *vino novello* – but also gives definition and edge to a more concentrated wine, enabling it to mature for decades.

Thick skins may produce considerable amounts of tannin, depending on how the wine is vinified, but not always a lot of colour since the skins are not heavily pigmented. Once again, the tannin can contribute to long life. Although reaching only average alcohol levels, Sangiovese has an attractive winey quality about it rather than the specific fruitiness which we associate with grapes such as Cabernet Sauvignon or Merlot. It can develop a rustic, farmyard feel, sometimes reminiscent of St-Emilion, and in mature Brunello di Montalcino it can be very complex indeed, showing tar, nuts, tobacco, woodsmoke and autumnal forest notes on top of the cherryish fruit.

Where next? Pinot Noir for the lighter aspects of Sangiovese and its vegetal, woodland smells. Cabernet Sauvignon shares its characteristics of quality, weight, power and concentration.

Sardinia

Carignan's finest hour

Grape varieties Cannonau, Carignano, Monica,
Cabernet Sauvignon

Style Robust, alcoholic, varying from rustic to really quite refined

Quality/Price *····⟩****/£····⟩£££££

High yields mean that most Carignano del Sulcis (France's Carignan), Cannonau di Sardegna (Grenache) and Monica di Sardegna, made from a variety believed to be of Spanish origin, are little more than easy-drinking, rustic wines. However, where producers cut their yields, the first two in particular can be extremely impressive. Some producers make a rich *passito* wine of varying sweetness levels from semi-dried Cannonau grapes. A few wineries also use Cabernet Sauvignon, either on its own or blended with Cannonau, to make rich, oaky wines which appeal to international palates but remain firmly Sardinian.

The Sardinian taste Basic Cannonau is robust, rustic stuff, with berry, plum and raisin flavours, while *passito* wines turn up the volume on both fruit and alcohol. Monica is softer, rounder and less long-lived, although still no wimp. Carignano del Sulcis at its best (from Santadi) is ripe, sweet and full of plum, prune and currant flavours with hints of bread.

Where next? Instead of *passito* **Cannonau**, try *amarone* or *recioto* from **Valpolicella**. As an alternative to straight Cannonau and Carignano del Sulcis, see how the two varieties perform in the **Languedoc**.

Sicily

Not red Marsala

Best-known wines Corvo Rosso

Grape varieties Nero d'Avola/Calabrese, Nerello, Frappato

Style Warm, soft Cerasuolo di Vittoria; cherry-and-chocolate Nero d'Avola

Quality/Price *····⟩****/£····⟩££££

With the exception of Corvo Rosso, a branded wine from Duca di Salaparuta rather than a DOC, Sicily doesn't boast any famous red wines – but that doesn't mean there are no good reds to be found on the island. Cerasuolo di Vittoria, made from Frappato and Nero d'Avola, could almost pass for a rosé, so light is its colour. Etna, by contrast, made from the Nerello Mascalese grape, is deep-coloured and full-bodied.

The finest wines are those made outside the DOC system, especially Regaleali's Rosso del Conte, Duca Enrico from Duca di Salaparuta and the varietal wines from the spanking-new Planeta winery.

The Sicilian taste Cerasuolo di Vittoria is warm, soft and full of ripe red-fruit flavours, with rather more substance than its light colour would suggest. Wines with a higher proportion of Nero d'Avola show flavours of cherries, currants, leather, tobacco and chocolate, with the best versions also having a decade's worth of tannins.

Tradition is the key to the character of Sicily's wine styles

Where next? Have a look at the rather different styles of wines being made on **Italy**'s other wine-producing island, **Sardinia**, then find what's new in mainland **Apulia**.

Somontano

Small, but with big ambitions
Grape varieties Cabernet Sauvignon, Tempranillo, Pinot Noir, Merlot, Garnacha
Style Varietals with a Spanish accent
Quality/Price **·····*******/£·····}££££

RECOMMENDED PRODUCERS
Enate
Bodegas Pirineos (Espiral)
Viñas del Vero

These wines are making a mark and the reason is simple. This is one of few regions where the local DO laws allow producers to plant foreign grapes such as Pinot Noir, Cabernet Sauvignon and Merlot on more than an experimental basis. The number of producers is few, but they are good.

The Somontano taste So far, the dominant flavour is of whatever varietal is being used. However, this comes with a Spanish accent, meaning that the plummy Cabernet Sauvignons and Merlots have a mellow, tobacco-y edge.

Where next? **Navarra** is the competition; **Rioja**, **Priorato** and **Ribera del Duero** the next step up.

Sonoma

No longer in Napa's shadow

Grape varieties Cabernet Sauvignon, Cabernet Franc, Pinot Noir, Merlot, Zinfandel

Style Rich, honest Zinfandel, sexy Pinot Noir, supple Bordeaux blends

Quality/Price ***·····⟩*****/££·····⟩£££££

Sonoma County is much larger and more diverse than its eastern neighbour Napa. The region splits into a number of distinct districts, and anyone looking for suitable conditions for growing virtually any variety will find at least one spot where it will thrive.

The Bordeaux varieties perform best in Alexander Valley, Knights Valley, Sonoma Mountain and Sonoma Valley. Zinfandel finds a home in the Dry Creek Valley, and producers from throughout California avail themselves of the fine old-vine fruit available in the district. Those looking for somewhere cooler to grow Pinot Noir will find Carneros (qv), Russian River Valley and Sonoma Coast to their liking. While there aren't as many wineries as in Napa, the quality is comparable, the prices often cheaper and the mood far more relaxed.

The Sonoma taste Given the wide range of growing conditions, it's difficult to speak of a generic Sonoma style for any variety. Cabernet and Merlot blends vary from dense, sweet, plummy and open-faced to rather tighter and more structured, yet still with rich, fragrant olive and currant fruit. Pinot Noir, at its best from the Russian River Valley, is an opulent, sexy wine, sometimes a little too oaky but packed with glorious, fragrant, silky fruit. Dry Creek Zinfandel is warm and welcoming, generously flavoured with berries and plums and seasoned with white pepper.

A glorious sunset over the Sonoma Valley

Where next? Napa Valley for **Cabernet** and **Merlot**, **Carneros** and the **Central Coast** for **Pinot Noir**, or check out the Australian competition from **Yarra Valley**, **Coonawarra** and **Margaret River**.

South Australia

Home of the Australian wine industry

Best-known wines Penfolds' Grange, Henschke's
Hill of Grace, Jacob's Creek...

Grape varieties Shiraz, Cabernet Sauvignon,
Grenache, Mourvèdre, Cabernet Franc, Pinot Noir

Style From world-class Shiraz to sup-me-quick,
bargain-basement blends

Quality/Price **····⟩*****/£····⟩£££££

South Australia merits its preeminent position as the Wine State whether we simply tot up the quantity or whether we adopt some formula for assessing quality. It is the home of Penfolds' Grange, which would register the maximum on any Richter scale of winemaking. This seminal wine was originally made on the Magill Estate near Adelaide, not far from where the state's first vines were planted in 1837. At the other end of the scale, wine gushes in torrents from the irrigated Riverland close to the borders with Victoria and New South Wales, ready to quench the thirst that barbies seem to bring on. If you have ever drunk an Australian "cask" wine (and why, incidentally, a plastic bag should have hijacked the term for a wooden barrel only an astute ad person would know), the chances are good that it will have originated in Riverland.

Between these extremes are two of Australia's best-known wine districts: the Barossa Valley and Coonawarra. The Barossa is the clearing house for much of the wine made in South Australia, and producers truck in vast amounts of wine from various parts of the state (and the other states) to be blended, bottled and then shipped out. However, there are also some excellent small estates making the most of old-vine Shiraz and Grenache, and the local Cabernet Sauvignons aren't bad, either. Coonawarra is the source of many of Australia's finest Cabernet Sauvignons, and the Shiraz can also be excellent. The region lies on a special type of *terra rossa* soil which is duplicated in several other parts of the south of the state, such as Padthaway, Robe and Mount Benson, and these areas may in the future enjoy the same prestige Coonawarra does today.

The Barossa lies to the northeast of Adelaide, but is not the only wine region close to the capital. To the south lie McLaren Vale, home of soft, chocolatey reds, and also Langhorne Creek, which supplies generously flavoured Cabernet and Shiraz to several wineries in the state, although a few producers are actually based here. East of Adelaide are the Adelaide Hills, home of some of the coolest vineyards and most elegant reds in the state. However, the best wine from the region is a Shiraz, from Henschke's

Hill of Grace vineyard. On the plains north of Adelaide, close to the urban sprawl, are a few wineries, the best of which is Primo Estate, but travel 70 km (43.5 miles) further and you hit Clare, home of more warm-hearted reds made from Cabernet, Shiraz, Merlot and Malbec.

Where next? **Victoria** offers an even greater diversity of styles, so follow the varietal route here first and then onwards to **New South Wales**. See also specific entries for **Adelaide Hills**, **Barossa**, **Clare**, **Coonawarra** and **McLaren Vale**.

Southwest France

An interesting corner of France
Best-known wines Madiran, Cahors
Grape varieties Tannat, Malbec, Negrette, Fer, Cabernet Sauvignon, Cabernet Franc, Merlot
Style Too diverse to get on one line
Quality/Price *····⟩****/£····⟩££££

If you ever wanted proof that France was a fascinating wine country, Southwest France is where you should look. Those looking for hundreds of high-class wines should start with Bordeaux and go no further. But anyone interested in the weird and the wacky should set off south and east from Bordeaux with their palates prepared for a broad and highly colourful spectrum of flavours.

The wines split into two groups: those which ape Bordeaux and the rest. The former category includes Bergerac, Buzet, Côtes du Brulhois, Côtes de Duras, Côtes du Marmandais and Pécharmant, and although there's little that the folk in the Médoc, Graves, St-Emilion and Pomerol need get too concerned about, there are several wines which are a cut above the vast majority of Bordeaux and Bordeaux Supérieur.

The non-apers are a disparate bunch, based on grape varieties which much of the rest of the world has never even heard of. Malbec is perhaps the most noble local variety, although only in Cahors does it play a starring role. Negrette is the driving force behind Côtes du Frontonnais, while Fer is responsible for the reds of Marcillac. Tannat is the main variety in Béarn, Côtes de St-Mont, and Tursan, but reaches its apogee in the usually tannic but occasionally very classy wines of Madiran. Straddling the dividing line between the two camps is Irouléguy, in which Tannat is blended with at least 50 per cent of the two Cabernets. The best producers are Brana and the local co-op, which makes Domaine de Mignaberry.

The Southwest France taste The entries for Bergerac, Cahors, Côtes du Frontonnais and Madiran will give you some inkling of what to expect from the Bordeaux-style wines and those based on Malbec, Negrette and Tannat, respectively. In Marcillac, the rustic Fer makes simple peppery, fruity wines which don't object to – indeed benefit from – 3 to 4 years of bottle age.

Where next? See also specific entries for **Bergerac, Cahors, Côtes du Frontonnais** and **Madiran.**

St-Emilion

Worth a detour

Region Bordeaux

Grape varieties Cabernet Sauvignon, Cabernet Franc, Merlot, Petit Verdot, Malbec

Style Sweet, plummy fruit, sometimes with cherry, raspberry and chocolate nuances

Quality/Price ***⋯⟩*****/££⋯⟩£££££

RECOMMENDED PRODUCERS

L'Angélus
Ausone
Beauséjour-Duffau-Lagarrosse
Belair
Bellefont-Belcier
Canon
Canon-la-Gaffelière
Cheval Blanc
Clos Fourtet
La Dominique
Ferrand-Lartigue
Figeac
Grand Mayne
Larmande
Magdelaine
Monbousquet
La Mondotte
Pavie
Pavie Decesse
Le Tertre-Rôteboeuf
Troplong Mondot
Trottevieille
Valandraud

St-Emilion is a bit of an oddball in the Bordeaux firmament. First of all, there is actually a place worth making a detour for, rather than the collection of shifty buildings huddled round a tiny square which passes for a village in other parts of the region. It is a very pretty wine town, on a hill with cobbled streets, ancient limestone cellars and medieval houses. Even the Romans were here: the poet Ausonius grew vines at what is today Château Ausone.

Secondly, there's a wide variation in soil types, with some having much in common with neighbouring Pomerol while others are more like those found in the Médoc, so the wines can vary quite markedly.

Thirdly, the appellation took it upon itself in 1958 to come up with its own classification of producers, which was to be revised every ten years (although in practice the intervals have been rather longer – 1958, 1969, 1985, 1996). But don't go thinking because you see the words "St-Emilion *grand cru*" on a bottle of wine that it will be among the region's best. There are hundreds of *grands crus*, very few of which provide anything remarkable. For better wine, you need to move up to *grand cru classé*. Following the 1996 classification, there are 55 *grand cru classé* properties, 11 *premiers grands crus classés* "B" and two *premiers grands crus classés* "A",

Cheval Blanc and Ausone. Fine, you think. Only some properties aren't included in the classification for various reasons. The two most obvious omissions are rising superstar Valandraud, ineligible due to not having produced wines for the ten years required by the classification panel, and Le Tertre-Rôteboeuf, which didn't bother to submit its wine to the panel. Perhaps they'll both be included in the next revision, perhaps not.

Merlot is the dominant grape in St-Emilion, although it doesn't have the same hold it has in Pomerol. Both Cabernet Franc and Cabernet Sauvignon are widely grown, with the former making up as much as 60 per cent of Cheval Blanc. The diversity of soils and of grapes used means that there's no such thing as a typical St-Emilion, and you're going to have to try several different châteaux' wines in order to get to grips with the appellation. The only problem with this will be that some of the most sought-after wines are made in tiny quantities; even if you can find them, you may not be able to afford them.

If St-Emilion all becomes a bit serious and complicated, and you yearn for the simple country life, four surrounding satellite villages borrow the suffix and oblige with straightforward wines. These are Lussac-St-Emilion, Montagne-St-Emilion, Puisseguin-St-Emilion and St-Georges-St-Emilion. Although most of these wines have precious little to do with St-Emilion proper, their mix of grapes may well be similar, and the soft, round fruit is attractive at around 3 to 5 years. Châteaux St-Georges, Maquin-St-Georges and Vieux-Château-St-André are among the best.

Château
Ausone in
St-Emilion
produces
memorable
Merlot wines

The St-Emilion taste The great attraction of St-Emilion is its easy, approachable drinkability and it is a good place to begin a tasting assault on the wines of Bordeaux. St-Emilions are generally among the lightest of the classic Bordeaux wines, maturing relatively swiftly, so most would be ready to drink within five years.

The more highly-ranked wines have rather more stuffing, with the sweet plummy fruit of lighter wines giving way to denser cherry, raspberry, cassis and chocolate flavours. They can be delicious at three or four years old, but they are built for rather lengthier ageing.

Where next? If you like the softness of St-Emilion with more weight of fruit, try **Pomerol. Fronsac and Canon-Fronsac**, Côtes de Castillon and Côtes de Francs are cheaper alternatives. For firmer wines, or **Cabernet Sauvignon**-based wines, continue to **Graves** or the **Médoc**.

St-Estèphe

The sturdy village of the Médoc
Region Bordeaux
Grape varieties Cabernet Sauvignon, Cabernet Franc, Merlot, Petit Verdot, Malbec
Style Tannic, earthy wines, showing blackcurrant and cigar-box tones with age
Quality/Price ***⋯⟩*****/£££⋯⟩£££££

RECOMMENDED PRODUCERS

Andron-Blanquet
Beau-Site
Le Boscq
Calon-Ségur
Chambert-Marbuzet
Cos d'Estournel
Cos Labory
Haut-Marbuzet
Lafon Rochet
De Marbuzet
Meyney
Montrose
Les Ormes-de-Pez
De Pez

St-Estèphe sits at the northern end of the Haut-Médoc. The gravel soil that underpins Margaux, St-Julien and Pauillac thins out here and lumpen clay takes its place. The result is that the wines don't have the elegance of Margaux or St-Julien, nor the breeding of Pauillac, but rather an earthy, stolid character. But give them 15 years or so and they do relax and show a bit of class. Classed growths aren't all that numerous here, but there are several *crus bourgeois* of note, headed by Haut-Marbuzet.

The St-Estèphe taste The wines are consequently sturdy, beefy, chunky, tannic, earthy, high in acidity, and sometimes even astringent in their youth. But with time, the tannic structure subsides and the fruit does emerge to give honest, rather than thrillingly complex, wines.

Where next? In the **Médoc**, Moulis and Listrac can be similarly sturdy. Compare St-Estèphe with **Pauillac** to see the latter's extra touch of class.

St-Joseph

Lightest of the northern Rhônes

Region Northern Rhône

Grape varieties Syrah

Style Forward blackcurrant and spice flavours

Quality/Price **⋯⟩****/££⋯⟩££££

It's hard to generalise about St-Joseph, as there is such a diversity of *terroirs*. The traditional core of the appellation was of well-exposed terraced slopes, but the boundaries were expanded in 1969 to 70 times more land, much of it rather less suitable flatter terrain. Wines from the good vineyards deserve their place in the northern Rhône Syrah firmament. Those from the lesser sites can be pleasant but really should either have a separate appellation or be content with being Côtes du Rhône. However, they are a good introduction.

The St-Joseph taste St-Joseph is the most transparently fruity of northern-Rhône Syrah wines, and bottles can be broached without fear of gum fatigue from their second birthday onwards. Good examples have Syrah's forthright spicy, blackcurrant flavour which is not obscured by a thick cloak of tannin, although the best wines will easily survive for ten years.

Where next? In the northern Rhône, **Crozes-Hermitage** is the next weightiest; after that, **Côte-Rôtie** and **Hermitage**; and finally, the biggest, **Cornas**. The southern Rhône will bring a warm, broad and easier style.

St-Julien

Benchmark claret

Region Bordeaux

Grape varieties Cabernet Sauvignon, Cabernet Franc, Merlot, Petit Verdot, Malbec

Style Refined, cedary, elegant plush wines

Quality/Price ***>*****/£££>£££££

Although St-Julien boasts no first-growth châteaux, it offers vividly delicious and harmonious wines and is an ideal place to start an exploration of the Médoc. As well as being the smallest of the famous Médoc villages, it is also the most consistent, thanks to the high quality of wine produced by the 11 classed-growth properties, the most impressive and expensive of which is Léoville-Las-Cases.

The St-Julien taste These are the most balanced, complete, all-round wines of the Médoc, with gentleness and approachability. There is an unmistakable surge of Bentley-like power under the bonnet, yet acres of soft leather in which to luxuriate, and a whiff of exotic enchantment in the lingering, cedary perfume. They are neither as opulently, voluptuously rich as Pauillac, nor as hauntingly fragrant as Margaux, yet they are adept at drawing together opposing elements of raw force and gentle persuasion.

Léoville-Poyferré is one of the châteaux in St-Julien – the Médoc's smallest village

Where next? Pauillac to the north is sterner, **Margaux** to the south is more perfumed – and more erratic. Or head outside France to see what **Tuscany, Coonawarra, Yarra Valley, Napa Valley, Sonoma, Stellenbosch, Hawke's Bay, Auckland** and **Maipo** can offer.

Stellenbosch

Leading light of the Cape
Grape varieties Cabernet Sauvignon, Merlot, Pinotage, Shiraz, Cabernet Franc
Style Rich, earthy Pinotage; increasingly complex Bordeaux blends
Quality/Price **⋯⟩****/££⋯⟩£££££

RECOMMENDED PRODUCERS

Alto
Altydgedacht
Beyerskloof
Clos Malverne
Neil Ellis
Grangehurst
Kanonkop
Meerlust
Meinert (Devoncrest)
Neetlingshof
Rustenberg
Rust en Vrede
Saxenburg
Simonsig
Stellenzicht
Thelema
Uiterwyk
Vergelegen
Vriesenhof
Warwick
Welgemeend

This is where most of South Africa's finest red wines call home, and it's also where most of the exciting activity in South Africa is happening at present. New producers who have no historical bondage to hold them back are pushing forward the quality barriers, and showing the rest of the world that South Africa is a force to be reckoned with.

The best of the traditional estates such as Meerlust and Kanonkop are keeping pace with them, and the results are first-class Bordeaux blends, Shiraz capable of taking on the Aussies and Pinotage which demonstrate that it is now a grape to be taken seriously. Yes, there are still some wineries that are underperforming, and yes, some of the vineyards are not as suitable for wine production as the Stellenboschers would have us think. However, thanks to the movers and shakers, Stellenbosch wines have improved more in the short time since apartheid was dismantled than in the 20 years before that.

The Stellenbosch taste With 50 different soil types and a diversity of winemaking styles, the taste of the wines is far from uniform. The finest Pinotage has a welcoming richness, with concentrated berry and banana flavours. Cabernet blends become more complex with each vintage, with riper fruit flavours backed up by less gawky, hard structures, so they should age even better than their predecessors have. Shiraz is also more refined, although no less powerful, with intense, berry and plum flavours infused with herby notes.

Where next? Still in **South Africa**, **Paarl** can offer similar quality, but not as many top-class producers.

Syrah/Shiraz

Beginning to get the respect it deserves
Style Dark berries, blackpepper, citrus peel, woodsmoke, chocolate and more
Grown in The Rhône, southern France, Australia, California, South Africa, Chile, Washington State, Italy

Cabernet Sauvignon is much more widely travelled. Pinot Noir sets more hearts fluttering. Yet, Syrah can proudly stand alongside these two varieties as one of the great grapes of the world, and manages to combine some of the best characteristics of both. It has the sturdiness, relative ease of cultivation and strong varietal thumbprint of Cabernet, together with – at its best – the perfume and gypsy wildness of Pinot. It is curious, then, that it isn't more popular, but this may have much to do with the fact that until comparatively recently, few people were even familiar with the variety.

The vine is thought to have originated, etymologically at least, from the town of Shiraz in present-day Iran, but it found its true home in the northern Rhône over 2,000 years ago. Some families there – the Chaves, for instance – have been growing Syrah on the Hermitage hillside for around 700 vintages.

Hermitage may be the most famous manifestation of Syrah, yet there's precious little wine made each year – Gevrey-Chambertin in Burgundy has four times more vineyards. Syrah is the power behind the other wines of the northern Rhône: Cornas, Côte-Rôtie, Crozes-Hermitage and St-Joseph. These vary in quality, weight and expense, and sometimes include small proportions of white grapes. Châteauneuf-du-Pape and other southern-Rhône wines include Syrah in the blend, but almost always in a supporting role to the dominant Grenache, as its forceful nature can make it presence felt rather strongly if too much is used. The only interest the rest of France has shown in Syrah until recently was in using Hermitage to beef up inferior claret during the 19th century. But today, producers in southern France are using it to good effect, either for 100 per cent varietal wines or in conjunction with other varieties. Mourvèdre and Grenache are often the favoured partners, but Cabernet Sauvignon has also been used to great effect, most notably at Domaine de Trévallon in Provence.

The Cabernet-Syrah blend is far more common in Australia, that other outpost of Syrah. Here, Shiraz, as it is almost always known, has been the most widely planted variety for many years, although it hasn't always been appreciated for the quality grape that it is. Time was in the early 1980s when many vineyards full of gnarled old Shiraz vines were grubbed up, abandoned or replanted with the more fashionable Cabernet Sauvignon. Today, fashion has swung back in Shiraz's favour, and many producers are cursing themselves for pulling out all those ancient vines, as the ones that remain are often providing the finest quality grapes. Australia shows how versatile Shiraz can be. It is the main variety in that giant, long-lived Australian classic, Penfolds' Grange, but it is just as adept at turning its hand to simple, fresh, fruity wines. Those looking for high-quality wines will find several styles from the peppery Rhône lookalikes of central Victoria to the huge chocolatey monsters of the Clare Valley.

It is Australia as much as France that has brought Shiraz/Syrah to the attention of many wine-lovers throughout the world. Today, more and more Syrah is being planted as producers look for another string to their red-wine bows beside Cabernet. California has now joined the ranks of those producing world-class Syrah, and to the north, Washington State has a small number of promising wines, as do Argentina and Chile to the south.

New Zealand, 15 years ago, was considered unsuitable for any red varieties, never mind Syrah, but today, Hawke's Bay produces a handful of Syrah wines, most of which are very good. South Africans call the grape Shiraz, and although the traditional wines have been rather clumsy, the current crop includes several wines which should keep the Aussies on their toes. Back in Europe, Syrah has appeared in vineyards in Tuscany, Piedmont and other parts of Italy, in various areas of Spain and in Switzerland.

The Syrah taste The grape's skin yields generous fruit, tannin and inky colour, and the juice provides good acidity. It therefore has great potential for making long-lived wines that are big, dry and intense, with a characteristic spicy and black-peppery smell. It looks (and, when young, can smell and taste) like the dark fluid that spilled out of inkwells in older readers' schooldays.

Some Syrah shares with Cabernet Sauvignon a taste of blackcurrants overlaid with blueberries, blackberries, plums and elderberries. Rhône Syrah can often show perfumed, orange-peel character; it takes well to oak ageing. The Australians favour American oak, which gives more roundness and vanilla-y softness to the wines. The French – naturally – prefer the less obvious character of French oak.

More mature wines can evoke tar, leather, liquorice, smoke and even burnt rubber, and older wines can be indistinguishable from claret. Mature, expensive wines are, however, in a minority. Syrah, being a good cropper and disease-resistant, makes plenty of light, easy, inexpensive drinking, both in France and Australia. The attraction of these wines is that, although they do not have the stature of classic Syrah, they are reliably good, full of raspberry and plum flavours. There is no need to send your nose on a delicate hunt-the-flavour mission; the fruit comes out to meet it.

Where next? For similar weight and power, try **Nebbiolo**, **Sangiovese** or **Touriga Nacional**, or try the new wave of **Priorato**s from **Spain**.

Tempranillo

Spain's greatest grape?
Style Spicy, with strawberry, toast, leather and tobacco tones
Grown in Spain, Argentina, Portugal

It is for its role in making Spain's Rioja that Tempranillo is considered a great grape. Here it typically makes up 70 per cent of the blend, along with Garnacha, Graciano and Mazuelo. It's often difficult to ascertain precisely what Tempranillo tastes like as the oak used is such an integral part of the wines. Unoaked 100 per cent Tempranillo Riojas can be disappointing, but this is often more a factor of high yields than the inherent quality of the grape.

Yet it is certainly true that the bolstering of the oak, and of the other grape varieties, brings a structure to Tempranillo which it can lack by itself. Rioja may be the most famous incarnation, but currently the best

Tempranillo is being made in Ribera del Duero, where it is known as Tinto Fino or Tinto del País. Up to 25 per cent of other grapes can be used in the blend, and Cabernet Sauvignon is a favoured variety for some producers (as it is in Navarra). However, others prefer not to blend, and the wines certainly demonstrate that, in the right conditions, Tempranillo can do very well without any help, thank you very much. The grape appears under a number of different guises – Cencibel, Ull de Llebre, Tinto de Toro – throughout Spain, and is displacing other lower-quality varieties from vineyards in places such as La Mancha and Valencia.

Outside Spain, it's rather more scarce. In the Douro, the Portuguese use Tinta Roriz in the blends for port and table wines, while Tinto Aragones is an ingredient in Dão. The Argentinians have extensive plantings, although so far there has been little beyond the clean, fresh and fruity. New World countries have yet to do much with Tempranillo, although there are plantings in Oregon and California.

The Tempranillo taste Unoaked Tempranillo, as the Argentinians and sometimes the Riojans make it, is simple, strawberry-ish and refreshing. To see how good it can be on its own when yields are kept low, go to Ribera del Duero. Here you have huge, dense, damson, cherry, blackberry and raspberry flavours with a spicy, earthy edge – wines which drink well from three or four years old but can last for 20 more.

Where next? Try **Pinot Noir**, which has something of the strawberry character of **Tempranillo**, or **Italy**'s Montepulciano.

Trentino-Alto Adige

Never mind the scenery, what about the wines?
Grape varieties Lagrein, Teroldego, Schiava, Cabernet Sauvignon, Merlot, Pinot Noir
Style Often light and dilute, but increasingly showing real personality
Quality/Price *⋯⟩****/£⋯⟩£££££

Italian-speaking Trentino is slightly warmer than German-speaking Alto Adige to the north. However, both places have much of interest in the way of red wines; indeed red grapes outnumber whites in both. Each is covered by a regional DOC which includes a number of different grape varieties. Some of these are familiar – Cabernet (Sauvignon

RECOMMENDED PRODUCERS
CV di Caldaro
Castello Schwanburg
CP Cortaccia
Foradori
Franz Haas
Hofstätter
Alois Lageder
Josephus Mayr
Maso Cantanghel
Josef Niedermayr
Pojer & Sandri
San Leonardo
CP Santa Maddalena
CS La Vis
Baron Widmann

The attractive Trentino Alto-Adige region in northeast Italy produces inspiring red wines

and Franc), Merlot (in Trentino) and Pinot Nero (aka Blauburgunder) – and although many wines made with these varieties are rather thin, good growers and the many splendid co-operatives (especially of Alto Adige) can produce splendidly concentrated wines, especially from the Bordeaux varieties. There are also several local grapes of interest. Schiava or Vernatsch is the most widely planted variety, with 60 per cent of the Alto Adige vineyards. Lagrein is used for reds and rosés, with the gutsier versions being labelled *dunkel* (dark). Teroldego makes mostly easy, Beaujolais-style quaffers, but some producers produce rather more serious oaked versions. Finally, Marzemino makes charming, aromatic wines in Trentino.

The Trentino-Alto Adige taste Full-flavoured wines used to be few and far between, with the overwhelming feeling being one of lightness and dilution of flavour. However, there are now more and more wines of real presence and personality, with the Bordeaux varieties being increasingly impressive, elegant and full of varietal flavour.

Of the local grapes, the plummy reds of Lagrein are chewy and flavoursome when young, turning into soft, smooth, smoky styles after a decade's ageing. Schiava makes light, inconsequential reds, instantly gulpable, with a slightly bitter and refreshing almondy edge. Marzemino is usually juicy and fresh in style, with fragrant raspberry flavours – equally attractive young or mature. The underrated Teroldego is used for dark, robust yet flower-scented wines with enough tannin to age five-plus years.

Where next? For Lagrein, try **Southwest France**'s **Côtes du Frontonnais** or **Cahors**. For Schiava, try **Burgundy**'s Passe-Tout-Grains or **Switzerland**'s Dôle. For Marzemino, try **Beaujolais** and for Teroldego, try **Dolcetto**.

Tuscany

Super Super-Tuscans, and more besides
Best-known wines Chianti, Brunello di Montalcino, Sassicaia
Grape varieties Sangiovese, Cabernet Sauvignon, Merlot, Syrah
Style Varies widely, but usually plenty of it
Quality/Price *······\}*****/£······\}£££££

RECOMMENDED PRODUCERS
Capezzana
Cantagallo
Frescobaldi
La Parrina
Il Poggiolo
Le Pupille

It's a toss-up between Tuscany and Piedmont as to which is Italy's finest red wine region. The most famous wines of both are based on just one grape variety: Nebbiolo for Barolo and Barbaresco in Piedmont, and Sangiovese for Chianti, Brunello di Montalcino and Vino Nobile di Montepulciano in Tuscany. But while the folks in Piedmont have Dolcetto and Barbera to play around with, not to mention other oddballs such as Freisa, Grignolino and Ruché, the Tuscans have little else of note. Or rather they *had* little else of note. Today, many of the region's finest wines contain no Sangiovese, and rely on Cabernet Sauvignon. Cabernet has been grown in Tuscany since the 18th century in the village of Carmignano, to the west of Florence, and this DOCG was for many years the only one permitted to use it.

However, restrictions on wines such as Chianti and Vino Nobile also stated that not only could no wine be 100 per cent Sangiovese but that white grapes such as Trebbiano and Malvasia had to be used in the blends. In the early 1970s, many Tuscan producers decided that they'd had enough of the restrictions and that if they couldn't make the wines they wanted within the DOC laws, then they'd go outside them. The result was a wave of wines which could only be labelled *vini da tavola* – table wines – soon to become known as the Super-Tuscans.

Some made 100 per cent Sangiovese wines, some opted for Bordeaux varieties and to a lesser extent Syrah and Pinot Noir. A third avenue was to mix the French and the Italian to make blends like Antinori's Tignanello. Sexy packaging, plenty of new oak and great quality of fruit soon put them in the very highest rank of Italian wines, with prices to match. From the 1996 vintage onwards, *vini da tavola* cannot state their origin, grape variety and vintage, and the Super-Tuscans now have three options. They can change to DOC status, either within an existing district where the laws regarding grape varieties and other issues

Carmignano ○ ○ Firenze
○ Pisa

Chianti ○
○ Chianti Classico

○ Bolgheri

○ Brunello di Montalcino
Vino Noble di ○
Montepulciano

have now been relaxed, or they can apply for their own DOC. Another avenue is to claim IGT Toscana status, which many feel carries more clout than any DOC name. An easy rule of thumb is that the best producers of Chianti, Brunello and Vino Nobile also make the best Super-Tuscans.

Carmignano lies within the Chianti Montalbano boundaries, and with its Cabernet content of 6 to 10 per cent was in some ways a forerunner of the Super-Tuscans. The wines are more refined than most Chianti, and there are also some lighter reds for early consumption made under the Barco Reale DOC. On the eastern side of Florence within Chianti Rufina is Pomino, a DOC created in 1983. Sangiovese is the main variety, but the two Cabernets and Merlot are also permitted. Morellino di Scansano and Parrina come from the southern reaches of Tuscany, and provide wines which – while never great – are good examples of honest Sangiovese. The regions of Bolgheri, Brunello, Chianti and Vino Nobile di Montepulciano have their own entries in this book.

The Tuscan taste Even with Cabernet-Merlot blends, the wines often have a certain slightly bitter, herby Tuscan-ity to them, although some of the top wines more closely resemble classed-growth claret. Sangiovese-based wines veer from pale and vaguely cherryish to powerful, plummy reds with a veneer of sweet oak to rather more old-fashioned and sturdy wines with almost savoury, prune-like flavours.

Where next? The Californians are beginning to make strides with **Sangiovese**, and have their own version of the Super-Tuscan blends. See also specific entries for **Bolgheri, Brunello di Montalcino, Chianti, Sangiovese** and **Vino Nobile di Montepulciano.**

Umbria

RECOMMENDED PRODUCERS
Adanti
Arnaldo Caprai
Castello della Sala
CS dei Colli Amerini
Fattoria dei Barbi
Lungarotti
La Palazzola
Palazzone

A desert with a few oases
Best-known wines Torgiano, Sagrantino di Montefalco
Grape varieties Sangiovese, Sagrantino, Cabernet Sauvignon, Pinot Nero
Style Tuscan-inspired Torgiano; spicy, blackberryish Sagrantino di Montefalco
Quality/Price *⋯⟩****/£⋯⟩££££

Umbria may be as pretty as Tuscany, but it's certainly not as well-endowed in the red wine department. However, it's not a complete desert. Some of the wines from Colli Amerini, usually but not always made from

Sangiovese, can be good and there are a few "Super-Umbrians" dotted about the province. The two DOCGs are Torgiano Riserva and Sagrantino di Montefalco.

Torgiano is virtually a one-horse town, managed with skill by the Lungarotti family. Sangiovese is the main grape, with Canaiolo, Montepulciano and Ciliegiolo in the blend. The basic wine, Rubesco (DOC), is overshadowed by the barrique-aged *riserva* (DOCG) from the Monticchio vineyard, which in the past has been able to hold its own against many a Super-Tuscan. Quality today is slightly more erratic.

Montefalco Rosso is another reasonable Sangiovese-based wine, but the real fireworks come with Sagrantino di Montefalco, Umbria's answer to the *recioto* and *amarone* wines of Valpolicella. It's made in the same way, using *passito* or dried Sagrantino grapes, and can be fermented to dryness or left a little sweet (*abboccato*).

Vine-training in Umbria follows a number of traditional methods

The Umbria taste Torgiano at its best provides the rich and slightly bitter, cherryish fruit of decent Chianti, but recent wines have seemed rather tired. Sagrantino di Montefalco is rich, densely fruity with blackberry notes, bittersweet and powerfully alcoholic. Drink it as an after-dinner treat as you would port, since most food will wither in its presence.

Where next? Tuscany instead of Torgiano; *recioto, amarone* (*see* Valpolicella), **Port** or France's **Vins Doux Naturels** instead of Sagrantino.

Valpolicella

A much-maligned name
Region Veneto
Grape varieties Corvina, Molinara, Rondinella
Style Bitter-cherry fruit in varying levels of intensity
Quality/Price *⋯⟩****/£⋯⟩£££££

Valpolicella is made in the Veneto, Italy's largest producer of DOC wine. Much of it is plain and boring, produced on an industrial scale and the vinous equivalent of muzak.

RECOMMENDED PRODUCERS

Accordini
Serègo Alighieri
Allegrini
Bertani
Bolla
Brigaldara
Dal Forno
Degani
Le Ragose
Masi

Bulk Valpol, from high-yielding vines planted on the fertile plains, has done absolutely nothing for the name of Valpolicella, the DOC system, Italy or the consumer.

Fortunately, there is more to Valpolicella than that. If you're prepared to pay a little more and hunt out the best producers and hillside vineyards, there are some absolutely wonderful wines to be enjoyed. The best are made in the Classico zone between the bumps (they are hardly hills) to the east of Lake Garda and north of Verona. One village to the north, Valpantena, is considered worthy enough to qualify for its own DOC, although the difference in taste between it and other Valpolicellas is marginal.

There are three different styles of Valpolicella: *normale, recioto* and *ripasso*. Variations in taste depend partly on which grapes are used. Corvina is the finest and brings structure to the wine, but it can only make up 80 per cent of the blend – there are a few 100 per cent Corvina wines which don't qualify for the DOC. Rondinella produces colourful juice with good acidity; Molinara is responsible for the softly fruity, easy-drinking styles. Then the winemaker has a choice of other varieties, including Rossignola, Negrara, Barbera and Sangiovese, up to 15 per cent. There is sufficient leeway in this mix to allow a wide variety of wines.

What principally determines the style, however, is the way the wine is made. The Valpolicella most often encountered is *normale*, which has been fermented to dryness in the normal way. *Superiore* versions have one degree more alcohol and are aged for a year, but, with a few notable exceptions, it hardly seems worth the bother. After all, the whole appeal of these light red wines (such as it is) is their freshness.

Recioto is made using dried grapes. The best bunches of grapes on an estate are picked 10 to 15 days earlier than the bulk of the crop in order to retain good acidity. They are then dried on straw-covered racks in cool, dry conditions for several months, during which they lose about one-third of their weight. The shrivelled grapes are crushed and a slow fermentation of the concentrated juice begins.

If the fermentation is stopped when the wine has reached around 13 per cent alcohol, some sweetness will remain and the wines, port-like in their sweetness, but much fresher-tasting, will be labelled *recioto*. If the wines are fermented to dryness, then the style is the big, powerful *amarone* with an alcohol level of around 15 per cent. Both styles are a million miles – no, make that *two* million – from commercial screw-top Valpolicella.

The third kind of Valpolicella, called *ripasso*, is somewhere between the other two in style. Once the *recioto* has fermented and been racked off the skins, ordinary Valpolicella is pumped onto these in the vat (hence *ripasso*), and the sugars and yeasts that are left behind begin a short re-fermentation. The process increases body and alcohol (13 per cent is common) and the result is a much more macho wine than straight Valpolicella. Trouble is, it doesn't always say *ripasso* on the label.

The Valpolicella taste *Normale* wines are light, fresh, youthful, crimson, cherry-like quaffers with a slightly tart edge to them, and should leave a gently bitter-almond finish like so many wines from this corner of the world. *Ripasso* versions (and the better single-vineyard *normales*) are altogether bigger, richer and fruitier, with a sweet 'n' sour liveliness.

Reciotos have intense, perfumed, plum and chocolate flavours and although sweet are not cloying, partly because of the acidity and partly because they have an edge of bitterness. In *amarones*, the fruit is so concentrated and the alcohol level so high that they give the illusion of being slightly sweet. They run a gamut of flavours from plums and chocolate to nuts and smoke, and they are so concentrated that a bottle will go a long way. Both *recioto* and *amarone* drink well from release but are capable of ageing for ten years or more.

Where next? For lighter styles, try **Bardolino**, Schiava from **Trentino-Alto Adige**, **Dolcetto** and lighter **Beaujolais**. For *recioto*, try Sagrantino di Montefalco (*see* **Umbria**) or **Port** (not tawny styles) and its imitators. For *amarone*, try **Priorato**, heavier styles of Cannonau di Sardegna (*see* **Sardinia**), **California Zinfandel** or Australian **Grenache**.

In Valpolicella, three types of grape variety are blended together to make red wines of great character

Veneto

Venice, Verona and Valpolicella

Best-known wines Valpolicella

Grape varieties Corvina, Molinara, Rondinella, Cabernet Sauvignon, Merlot, Wildbacher

Style From pleasantly gulpable to mellow and fruity to aromatic and herbaceous

Quality/Price *···⟩****/£···⟩£££££

Extending from Venice on the Adriatic coast inland to Lake Garda, the Veneto produces wine in vast quantities and makes more DOC wine than any other part of the country. It's a push for most people to think of any reds from this corner of northeastern Italy apart from Valpolicella, but there are some to be found.

Bardolino is Valpolicella's little brother, and the other main DOCs are Breganze, Colli Berici, Colli Euganei, Lison-Pramaggiore (which spills over onto Friuli-Venezia Giulia), Montello e Colli Asolani and Piave. The best wines in these are usually made from imported grapes, especially Cabernet and Merlot, but there are some native varieties of note, such as the rich and tannic Raboso of Piave and the aromatic Wildbacher. Native grape varieties such as Corvina, Rondinella and Molinara go into the region's two most famous wines, Bardolino and Valpolicella, and the rich and tannic Raboso del Piave matures with a warm, mellow glow. Imports include some fine Cabernets, Merlots and Pinot Noirs. A classic Bordeaux mix is used to make Venegazzù della Casa from Conte Loredan-Gasparini.

The stunning geology of the Veneto, a region that produces a number of red wine styles

The Veneto taste Bardolino is toned-down Valpolicella. It can be pleasantly gulpable, but almost never excites. Raboso is warm, mellow and fruity and benefits from a short period of bottle-age, while Wildbacher is aromatic and herbaceous. The Cabernet blends can be very impressive, with smoky, berry and blackcurrant fruit shining out.

Where next? When you've drunk the Veneto dry, go east to **Friuli-Venezia Giulia** or west to **Trentino-Alto Adige**.

Victoria

Splendidly diverse

Best-known wines Yarra Valley Pinot Noir
Grape varieties Shiraz, Cabernet, Pinot Noir, Merlot, Durif
Style Everything from light Pinot Noir to blockbuster Durif
Quality/Price **····⟩*****/££····⟩£££££

Variety is the hallmark of Victoria. No other Australian state has so many small wineries making such a variety of different wines in so many different ways. Sadly, few of its producers are of such a size as to make a large impact in the export markets, but now that several of Australia's largest companies are investing in the state, this could change.

The Yarra Valley to the east of Melbourne is perhaps the best-known district. This was one of Australia's premium wine regions in the late 1800s, but its modern history dates from the early 1970s, when several small wineries were established. Pinot Noir is the most highly rated variety, but Cabernet Sauvignon and Shiraz also do well, and Merlot shows promise. Pinot is the favoured red variety in the marginal Mornington Peninsula, although some wineries persist with Cabernet and Shiraz. To the west of the bay, Geelong favours the same three varieties.

North of Melbourne are Sunbury and the Macedon ranges which are most definitely on the chilly side. Again, this is, or should be, Pinot country, but the best wines from the region are Craiglee Shiraz and Virgin Hills, a Bordeaux blend. Gippsland is a vast, cool region east of the Yarra where the few wineries are spread far and wide, and where Bass Phillip makes one of Australia's finest Pinots. In the far southwest of the state lies Drumborg where, perhaps curiously, Cabernet is the favoured variety.

To the north of the Great Dividing Range in Central Victoria it is decidedly warmer, and Shiraz comes into its own. The most westerly region is Great Western, or the Grampians as its known to the locals. Some of the Shiraz vines date back to the 19th century, and the variety is still the region's best, although Cabernet, Pinot Noir and even Dolcetto and Pinot Meunier are grown. To the northeast is another outpost of first-class Shiraz, the Pyrenees, although once again the Cabernet can be equally fine. Both are among the most long-lived wines made anywhere in the country.

Bendigo and Heathcote lie eastwards from here and the wineries are widespread and few in number, but the quality is excellent, with Shiraz being the star variety. Still further east is the Goulburn Valley, where Chateau Tahbilk has a vineyard dating from 1860. Yes, it's Shiraz, but

RECOMMENDED PRODUCERS

Bannockburn
Bass Phillip
Best's
Brown Brothers
Chateau Tahbilk
Craiglee
Dalwhinnie
Dromana Estate
Giaconda
Jasper Hill
Mitchelton
Mount Langi Ghiran
Nicholson River
Paringa
Passing Clouds
Scotchman's Hill
Seppelt
Taltarni
Virgin Hills
Water Wheel

again, the Cabernet from the region can be just as good. The best wines of northeast Victoria are the luscious Liqueur Muscats and Tokays. However, some producers use the hot conditions to make massive Cabernets and Shiraz, and you'll also find some rip-snorting wines made from Durif, which may or may may not be California's Petite Sirah. There are several higher-altitude sites which can produce rather more elegant wines, as Brown Brothers and Giaconda show.

To the west between Mildura and Swan Hill are the irrigated vineyards of the Murray River, the source of vast quantities of unambitious wines and the occasional more concentrated surprise.

The Victoria taste Shiraz varies from the perfumed, cracked-pepper and blackberry of the cooler southern vineyards through rich, spicy, earthy, tannic and packed with berry flavour in Central Victoria to massive, almost port-like and often rather volatile around Rutherglen in the northeast.

Cabernet shows a similar diversity of style, with some wines being green and scarcely ripe, while others are full-bodied with berry and damson rather than blackcurrant flavours. The best Pinot Noirs are balanced and full of raspberry fruit, and now show the velvety texture and exotic aromas which they often lacked in the 1980s.

Where next? For other cool-climate wines, try neighbouring Tasmania (*see* **Australia**); compare **Yarra Valley Pinot Noirs** with one from **Oregon**. For more statuesque **Cabernet**, try the **Margaret River**; for more juicy, succulent styles try **South Australia**.

Vin Doux Naturel

Don't mind if I Doux
Region Southern France
Grape varieties Grenache
Style France's answer to port
Quality/Price **⸱⸱⸱⸱⸱>****/££⸱⸱⸱⸱>£££££

The best-known *vins doux naturels* (VDNs) of France are generally Muscat-based whites. The reds are also fortified wines whose fermentation is stopped by the addition of grape spirit. The process is similar to that used in making port, and VDNs reach a similar strength (around 20 per cent alcohol) and are sweet because of the unfermented grape sugar that remains. Banyuls, made down near the Spanish border, is the best-known, while other

VDNs from Roussillon include Rivesaltes and Maury. Like this trio, Rasteau from the southern Rhône is also based on Grenache, and although not as classy as the Muscat from neighbouring Beaumes de Venise, can still be warming and satisfying.

Wines labelled *rancio* have been kept in barrel (often in warm conditions) for an extended period.

RECOMMENDED PRODUCERS

Mas Amiel
Cazes
Des Chênes
De Jau
Maurydoré
Rabasse-Charavin
Sarda-Malet
Cave des Vignerons de Rasteau

The Vin Doux Naturel taste VDNs are rarely in the same class as port, being rather heavy and coarse, particularly after being left out in barrels to mature under the hot southern sun. They can retain deep, plummy flavours, but most develop a raisiny character. Extra open-air ageing brings on an oxidised character and a tawny colour to the wines.

Where next? Port, *recioto* (*see* **Valpolicella**), Cannonau from **Sardinia**, Sagrantino di Montefalco from **Umbria**, Mavrodaphne from **Greece**.

Vino Nobile di Montepulciano

Not as noble as it would like to be
Region Tuscany
Grape varieties Sangiovese, Mammolo, Canaiolo
Style Chunky and chewy, with cherry and blackcurrant fruit
Quality/Price **······⟩****/£££······⟩£££££

RECOMMENDED PRODUCERS

Terre di Bindella
Podere Boscarelli
Le Casalte
Fattoria del Cerro
Dei
Podere Il Macchione
Poliziano
Villa Sant' Anna
Tenuta Trerose
Tenuta Valdipiatta
Vittorio Innocenti

A slightly confusing beast, this, in that it is made largely from Prugnolo Gentile (a clone of the Sangiovese grape), and has nothing to do with the Montepulciano of Abruzzo, the Marches and Molise. Montepulciano in this instance is a rather pretty village to the south of Siena, and the noble DOCG wine from here should be like smart Chianti. This has not always been the case, though, and despite vast improvements in recent times and some top-class estates such as Poliziano, the finest Vino Nobile is still outclassed by the top *riservas* from Chianti Classico and Chianti Rufina. Vino Nobile must be aged for two years in cask, and producers have the option of the Rosso di Montepulciano DOC for wines that don't meet this requirement.

The Vino Nobile di Montepulciano taste Vino Nobile has the slightly bitter-cherry fruit of Tuscan Sangiovese, which is often accompanied by hints of blackcurrants. In its youth, the wines, although never as forbidding as Brunello di Montalcino, can be quite tannic, but they soften with age to a robust pepperiness.

Where next? Try Brunello di Montalcino, Chianti, Carmignano (*see* Tuscany).

Volnay

The silky one

Region Côte de Beaune
Grape varieties Pinot Noir
Style Silky, sweet, fragrant strawberry and cherry fruit
Quality/Price ***····⟩*****/£££····⟩£££££

Rustic Burgundian cuisine is a perfect match for the region's red wines

If you want a wine that is ethereal and seductive, then Volnay could be your perfect choice. In neighbouring Pommard, the soils tend to be rich in clay and the wines are on the sturdy side, but in Volnay, there is plenty of limestone in the soil, which brings finesse. There are no *grands crus* here, but several *premiers crus*, the finest of which are Cailleret Dessus, Clos de la Pousse d'Or, Clos de Chênes and Taillepieds. Volnay spills over into Meursault, with some wines being labelled Volnay-Santenots if they are red, Meursault if they are white.

The Volnay taste Some wines sing with light, sweet, fragrant strawberry and cherry fruit in youth, developing into elegant wines with moderate ageing (five years at most); the texture evokes silk and lace.

Others are bigger and more powerfully structured, with a greater weight of fruit that needs almost a decade to blossom, although they seldom reach the chunkiness of Pommard.

Where next? For more silky **Burgundy**, **Chambolle-Musigny** and **Vosne-Romanée** in the **Côte de Nuits** are good places to start – and finish.

Vosne-Romanée

Home of the finest Pinot Noir in the world

Region Côte de Nuits

Grape varieties Pinot Noir

Style Opulent, plummy and sensuous, with notes of chocolate and figs

Quality/Price ***·····⟩*****/£££·····⟩£££££

The Côte de Nuits reaches its greatest heights of quality, excitement and prices in Vosne-Romanée. One estate has traditionally dominated the quality end of the market. The Domaine de la Romanée-Conti – DRC to those in the know – is sole owner of the *grands crus* Romanée-Conti and La Tâche, and also has vineyards in Romanée-St Vivant, Richebourg, Grands-Echézeaux and Echézeaux. For years it stood unassailed as Burgundy's finest domaine, until its co-owner Lalou Bize-Leroy bought an existing domaine with vines in many of the same vineyards as DRC and changed its name to Domaine Leroy. Both now make tiny amounts of stunning wines at hideous prices. Fortunately, there are other growers here whose wines are more affordable, though not cheap.

In addition to the six *grand crus* mentioned above, Vosne has a further two, La Grande Rue and La Romanée. Grands-Echézeaux and Echézeaux are officially part of the village of Flagey-Echézeaux, which sells its ordinary wine as Vosne-Romanée – wouldn't you, with a name like that? Vosne *premiers crus* of note include Malconsorts, Boudots and Suchots. Compared to other villages, the *premiers crus* and village wines here can be exceptional.

The Vosne-Romanée taste The Vosne *grands crus* are so big, spicy and intense that you could mistake them for northern Rhône, until faced with the unmistakable sweet and savoury contrasts of Pinot Noir in a rich, fleshy and concentrated cloak of plummy fruit and ripe figs.

Texture counts, too, as with any good burgundy; their smooth, sensuous softness evokes cream for some, silk and velvet for others, and they become even more alluring with 15 to 20 years of age. In lesser wines, the ripe plums, hint of cinnamon spice, whiff of smoke and echo of chocolatey richness are like a pastel sketch of the boldly coloured oil canvas of the *grands crus*.

Where next? After the other outposts of **Pinot** greatness in the **Côte de Nuits** such as **Chambolle-Musigny** and **Gevrey-Chambertin**, it's downhill whichever way you look from here.

Washington State

Too good for apples

Best-known wines There'll be dozens of them in 100 years
Grape varieties Merlot, Cabernet Sauvignon, Cabernet Franc,
Syrah, Lemberger
Style Impressive, whatever the variety
Quality/Price **⋯⟩*****/££⋯⟩£££££

In 1984, Riesling was the most widely planted variety in Washington State, followed by Chardonnay and Chenin Blanc. Red grapes took up less than 20 per cent of the vineyards, largely because few believed that the state was capable of making any decent red wine. Today, the picture is rather different. The vineyards are split roughly 50/50 between red and white varieties, and while the Riesling and Chardonnay can be very good, it is the red wines for which Washington is making its name. Cabernet Sauvignon and Merlot lead the way, but Cabernet Franc and Syrah are also being planted as fast as irrigation rights can be obtained, which often means contending with the local apple farmers.

Bordeaux blends can already hold their own against those produced further south in California, and there is no reason why they shouldn't get better. The Syrah, sitting nicely between the Rhône and Australia in style, also looks like being a world-beater in the future. And although the plantings of Mourvèdre, Nebbiolo and Sangiovese are just experimental at present, it would come as little surprise to see them thrive in this state of excitement.

An irrigation
canal provides
water for vines
in Washington
State

The Washington State taste The Bordeaux-inspired wines ooze class, and are never too showy and aggressively extracted in the way that California wines can be. Cabernet Sauvignon is succulently textured with sweet, fleshy, berry and currant fruit and hints of olives. The best Merlot is spicy and supple with fragrant mulberry and blackberry flavours. Both styles are delicious young but can age supremely well. Syrah has the perfume and orange-peel character of the Rhône with the open, honest fruit flavours of Australia, and again is very amenable as to when you drink it. The spicy, perfumed Lemberger is capable of some gutsy, age-worthy wines, but is never going to be more than an interesting oddity.

Where next? California to see the main rivals for **Cabernet** and **Merlot**.

Western Australia

Quality rather than quantity
Best-known wines Margaret River Cabernet
Grape varieties Cabernet Sauvignon, Shiraz, Cabernet Franc, Pinot Noir
Style More elegant than the folks back east
Quality/Price ***⋯⟩****/££⋯⟩£££££

RECOMMENDED PRODUCERS

Alkoomi
Capel Vale
Chateau Barker
Chatsfield
Evans & Tate
Forest Hill
Goundrey
Houghton/Moondah Brook
Howard Park
Plantagenet
Salitage
Sandalford
Wignalls

Australia's largest state is not a major producer of wine, but what it does make is of a very high standard. The vineyards all hug the southeast corner of the country, where the Indian Ocean brings not only cool temperatures but drying winds that demand extensive irrigation to compensate. The hot Swan Valley region to the northeast of Perth, where the harvest typically starts in January, has traditionally been the source of much of the state's wine, most of it simple and fruity. But today, less than a quarter of Western Australian wine comes from the Swan Valley, and it is the higher quality districts which are expanding.

Foremost among these is Margaret River, home of some of Australia's most elegant Cabernet Sauvignon. Gaining in importance is the Great Southern region, which covers a large area close to the southern coast around the towns of Albany, Denmark, Frankland and Mount Barker. The Cabernet Sauvignon and Shiraz can match Margaret River for flavour and elegance, and the Cabernet Franc is also promising. Pemberton lies between here and Margaret River, and though only a recently developed region, has already made some excellent Pinot Noir. Between Margaret River and Perth is Geographe, where Capel Vale and a few other wineries make worthy wines.

The Western Australia taste Shiraz from the Great Southern region is richly flavoured with peppery blackberry and plum fruit, but has a structure that is quite tight and Rhône-like.

Cabernet Sauvignon can be very refined with the cedary, blackcurrant flavours normally associated with Bordeaux. Pinot Noir from here and Pemberton has strawberry and raspberry fruit, sometimes with a slightly peppery overtone.

Where next? **Victoria** can offer similar quality and styles of wine, but why not take a look what is happening in the Pacific Northwest of the **United States**, where **Oregon** and **Washington** are making wines to challenge the Californians. See also the entry for **Margaret River**.

Yarra Valley

RECOMMENDED PRODUCERS

Coldstream Hills
De Bortoli
Diamond Valley
Domaine Chandon
(Green Point)
Mount Mary
Oakridge
St Hubert's
Seville Estate
Tarrawarra
Yarra Ridge
Yarra Valley Hills
Yarra Yering
Yeringberg

Where rich Melbourne folk come to make wine

Grape varieties Pinot Noir, Cabernet Sauvignon, Shiraz, Merlot
Style Supple, fruity and fragrant Pinot; peppery Shiraz; elegant Cabernet
Quality/Price ***····⟩*****/£££····⟩£££££

The Yarra Valley is one of Australia's coolest growing regions, and has a range of soils to which different grape varieties will respond. Cabernet Sauvignon and Shiraz perform well, but anywhere that can make a passable Pinot Noir gets the bended knee and bared-head treatment from reverential drinkers. The 1980s saw prices outpace the quality of many Pinots, but the maturity of both vines and winemakers has shown through since then. The few Merlots produced show great promise, while there are even a few vines of Touriga Nacional with which Yarra Yering makes tiny quantities of very impressive port.

The Yarra Valley taste Yarra Valley Pinots have an impressive weight of strawberry-to-raspberry-to-cherry fruit, a richness of texture, and sometimes even a hint of the gaminess which is the hallmark of classic Pinot. Cabernet blends are elegant with supple tannins and rich, sometimes almost savoury, berry, plum and damson fruit. Shiraz has the peppery edge of the northern Rhône, together with ripe, full, blackberry flavours.

Where next? **Margaret River** for the **Cabernets**, **Adelaide Hills** for **Pinot Noir** and Great Southern of **Western Australia** for **Shiraz**.

Zinfandel

The spicy side of California
Style Spicy blackberry, cherry and damson, with a sprinkling of white pepper
Grown in California, Arizona, Chile, Australia, South Africa, Italy

It is remarked that California's favourite son is in fact adopted and is actually the Primitivo of southern Italy. However, the Italians have never exploited their grape to remotely the same extent that they have Stateside, where they make pink wine, fortified wine, dessert wine and – thankfully – normal table wine from Zinfandel.

After a lull in the 1980s when no one seemed interested in it, Zinfandel is currently enjoying renewed popularity, and demand is high for fruit from the old vines of the stuff which can still be found in California, especially in the Dry Creek region of Sonoma. Other countries have experimented with the grape, usually with good results, but the number of wines remains few.

Zinfandel isn't the easiest grape to grow, and often the same bunch will contain both unripe and overripe grapes. Some Californian growers blend in a small amount of other varieties such as Petite Sirah to give a little more structure. Others prefer to let the grape speak for itself, and this can result in wines with alcohol levels as high as 17 per cent. Zin is also the type of grape to which not a few winemakers become rather emotionally attached – the evidence can be found by looking for the Zin Prayer on the back label of a bottle of Cline Zinfandel.

The Zinfandel taste A good young Zinfandel has lively, peppery fruit which may say "cherries", "blackberries" or "raspberries"; it will also say "drink me". Yet with its amazing potential for ageing it can produce tannic, concentrated, deeply coloured wines, packed with enough sustaining fruit to see them on a very long journey.

After 20 to 30 years in bottle they will be challenging clarets of similar vintage. The 17 per cent monsters need time to calm down, although it's debatable whether they will ever be as well balanced as less potent versions.

Where next? For big fruit and big flavour, **South Australia** is the first stop for **Shiraz** and **Grenache**. After that, try **Châteauneuf-du-Pape**, **Priorato** and the bigger southern Italian reds such as Castel del Monte. And after all that, have a glass of fizzy water.

158 FRA

Red wine by country

France

Le Boss

Best-known wines Hermitage, Margaux, Chambertin, Châteauneuf-du-Pape

France appears to have everything. The wines are varied in style and cover the whole price range. There is something for everybody, from raspberryish Cabernet Franc in the Loire, to deep, blackcurranty Cabernet Sauvignon in the Médoc, from mainstream burgundy to odd little *vins de pays* made from odd little grapes in odd little parts of the Southwest.

Many of them are more than just wines; they are models that have been copied and reproduced in most grape-growing countries. It looks deceptively simple to grow the same grape variety in a similar climate half-way around the world, then stand back and wait for the money to roll in. But producers who embark on such projects soon realise there is more to it than that. France has the class, the charm, the sophistication and the chic, as well as the nuts and bolts. Everybody respects France.

France occasionally replies to the accolades with a rather smug and self-satisfied grin, but more often nowadays by turning the tables and naming some wines after the grape variety, opening out the fruit and easing back

FRENCH WINE LAW

French wine law splits the country's wines into four categories.

• Largest, best known and theoretically best is the *appellation d'origine contrôlée*, known as AOC or simply AC. The AC does not guarantee quality, but it does (or should) guarantee that a wine comes from where the label says it does, is made from certain grapes and is produced in a certain way.

• Below this are *vins délimités de qualité supérieur* (VDQS), with similar controls to AC but for separate regions. This category has all but

disappeared as most have been promoted to AC.

• Less strictly controlled, *vin de pays*, or country wines, say on the label where they come from and (if the producers choose) what grapes they are made from – vary from simple to modern classics.

• *Vin de table*, the everyday plonk of the working man, can be made from more or less any grapes, grown nearly anywhere; indeed, any indication of such things on the label is strictly forbidden.

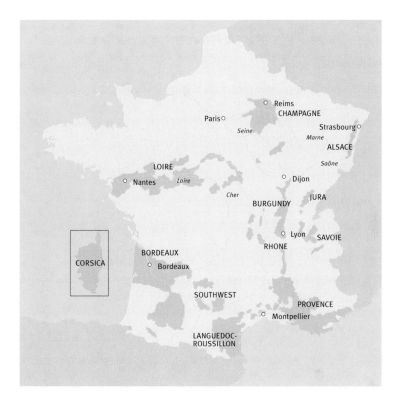

on the oak, just like they do in the New World. France is adaptable, and that is a strong card. It means that some wine styles are changing; not as fast as they are in California or Australia perhaps, but surely and steadily.

France is the single most important wine-producing country in the world. It is usually topped by Italy not only for sheer quantity, but often for blistering whatever-next? excitement. And countries such as Australia and California have pulled models of France to bits and stuck them together with their own pot of glue, threatening France's supremacy. In addition, that smugness mentioned earlier is often combined with a blinkered outlook that seems to ignore the vast quantities of mediocre wines being produced in some regions which really should be doing better. Yet the variety of styles, the profusion of classics, the fascinating nooks and crannies, make it a country to return to time and again. When you are tired of France, you are tired of wine.

Where next? See the specific entries for **Alsace, Anjou-Saumur, Bandol, Banyuls, Beaujolais, Beaune, Bergerac, Bordeaux, Bourgueil and Chinon, Burgundy, Cahors, Chambolle-Musigny, Châteauneuf-du-Pape,**

Corbières, Cornas, Corsica, Costières de Nîmes, Côte Chalonnaise, Côte de Beaune, Côte de Nuits, Côte-Rôtie, Coteaux du Languedoc, Côtes du Frontonnais, Côtes du Rhône, Côtes du Roussillon, Crozes-Hermitage, Fitou, Fronsac and Canon Fronsac, Gevrey-Chambertin, Gigondas, Graves, Hermitage, Languedoc-Roussillon, Loire, Madiran, Margaux, Médoc, Minervois, Morey-St-Denis, Nuits-St-Georges, Pauillac, Pessac-Léognan, Pomerol, Pommard, Provence, Rhône, Southwest, St-Emilion, St-Estèphe, St-Joseph, St-Julien, Vin Doux Naturel, Volnay and Vosne-Romanée.

Italy

Stylish from top to toe
Best-known wines Chianti, Brunello di Montalcino, Barolo, Valpolicella

Italy is the most exciting wine-producing country in Europe. Its quirky A–Z of grape varieties, grown in every sort of climate imaginable – from the snows of the Alps to the heat of the south as far as the island of Pantelleria near Tunisia – yields a positive cornucopia of wine flavours and styles.

Most years Italy tops the league table for quantity, producing around one fifth of the world's wine. Much of this is plain drinking, some of it going anonymously abroad for blending, some bearing a well-known label – Bardolino, Chianti, Lambrusco – which is often more memorable than the contents. Barolo, Barbaresco, Brunello di Montalcino and the Super-Tuscans (*see* **Tuscany**) are among the best wine styles, but they account for a comparatively tiny quantity of Italy's total wine production.

Italy used to suffer badly by comparison with France. Traditional, fusty drinkers outside Italy felt that if a wine didn't taste like either claret or burgundy there must be something wrong with it. Very little in Italy, at the time, tasted remotely like claret or burgundy, and, to be fair to the old buffers in their clubs, much Italian wine was oxidised, tannic, and virtually undrinkable outside the neighbourhood in which it was born and, thankfully, often died. But then two things happened: drinkers changed, and Italy changed.

We, for our part, began to expand our horizons. We might never be able to reel off all the *grands crus* of Burgundy, but we learned to recognise a ton of flavour when it hit us in the mouth. And we could work out that, since some of the new wines often cost only a fraction of the old, we should not find it difficult to put our money where our ton of flavour was coming from. As soon as Australia and California took the mystery out of French wine, the door was open for Italy to step through and charm the socks off us.

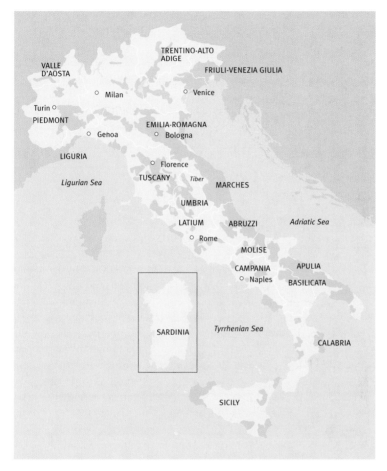

Italy rose to the occasion magnificently, and is still rising. The technical trappings of stainless steel and temperature-controlled fermentation swept through the country much faster than in Spain and Portugal. Most importantly, Italy has not put all its grapes, so to speak, in one basket. It has hung onto Sangiovese, Dolcetto, Nebbiolo, Montepulciano and many others, while warmly embracing Cabernet Sauvignon and its international travelling companions.

The most go-ahead regions for red wine are Tuscany and Piedmont, with the northeast (*see* **Trentino-Alto Adige**, **Friuli-Venezia Giulia** and **Veneto**) not far behind. Southern Italy and the islands, once content to churn out large quantities of pap, now have more smaller, quality-minded wineries joining the large co-operatives which still dominate the region. Both are using local grapes such as Aglianico, Aleatico, Gaglioppo, Negroamaro,

Primitivo and Uva di Troia to make everything from simple, everyday quaffers to full-bodied, age-worthy and very attractive reds. Throughout the 20 provinces, in fact, wine quality is higher than it has ever been. For more details of the regions mentioned above and of Lombardy, Apulia, Sardinia, Sicily and Umbria, turn to the relevant sections in the A–Z section of this book.

Valle d'Aosta lies between Piedmont and the Alps, and the regional d'Aosta DOC allows a range of varietal wines including Pinot Nero and Nebbiolo as well as blends. Producers to look out for include Charrère and Les Crêtes. Those who visit Liguria on the other side of Piedmont are usually more interested in the Riviera than the wine, although the occasional Rossese di Dolceacqua from Cane or Terre Bianche can be good.

In central Italy just south of Tuscany, Latium has no red equivalent of Frascati, or indeed any red DOCs of renown. However, a number of producers do stand out, namely Casale del Giglio, Colacicchi, Falesco (fine Merlot), Paulo Di Mauro and Castel di Paolis. On the opposite coast, Sangiovese is the main red grape of Emilia-Romagna in the DOC Sangiovese di Romagna. The DOCs of Colli Bolognesi and Colli Piacentini both allow varietal Barbera and Cabernet Sauvignon plus Merlot in the former and Pinot Nero in the latter, as well as blends. In Colli Piacentini, Bonarda is blended with Barbera to make Gutturnio. Many producers choose to work outside the DOC regulations, and this is where most of the best wines are found. Look out for wines from Casa Chiara, Castelluccio, Fattoria Paradiso, La Stoppa, Tenuta Bonzara, Tenuta la Palazza, Tre Monti, Terre Rosse and Zerbina.

Sangiovese is also important in the Marches region further down the Adriatic coastline. However, this is where the deep, spicy Montepulciano grape begins to make its presence felt, with the two varieties being blended together for Rosso Piceno, while Montepulciano gets the upper hand in Rosso Conero. The best producers are Boccadigabbia, Garofoli, Mecella, Moroder, Le Terrazze, Umani Ronchi and Villa Pigna. Montepulciano d'Abruzzo is the only wine of note in Abruzzi, but Illuminati, Masciarelli, Montori, Tollo, Umani Ronchi and Valentini all make admirable versions.

The powerful, well-structured, cherry-and-chocolate Aglianico is the great grape of Campania and Basilicata. In Campania, Taurasi is the best and best-known wine, thanks to the efforts of Mastroberardino, but the wines from Caggiano and Feudi di San Gregorio are also good. Other Aglianico-based wines include Falerno del Massico (look for Villa Matilde and Michele Moio) and Taburno (Ocone's is the best). Aglianico also plays a small part in Montevetrano's excellent wine, along with Cabernet Sauvignon and Merlot. In Basilicata, Aglianico del Vulture is the only wine of note. The best comes from D'Angelo, with Paternoster and Sasso also making fine versions.

In Calabria, the toe of Italy's boot, the Gaglioppo grape is used for the region's best-known wine. The full-bodied Cirò, especially in the hands of Librandi, can be very good. Savuto, in which Gaglioppo once again plays a part, is somewhat lighter, with producers such as Odoardi making pleasant rather than great wines.

Italy's strength is its diversity, brought about on a heroic scale by sheer disregard for conformity. Each of its many thousands of winemakers is determined to show how original he is, how different from his neighbour, how unconcerned he is about slotting comfortably into somebody else's grand scheme. It looks a mess, but the wealth of creativity produces exciting wines that reward exploration. Please do not give up. Persevere, and Italy will both surprise and delight.

Where next? See specific entries for **Apulia, Barbaresco, Barolo, Bolgheri, Brunello di Montalcino, Chianti, Friuli-Venezia Giulia, Lombardy, Piedmont Sardinia, Sicily, Trentino-Alto Adige, Tuscany, Umbria, Valpolicella, Veneto** and **Vino Nobile di Montepulciano.**

ITALIAN WINE LAW

The DOC system, introduced in the mid-1960s, is an attempt to impose some sort of order on thousands of individualists. Originally, all wines fell into one of three categories:

• *Denominazione di origine controllata e garantita* (DOCG), supposedly the peak of vinous perfection, of which there are currently 14. The regulations stipulate means of production, grape varieties and origin, and *garantita*, in theory, guarantees quality.

• *Denominazione di origine controllata* (DOC) is the next step down, DOCG minus the guarantee: there are over 250 DOCs.

• Other words you might see on DOC and DOCG wines are – *classico*: theoretically the best wines the region has to offer; *superiore*: generally a wine with slightly higher natural alcohol, although it, too, may refer to the area of production; *riserva*: which applies to higher-quality wines of a DOC or DOCG that have been aged for longer than usual.

• *Vini da tavola*, or table wine, is officially the lowest of the low. However, from the 1960s onwards, several producers, especially in Tuscany,

decided that they wanted to make wines which did not fit into the framework of the DOC laws.

Although these soon became some of Italy's finest and most expensive wines, they could only be called *vini da tavola*. New legislation in the 1990s has meant that from the 1996 vintage onwards, *vini da tavola* are forbidden to state their origins, grape varieties and vintages.

This latest development has given the producers of the *vini da tavola* two options. They can change to DOC status, either within an existing district where the laws regarding grape varieties and other issues have now been relaxed, or they can apply for their own DOCs. Alternatively, they can be classed as...

• *Indicazione geografica tipica* (IGT), the equivalent of the French *vin de pays*. Many of the *vini da tavola* now come under the IGT Toscana, for example.

RECOMMENDED PRODUCERS

Graf Adelmann (Württemberg)
Friedrich Becker (Pfalz)
Bercher (Baden)
Dautel (Württemberg)
Rudolf Fürst (Franken)
Dr Heger (Baden)
Bernard Huber (Baden)
Karl-Heinz Johner (Baden)
August Kesseler (Rheingau)
Knipser (Pfalz)
Koehler-Ruprecht (Rheinpfalz)
Laubenstein (Rheinhessen)
Lergenmüller (Pfalz)
Lingenfelder (Pfalz)
Mayer-Näkel (Ahr)
Messmer (Pfalz)
Thomas Siegrist (Pfalz)
Vollmer (Pfalz)

Germany

Not all white, all right?

Best-known wines Baden Pinot Noir

White wines predominate in Germany, with only around 15 per cent of production being red. Even so, why don't we hear more about the German reds? Quite simply because the vast majority are not very interesting. The climate is the problem. All grapes need sun to ripen, and red ones in particular need it to produce the colour, tannin and flavouring components that are found on, or just under, the skin. Germany is up at the northern limit of viticulture; in fact, it straddles the leading edge at 50° north, so unless a vineyard is especially favourably sited, the grapes will be pale in colour, high in acid and low in flavour, and the resulting wines will never amount to much.

Yet the wines from the more favoured sites can be very good. Hardly any of these sites are warm enough for grapes such as Syrah and Cabernet Sauvignon, although Pinot Noir (Spätburgunder) thrives in many vineyards, producing more interesting wines than those made with Blauer Portugieser, Limberger/Lemberger, Trollinger and others. A relatively recent crossing, Dornfelder, is also turning out impressive wines.

Wherever red wine is produced in Germany, it really does take an enthusiast to make something of it. Since a concentrated wine requires low yields, it is likely to deter anybody who thinks purely in terms of economics and accountancy. But long skin-contact and *barrique*-ageing are bringing more character to many of the reds. The system of categorising the wines according to must-weight (natural sugar level) is adopted for both reds and whites, although a red *spätlese* is much less likely to be sweet than a white one; the word *trocken* confirms that the wine is dry.

Curiously, the sunniest parts of Germany are not always the ones where red wine is made. The Ahr, one of the northernmost regions, is well known for reds, or at least for darkish, slightly sweet rosés made from Spätburgunder. Assmannshausen, on the edge of the Rheingau, has a reputation for reds which are more highly regarded in Germany than abroad; if they are sought after, though, it is probably because there is precious little to go around. The warmer regions of Rheinhessen, Pfalz, Baden and Württemberg all have red wine traditions in varying degrees. Württemberg's Schillerwein is a local blend of red and white grapes, and Baden's slightly sweet Rotling is a blend of Spätburgunder and Pinot Gris. Koehler-Ruprecht makes a Spätburgunder Eiswein as a curiosity.

The German taste Most of the reds resemble nothing more than dark rosé. They generally have gentle, wispy, strawberry scents and flavours rather than full-blooded ones. They are high on freshness – if you catch them young enough – but low on flavour, tannin and stuffing, and are generally for drinking young.

Most Spätburgunder falls into this broad category, but good winemakers manage to make richer, fruitier, fuller-bodied wines which can be excellent, if occasionally slightly over-oaked. The deep-coloured Dornfelder can also impress, whether it is made in a light, spicy, cherryish Beaujolais style or in a richer, throatier vein with oak influence.

Where next? Pinot Noir from **Alsace**; or the **Loire**; **Beaujolais** and Mâcon; **Dolcetto**, Bardolino and **Valpolicella**.

Spain

Hot (and sometimes very hot) bed of activity

Best-known wines Rioja, Ribera del Duero, Navarra

Spain is the world's third largest producer of wine and has the largest area under vine of any country on earth; it accounts for half the vineyards of the European Union.

The arid climate largely prevents this being converted into a commensurate amount of wine, but it is still the sort of potential that puts the wind up its competitors. Until recently, much of this potential was unrealised, but the Spaniards are now availing themselves of the wonders of modern technology and making better wine than they have ever done before.

Rioja has been waving the Spanish quality flag for decades, but it now has competition from other regions such as Ribera del Duero and Priorato, with Navarra, Penedès (*see* **Catalonia**) and Somontano also improving rapidly. Ribera del Duero's neighbours in Castilla-Léon include Toro

SPANISH WINE LAW

Spain's wine classification has similarities with those of Italy or France.

• *Denominación de origen calificada* (DOCa) is a comparatively recent introduction used to denote the superior DOs, and is equivalent to Italy's DOCG.

• *Denominación de origen* (DO) specifies the source, grape varieties and means of production, much as France's AC and Italy's DOC do.

• *Vino de la tierra* is more flexible than a DO, roughly equivalent to the French *vin de pays*.

• *Vino comarcal*, or "regional wine", applies to wine made in 21 *comarcas*, or regions, which show some individual regional character.

• *Vino de mesa* is the lowest level, equal to France's *vin de table*, but there are some good wines.

and Cigales, both of which can make easy, fresh, Tempranillo-based wines. Bierzo, in the northwest, home of some increasingly interesting wines based on the Mencía grape, is technically part of the same province, although it has more in common with Galicia. Somontano's compatriots in the northeast in Aragón are Campo di Borja, Cariñena and Calatayud. Garnacha, Mazuelo and Monastrell – or Grenache, Carignan and Mourvèdre, if you're French – are the main varieties here, although Cabernet Sauvignon and other foreign imported varieties are making their presences felt.

All these regions lie in the cooler northern districts of the country. Admirable as the improvement in such places is, just as significant is what has been happening in warmer areas to the south. Fresh fruit is appearing where once there was just flabbiness, oxidation and evidence of dirty old barrels. The huge Castilla La Mancha plain in south-central Spain will never be a fine-wine region, but the reds made from Cencibel – the local name for Tempranillo – can be fresh, juicy and great value, especially those from Valdepeñas.

To the east lies Valencia and the DOs of Yecla, Almansa, Utiel-Requena, Jumilla and Alicante, where the grapes used include Bobal, Monastrell, Garnacha and Tempranillo. There are few wines of note from the islands, with the exception of Binissalem from Mallorca which is made mostly from the rare Manto Negro grape.

You still get the feeling that Spain must have more to offer in the way of indigenous grapes. The country boasts over 600 different varieties, and the innovative Miguel Torres has an experimental vineyard in Penedès in which over 120 of them are planted. However, even with the recent advances in quality, only Tempranillo has truly shown that it can offer top-class wines with any consistency.

Where next? See the specific entries on **Catalonia**, **Navarra**, **Priorato**, **Ribera del Duero**, **Rioja** and **Somontano**.

RECOMMENDED PRODUCERS

Portugal

Quinta de Abrigada
Almeirim Co-op
Bela Fonte
Quinta da Boavista
Bright Brothers
Casa do Valle
JM da Fonseca
Quinta da Foz do Arouce
JP Vinhos
Quinta da Lagoalva
José Neiva
Quinta das Pancas
Ponte de Lima Co-op
Redondo Co-op
Reguengos Co-op
Sogrape

It's getting better all the time...

Best-known wines Port, Dão, Bairrada

Port and Madeira are famous the world over. Portuguese table wines aren't. Why? In the past, there have been two main reasons. Firstly, the domestic population has had a very healthy thirst, putting them in the top three of the European drinking chart. Secondly, the wines haven't been up to scratch. The two facts are related. Portuguese wine drinkers have traditionally equated quality with lengthy ageing in large, old and often rather dirty oak casks. Add to that the fact that the wines which went into those casks in the first place were hugely tannic, and the only surprise is that anyone could find wines made in such a fashion palatable. The occasional Dão or Bairrada managed to have enough fruit to survive such treatment, but on the whole, standards left a lot to be desired.

Then, in the 1980s, things started to change. A few of the larger companies had already invested in winemaking equipment and the odd new barrel or two, but the really crucial event was in 1986, when Portugal joined the European Community (EC). With the help of EC grants, existing cellars were refurbished and new ones built, and the improvement in the wines since then has been rapid. Palates used to Cabernet Sauvignon and Merlot have thrilled to the very different flavours of Portugal's indigenous grapes, some of which – Baga and Touriga Nacional especially – show real class. There are French grapes, but producers mainly stick to local varieties.

However, while some of Portugal's winemakers have shown that they have what it takes to compete on an international stage, there is still a lack of skilled personnel both when it comes to growing grapes and making wines. Input from foreigners has been rare, with the exception of a handful of very talented Australians who have set up base in the country. With more outside help, could the learning process speed up even more?

PORTUGUESE WINE LAW

Portugal's wine classification has many similarities to that of France.

• *Denominação de origem controlada* (DOC) specifies the source, grape varieties and means of production, much as France's AC does.

• *Indicação de proveniência regulamentada* (IPR) is the equivalent of France's VDQS classification.

• *Vinho regional* (VR) is a more flexible classifiction than a DOC, and is equivalent to the French *vin de pays*.

• *Vinhos de mesa* is the equivalent to the French *vin de table*.

Port is, of course, the best-known wine from Portugal, but no table wine enjoys such renown. Dão and Bairrada have traditionally been considered the sources of the finest wines, but standards in both are rather wayward, the top reds having little in common with some of the old-fashioned dishwater which goes by the same name. So in other words, it's more important to look for the name of the producer than the region, something that is true throughout Portugal, with only the Douro showing any sort of consistency (and even then not a great deal).

Take, for example, the Alentejo, the vast region that occupies over a third of mainland Portugal. Much of what is made here is dreadful, but Esporão and Pera Manca are among Portugal's finest producers. The Algarve region to the south of Alentejo has little of interest, but Terras do Sado to the west, which takes in the Setúbal peninsula, offers several excellent wines, thanks largely to the efforts of JM da Fonseca and JP Vinhos.

North of here is the Ribatejo, which literally sits on the banks of the Tagus (Tejo). This is Portugal's second-largest producing region, a land of co-operatives, of wine sold in bulk to bottlers both inside and outside the region, with no more than a few rare flashes of quality. The most productive wine region is Estremadura, sometimes referred to as Oeste, which lies between Ribatejo and the coast. As in the Alentejo, cheap quaffers are the order of the day, but there are also some fine and innovative estates such as Quinta das Pancas and Quinta da Boavista. Best of a number of demarcated regions (IPRs) are Alenquer, Arruda and Torres Vedras.

Within Estremadura are two DOCs of interest, as much for the stories behind them as for the quality of the wine. Carcavelos is a sweet, fortified wine made from a blend of red and white grapes which was famous in the 18th century but today boasts just one producer: Quinta dos Pesos. The resolutely tannic wines of Colares are made from *phylloxera*-free Ramisco vines planted in sand near Sintra on the Atlantic coast. With the current standards of winemaking, it's an historical curiosity rather than a style that is going anywhere in particular.

Beiras covers central Portugal, taking in the DOCs of Dão and Bairrada, and as in those two districts, standards vary enormously. The north of the country is split between Trás-os-Montes, within which lies the Douro, and Rios de Minho, which takes in Vinho Verde. Blends from the Douro which also include grapes such as Cabernet Sauvignon come under the Trás-os-

Montes heading. Red Vinho Verde, made from a variety of grapes, the best of which are Vinhão, Azal and Espadeiro, is a bracing experience, with peppery fruit and a slight prickle to it.

The Portuguese taste The traditional style of Portuguese wines – old and oxidised with whatever fruit there is masked by a tannic overcoat – has given way to something altogether more appealing. Fruit flavours usually veer towards the blackberry, damson, plum and blackcurrant spectrum, and there are often hints of tobacco, spices, vanilla and leather. Some wines still carry a hefty amount of tannin, but the fruit is (usually) the dominant feature. Some winemakers still have to get to grips with oak handling, especially with the cheaper wines, where excessive use of oak chips often adds coarse, dusty flavours, swamping the lovely fruit. But, given the choice between this and the dried-out old bones of the past, I know what mine is.

Where next? See specific entries for **Alentejo**, **Bairrada**, **Dão**, **Douro**, **Port** and **Touriga Nacional**.

Switzerland

Steep slopes, steep prices
Best-known wines Ticino Merlot

Switzerland, like Austria, is dominated by white wines, but makes some very attractive light reds, mostly from French grape varieties. The cool climate suits Pinot Noir, which thrives near the area of Neuchâtel and –

as Blauburgunder or Spätburgunder – in the German-speaking north. Dôle is the blend of Pinot Noir and Gamay made in the Valais region. Perhaps the most interesting wines are the Merlots from Ticino in the south of the country. Those marked "VITI" have passed the requirements of an official tasting panel and should be the best, although it often just means that the wine has been aged for a certain amount of time.

The Swiss taste Ticino Merlot can be very pleasant and plum-and-cherry fruity, with a slightly grassy edge. Where oak has been used, a few producers have managed to make more serious wines, but we're not talking Pomerol here.

Where next? Try other light **Pinot Noirs** from **Alsace**, **Sancerre**, the northern reaches of **Burgundy** and **Germany**. As an alternative to Swiss **Merlot**, try **Dolcetto**.

Austria

And very good they can be, too
Best-known wines Nothing at present, but wait and see...

Austria will always be better known for its white wines than for its reds. However, the reds have come along in leaps and bounds in recent years. Mittelburgenland in Burgenland and the Thermen region in Niederösterreich are where most of the best come from. If such names hardly trip off the tongue, neither do those of the grape varieties involved, including Blauburgunder (aka Pinot Noir), Blaufränkisch (aka Lemberger or Kékfrankos) and Blauer Portugieser, Zweigelt and St Laurent. Some Merlot and Cabernet Franc are grown, but Cabernet Sauvignon is the foreign import that has enjoyed the greatest success, either by itself or in a blend with the Austrian varieties.

RECOMMENDED PRODUCERS
Paul Achs
Juris-Stiegelmar
Pöckl
Reinisch
Ernst Triebaumer
Josef Umathum

KAMPTAL
KREMSTAL
WACHAU
TRAISENTAL
Danube
WEINVIERTEL
DONAULAND
VIENNA ○ Vienna
CARNUNTUM
THERMENREGION
NEUSIEDLERSEE
Neusiedler See
NEUSIEDLERSEE-HUGELLAND
MITTEL-
BURGENLAND
Mur
SUDBURGENLAND
WEST STYRIA
SOUTHEAST STYRIA
STYRIA

The Austrian taste Zweigelt is bright and zippy with ripe, berry flavours, while Blaufränkisch is Austria's answer to Beaujolais: fresh and tart with spicy cherry fruit. St Laurent can develop earthy, red-berry flavours and a lush texture not dissimilar to Pinot Noir. Pinot Noir itself, as Blauburgunder, seldom impresses, but Cabernet Sauvignon can be surprisingly rich and fruity, with plums and blackcurrants to the fore.

However, where producers have gone out of their way to extract as much flavours as possible from their grapes, there can be a stewed fruit, vegetal, tomatoey note in the wines.

Where next? Try **Trentino-Alto Adige** reds, especially Teroldego, for more light fruit and perfume. Blaufränkisch is found as Kékfrankos in **Hungary**, and Lemberger in **Germany** and **Washington State**. Some of the flavours in the **Bordeaux**-inspired wines find echoes in **New Zealand's Cabernets.**

RECOMMENDED PRODUCERS

Chapel Hill
Tibor Gal
Thummerer

Hungary

Land of the anaemic bull
Best-known wine Bull's Blood

Unfortunately, Hungary has no red wine to match its glorious Tokáji whites. The best-known wine is Bull's Blood (Egeri Bikavér), made from Kékfrankos (known as Blaufränkisch in neighbouring Austria), but this is hardly the fierce, legendary, barbaric experienceimplied by the name.

The Kékfrankos grape is grown in Sopron in western Hungary. And, Kadarka, which is the country's most widely planted grape variety, makes red wines varying in style from light to full-flavoured. There are also imported grapes, such as Cabernet Franc, that can do well in some cases, but there's still nothing to make you hold your breath.

The Hungarian taste

The Kékfrankos grape makes light and lively red wines, while the Kardaka makes a style that has a little more edge and fire. International varieties, such as Cabernet Franc can be juicy and fresh when they are well made.

Where next? Similarly rustic styles can be found in **Bulgaria**. Australian **Shiraz** would be ideal for the blood-transfusion Hungary's bulls seem to need.

Bulgaria

RECOMMENDED PRODUCERS
Vinis Iambol
Perushtitza
Vinprom Russe
Vinprom Shumen
Menada Stara Zagora
Lovico Suhindol

We live in hope...

Best-known wines Suhindol Cabernet Sauvignon,
Haskovo, Merlot

At a time when it seems that every country in the world is improving its wines, it's hard to say the same about Bulgaria. In the 1980s, Bulgarian Cabernet Sauvignon was a huge success because it offered more juicy, earthy, blackcurrant flavour, more bang for your buck than any other wine around. Exports rocketed from 50,000 cases at the beginning of the decade to over 1.5 million by the end of it, and have since risen even further.

However, if you think that the wines which are on sale today are not as good as those from the original wave, you're not alone. Even the Bulgarians acknowledge that they struggle to maintain standards, and it's easy to see why. The vineyards are in an atrocious condition. In the days of communism, the state looked after them, but now they are often neglected or abandoned. Few wineries have any vineyards of their own, so they have to scrabble for what fruit is available, sometimes regardless of its state of health. The wineries themselves, many now privatised or run as independent co-operatives, are still rather primitive by modern standards, but they are better equipped than they have ever been. Visiting consultants have been put to good use, giving advice on how to improve all the winemaking.

Unfortunately, several wineries have interpreted this advice as meaning that what the consumer wants is wines with more new-oak character. This is fine when there is flavour to back it up, but with the fruit quality falling, the wines are often out of balance. Taste through a winery's range, and the quality seldom bears much relation to the price.

The young unoaked wines are often the best and the occasional older wine which has spent time in large old barrels can also be very good. This was the style which attracted wine-lovers to Bulgaria in the first place. However, it is the wines with upfront new oak and not enough fruit that the wineries, or at least those selling to foreign markets, consider to be their best. Bulgarian labels can be confusing. The wineries are usually named after the region

they are in, but there's nothing to stop each buying fruit from other parts of the country. Hence the Sliven winery can make Iambol Cabernet, while the Iambol winery can make Sliven Cabernet. Certain regions have reputations for different varieties. The best Merlot comes from Haskovo, especially Stambolovo, while Assenovgrad, Stara Zagora (particularly Oriachovitza), Svischtov, Suhindol and Iambol make fine Cabernet. For the local varieties, Gamza's home is Suhindol, Mavrud's thrives in Assenovgrad, Perushtitza and Plovdiv, while Melnik is the speciality of Damianitza.

The Bulgarian taste Cabernet Sauvignon produces solid, workmanlike wines, the best of which have a rich, blackcurrant flavour. The finest Merlot is sweet and plummy with a lush, creamy texture. Unoaked versions of both are sappy and vibrant, while wines which have aged in old oak are rounded and velvety. Where new oak is used, it's often hard to see far beyond it.

Melnik, a thick-skinned variety (and also a place to confuse matters), produces deeply coloured, highly tannic, strong and age-worthy wines with hints of tobacco. Mavrud makes typically dark, plummy and spicy wines and again is reasonably long-lived. The Hungarians claim that Gamza is their Kadarka grape, but with its spicy, black-fruit flavours, it could almost pass for Zinfandel.

Where next? Chile and southern France have taken over the role of providers of cheap-and-cheerful Merlot and Cabernet, and both can also offer higher rungs on the quality ladder. Stay in southern France for alternatives to the spicier Mavrud and Melnik.

Romania

Frustratingly erratic
Best-known wines Dealul Mare Pinot Noir

Every so often, Romania gives you a glimpse of just how good it could be if only it had the money to give its wine industry the complete overhaul it so badly needs. There are mature vineyards planted with in-demand varieties such as Pinot Noir, Cabernet Sauvignon and Merlot, as well as interesting local grapes like Feteasca Neagra, which, although rather unruly, could be revived with not too much difficulty. However, the wineries for the most part are filthy and poorly equipped. Good batches of wine are being made, but they are often lost in blending or – which is even sadder – simply sit decaying slowly in a tank because there isn't enough money to bottle them. Where flying winemakers have waved their magic wands, the

ROMANIA

Prut

○ Timilisoara

Olt

Danube

Bucharest ○

Danube

wines can be good, although over-oaking is a problem. Better are the slightly more old-fashioned wines which have been in large old-oak casks, but not for too long. The Dealul Mare region is the source of many of the better reds.

The Romanian taste One bottle of Romanian Pinot Noir can be rich, savoury and full of plummy fruit. The next ten can be thin, coarse or astringent – and sometimes all three. The better Cabernets and Merlots have ripe, rich, red, fruit flavours and a soft, mellow structure.

Where next? After seeing what **Hungary** and **Bulgaria** can offer, follow the grape varieties to the more reliable **Languedoc**.

Greece

Watch out for the phoenix
Best-known wines Château Carras

Thankfully, there is no red equivalent of Retsina (although a few pinkish ones do exist). Even so, most people would struggle to come up with the name of *any* Greek red wine, but they do exist. Though diplomatic mutterings about "unrealised potential" still go on, there are a number of producers – a smallish number it must be said, but still a number – who are producing some very pleasant wines. The wineries are at last being updated, while the grapes being

RECOMMENDED PRODUCERS
Achaia Clauss
Antonopoulos
Boutari
Château Carras
Gerovassilou
Hatzimichali
Kourtakis
Château Lazaridi
Domaine Mercouri
Papantonis
Skouras
Tsantali
Tselepos

GREECE

Thessaloniki

Aegean Sea

Patras

Athens

used are an eclectic mix of local and foreign varieties. Xynomavro, Agiorgitiko (St George) and Mavrodaphne are the most prominent of the former. Cabernet Sauvignon and Merlot are the most popular of the latter.

Xynomavro is the power behind Goumenissa and Naoussa, while Nemea from Corinth is made with Agiorgitiko. Mavrodaphne is pressed into service in Goumenissa, Naoussa, Nemea and Patras to make *vin doux naturel* (*qv*). However, the imported grapes are excluded from nearly all of these, so Cabernet Sauvignon and Co have to be labelled "Topikos Oenos" (*vin de pays*) or "Epitrapezii" (*vin de table*). Cava is not a sparkling wine but an aged table wine.

The Greek taste Oxidation and dirty old oak still form the lasting impressions of many Greek wines, but this is changing. The best wines come from the smaller estates, and their flavours are dictated by the grape variety and winemaker rather than by the region of origin.

Xynomavro has moderate tannin and high acidity, with berry and cherry fruit flavours, and ages to spicy complexity. Agiorgitiko is velvety with berry fruit – not dissimilar to Merlot, which explains why some producers blend it with Cabernet Sauvignon. When the Bordeaux varieties are used by themselves, the wines are very much like Rioja meets Bordeaux: soft and mellow yet fragrantly fruity. Mavrodaphne is also best described as a halfway house – the fragrant fruit, with the soft, warm structure of a tawny port. The wines are never as good as either but are excellent value.

Where next? Portugal and Italy to see where Greece might go next.

RECOMMENDED PRODUCERS
Château Kefraya
Ksara
Château Musar

Lebanon

No longer a one-horse town
Best-known wines Château Musar

In most people's wine-minds, Lebanon *is* Château Musar. The conditions under which Serge Hochar makes his blend of Cabernet Sauvignon with some Cinsault and Syrah have been difficult in the past, to say the least.

Don't go looking for the 1984; the grapes never made it through the war zone from the vineyard. Given such an environment, it's surprising the wine is so good, rather like a claret with a dollop of something from the southern Rhône. Full-bodied, well-structured, with sweetly plummy fruit and an exotic whiff of resin and spice, it has great ageing potential and is best around 10 to 15 years old.

But don't write off Lebanon as a one-horse, well, one-winery country, otherwise the folks at Château Kefraya and the handful of other producers would take issue. The inaugural vintage, 1996, of Comte de M, Kefraya's new blend of Cabernet, Mourvèdre and Syrah, is very classy, sweet and spicy with plum and cherry fruit and hints of leather. Many feel it's a better wine than Musar, but whether it will be as consistent remains to be seen.

Where next? Bordeaux, the southern **Rhône** and **Provence**.

England

Pink, white and blue
Best-known wines The best red grapes end up in white fizz

RECOMMENDED PRODUCERS
Boze Down
Chapel Down
Hidden Springs
Thames Valley Vineyard
Wooldings
Wyken

Too much rain, not enough sun, too many late frosts... you name it, the wine producers are up against it. The generally accepted limit for sensible viticulture is 50°, and it runs through the very southern tip of the country, and then only in places. Some red grapes will just about ripen, but Triomphe d'Alsace, Dornfelder and Dunkenfelder are hardly the sexiest of varieties.

Beenleigh Manor in Devon has some Cabernet Sauvignon grown under plastic covers, but the best use it has been put to so far has been to make a rather pleasant rosé. Pinot Noir can ripen in good years, but if Champagne can't do it, what hope is there in the Home Counties? Sorry Brits, it's all very well being patriotic and all that, but if you're going to grow red grapes, stick to making rosé or sparkling wines.

The English taste Too often, the wines are over-macerated in order to extract more flavour, and as the grape skins are unripe, this means extracting lean, green, mean flavours. The better wines have some earthy damson and blackberry fruit, but there's almost always a hint of unripeness lurking in the background.

Where next? Try cool-climate **Pinot Noir** northern **Burgundy** (Chablis), **Alsace**, **Switzerland** and **Germany**. Also reds from **Trentino-Alto Adige**.

AMERICAN WINE LAW

America has over 100 designated AVAs, or American Viticultural Areas. The only rules governing their use on wine labels is that 85 per cent of the grapes must have been grown in the region concerned. Some AVAs, such as Napa Valley, are huge, with many producers as well as several smaller AVAs within their boundaries. Others are tiny – North Yuba has one winery, for instance. Unlike the European appellation systems, there are no regulations as to which grape varieties are grown, nor to the way in which they are grown and vinified.

United States

The pioneer spirit lives on

Best-known wines Napa Valley Cabernet Sauvignon

California is and probably always will be the largest wine-producing state in America. However, where once it was the only one making quality red wines, there are now a number of other states which are capable of making wines which can compete with, and occasionally out class the Californians. Oregon with its Pinot Noir and Washington State with its Cabernets and Merlots are the most important of these, but in the future they may not be the only competition. Washington Syrah already shows promise and New York State Merlot can also be very good. But what about Merlot and Cabernet Franc from Virginia? Cabernet Sauvignon from North Carolina? Even Zinfandel from Arizona? They exist today and the best examples are very good. Twenty years ago, Washington State was considered fit only for apples, and look where it is now. Watch this space closely, as it could be very interesting in the coming years...

Where next? See specific entries for **California**, **Carneros**, **Central Coast**, **Monterey and San Francisco Bay Area**, **Napa Valley**, **Sonoma**, **New York State**, **Oregon** and **Washington State**.

Canada

The not-so-frozen north

Best-known wines Watch out for Merlot and Pinot Noir in future

RECOMMENDED PRODUCERS
Calona
Château des Charmes
Hawthorn Mountain Vineyards
Henry of Pelham
Inniskillin
Inniskillin Okanagan
Lakeview Cellars
Marynissen Estates
Mission Hill
Nichol
Quails' Gate
Southbrook Farm
Thirty Bench
Tinhorn Creek

Canada's serious wine industry is still very much in its in fancy. Even so, there have been wineries here for many years churning out wines made from *Vitis labrusca* and hybrid varieties under names such as Cold Duck, Luv-A-Duck, Gimli Goose and Pussycat.

Vinifera vines began to be planted in the 1970s, since when progress has been rapid. While whites lead the way, reds are beginning to make an impact, and several of the wines show great promise for the future. The main areas for reds are the southern half of the Okanagan Valley in British Columbia and the Niagara Peninsula in Ontario. Most of the effort is concentrated on the Bordeaux varieties, but there's also some palatable Syrah and Pinot Noir, and even Petite Sirah from Marynissen in Ontario. Wines from the hybrid varieties are slowly disappearing, but the occasional Baco Noir and Marechal Foch can still be rustically tasty.

At present, the wines have much in common with what New Zealand was making in the 1980s. The winemakers have often trained in Germany and lack experience with red varieties in particular. It's no coincidence that two of British Columbia's best wineries – Quails' Gate and Mission Hill – both have winemakers of Antipodean origin. However, as the vines and the winemakers mature, the wines have will have great potential only to get better.

The Canadian taste

Canadian Cabernet Sauvignon tends to have blackcurrant and blueberry flavours, Cabernet Franc has an earthy, berry quality, while Merlot can be plummy and slightly minty.

The structure of all the Bordeaux-inspired wines is often rather hard and raw, but with any luck improvements in winemaking should be able to deal with that. Pinot Noir varies from jammy and soupy through leafy and vegetal to supple and silky with plenty of raspberry fruit and finesse. In capable hands, Baco Noir and Marechal Foch produce rich, spicy wines with inky berry and chocolate flavours, but many versions are rather sickly and coarse.

Where next?

From a similar standing start, **New Zealand** has made great progress with its red wines in recent years. Not many other countries make such an array of hybrid-based wines.

Argentina

Plenty up its sleeve, but slow to unbutton its cuff

Best-known wines Malbec

Because they are neighbours, it's easy to think of Chile and Argentina as producing similar wines. However, the two countries and their inhabitants are very different. Chileans historically are not wine drinkers, so the producers go out of their way to make wines which are acceptable for foreign palates. Argentinians, on the other hand, are, so wine companies cater first and foremost for the national taste, which is for old-fashioned, over-aged red wines and tired old whites.

As in Chile, the wine regions would normally be considered too dry, but viticulture is possible due to the melting snow draining from the Andes and providing plentiful irrigation water. And as in Chile, the growers still use rather too much of that water in their vineyards, with the result that flavours are not as concentrated as they could be. Even so, foreign winemakers who have worked in Argentina say that the vineyards are in a fairly healthy condition, and there are few problems with the grapes that arrive at the winery. However, the wineries themselves are often filthy and poorly equipped, and producing wine in such conditions is difficult to say the least. Fortunately, there is a growing number of wineries which are keen to make an impact in overseas markets, and these are updating their facilities accordingly. It's also interesting to see the number of Chilean companies that are investing in the country.

The three most widely planted grapes are Criolla Chica, Criolla Grande and Cereza, and the pale pink wines made from these are instantly forgettable (until the morning after). The rest of the vineyards are an eclectic mix of varieties of varying origins. When the Italians settled, they brought Dolcetto, Barbera, Nebbiolo, Bonarda and Sangiovese, while the Spanish legacy is Tempranillo and Garnacha. The Bordeaux varieties are also here, but the one that has adapted best to the conditions is Malbec, which makes wines of a stature and complexity not repeated anywhere else in the world.

Around two-thirds of the vineyards are in Mendoza province, with the best of these being the higher vineyards in the west of the region. Promising sub-regions include Luján de Coyo, Maipú, Tupungato and Agrelo. The other regions making good reds are all north of Mendoza but still clinging to the Andes. Cafayate, in the province of Catamarca, has some decent

Cabernet, while the high altitude vineyards of Salta can make some of Argentina's most characterful wine.

The Argentinian taste It's still the winemaker who calls the shots here. There are probably some wines being made today which in years to come will be held up as shining examples of *terroir*-driven reds, but the only common thread running through the best reds of today seems to be fruit from higher-altitude, low-yielding vines. The Italian varieties seldom perform as well as they do in their natural habitat, with the exception of the spicy, fragrant Bonarda. Syrah and Tempranillo will be very good when yields are reduced, while Cabernet is also successful, showing rich, inky, blackcurrant flavours.

Malbec is the star variety, displaying perfumed plummy fruit wherever it goes. Dress it up in oak and it struts proudly around, looking handsome and well-built. It's not always easy to pigeon-hole, though. Catena makes it seem like a cocky Cabernet, while Weinert fashions something akin to great old-fashioned Rioja from it. Malbec makes a fine blend with Cabernet, too – Colomè's Viñas de Davalos Tinto from Salta could pass for a Châteauneuf-du-Pape.

Where next? Try **Cahors** to see how far in advance Argentina is with **Malbec**. Compare the **Cabernets** with those of **Chile** to see how different they are.

Brazil

What Renaldo drinks when recovering from injury
Best-known wines Val-Pele-cella?

Brazil comes third in the South American production league after Argentina and Chile, but it lags way behind in quality. Its hot, humid conditions are exactly what a vine doesn't need. Even so, there are a few spots in the extreme south of the country which grow a wide range of grapes, most of which are *labrusca* or hybrid grapes, but with a few better-known *vinifera* varieties such as Cabernet Sauvignon, Merlot and Barbera. High rainfall means that rot is an ever-present problem, but some of the wines made by Forestier, Palomas and Vinicola Aurora have shown that there is potential.

Where next? How about **Uruguay**, which lies just to the south of Brazil?

Chile

The long, thin one

Best-known wines Heart-friendly, user-friendly Cabernet

To understand Chile's vineyard regions, you need to rethink your wine geography. You'd think that in a southern-hemisphere country, such as Chile, the further north you went, the warmer it would be. And, yes, if you travel far enough, this is certainly true. However, in the Central Valley, home of most of Chile's vineyards, there's not a huge difference in the climate.

Travel from east to west, however, and the situation is rather different. The Central Valley is flanked by the mighty Andes to the east and the much smaller coastal range of mountains to the west. The higher up the Andes you climb on the east side of the valley, the cooler it gets. Head west and as well as the climate becoming warmer, what slopes there had been give way to large expanses of flat, fertile land. Enthusiastic use of irrigation, still a problem, means that some vineyards are just too fertile, and the grapes often lack concentration. Carry on west and you hit the slopes of the coastal range, where once again the ground is less fertile and therefore better suited to wine grapes. Unlike regions to the east, there is actually some rainfall here, so irrigation is not always necessary. Sea breezes drifting through the hills begin to exert their influence, and it's cool once more.

Chile's red wines are among the best value on the planet, and extremely gluggable. This hasn't always been the case. Throughout the 1980s, there were lots of rumours that Chile was about to do something big, but little materialised. Then, around 1992, it was almost as if the whole country woke up and said, "Let's make some wine." Out went the large, old picturesque but grubby casks, in came the stainless steel and the pristine new-oak barrels. Almost overnight, the wines changed from well-meaning but dull to exciting, vibrant and – whoops, I seem to have finished the bottle.

Cabernet Sauvignon led the way, but close behind was some of the yummiest Merlot going. Well, at least that's what it said (and usually still says) on the bottle. The truth is that at least 60 per cent – and some say 90 per cent – of what Chile calls Merlot is actually an obscure Bordeaux variety called Carmenère. With Carmenère and true Merlot often interplanted in the same vineyards, it will be many years before anyone is fully sure that a bottle labelled Merlot is actually Merlot. And even when the vineyards have been sorted out, there are the commercial considerations to think about – Carmenère may provide the better wine, but Merlot sells better.

Most wines are still at the cheap and cheerful end of the market. But Chile is also muscling in very successfully on the slightly higher ground which Australia has ruled for so long, and not just with Cabernet and Merlot/Carmenère. Pinot Noir has proved successful, as have Malbec and Zinfandel, and the few Syrahs that exist show great potential.

At a higher level still, Montes Alpha "M" (Montes), Seña (Caliterra and California's Robert Mondavi) and Alma Viva (Concha y Toro and Mouton-Rothschild) all wear price tags more often seen on classed-growth claret. They're good wines, but they should be half the price. Yet isn't this a sign that an up-and-coming wine country has finally arrived, when impoverished wine writers begin to complain about the prices?

Chile has been divided into wine districts, but it still makes more sense to talk about which are the best producers, especially as the decision of how much to irrigate has such a crucial effect on wine quality. Furthest north and one of the newest wine areas is the Valle de Limarí, where the Francisco de Aguirre winery is showing the potential. Aconcagua splits into two regions, the Aconcagua Valley itself, where Errázuriz is the only producer of note, and the Casablanca Valley. The main districts of the huge Central Valley are (from north to south): Maipo, Rapel, Curicó (*see* specific entries) and Maule, which is a huge region known mainly for white wine, but with some good Merlot coming from near Talca. The Southern Region may one day contain more than experimental plantings.

The Chilean taste See the specific entries for Casablanca, Maipo, Rapel and Curicó. Until more producers make wine with fruit from the Aconcagua Valley, it doesn't make any sense to speak of a regional style, only the style of Errázuriz, arguably the finest estate in Chile.

Where next? Follow **Cabernet** and **Merlot** around the New World (you won't find much Carmenère). See **Casablanca**, **Curicó**, **Maipo** and **Rapel**.

Mexico

Olé, anybody?
Best-known wines LA Cetto Petite Sirah

RECOMMENDED PRODUCERS
Casa Pedro Domecq
Casa Madero
LA Cetto
Monte Xanic
Santo Tomas

With a population that drinks tequila and beer in preference to wine, and with California's huge and very efficient Central Valley not so far away, the Mexican wine industry is always going to have a tough time. You'd think it might be too hot to grow vines here, but the altitude and the ocean breezes keep the vineyards cool enough for varieties such as Cabernet Sauvignon, Petite Sirah, Nebbiolo and Zinfandel.

The Mexican taste At this point in time it is difficult to define what a Mexican style is as there are so few wineries in this country. However, if your taste buds are demanding a taste of what Mexico can produce, try LA Cetto's gutsy, spicy Petite Sirah.

Where next? Compare Mexican wines with those of **California's** Central Valley.

Uruguay

RECOMMENDED PRODUCERS

Juanicó
Castel Pujol

Why Tannat?
Best-known wines Nothing as yet

You may not have realised that Uruguay made wine. If you did, you probably weren't aware that it made one million hectolitres of the stuff each year. Much of it is (thankfully) consumed *in situ*, but the reds which do escape are usually based on the sturdy Tannat of Madiran and other wines of southwest France which were introduced by Basque settlers in the late-19th century. So far, the wines have not shown much that the Chileans and Argentinians need worry about, but they do on occasion rise above the "interesting" level to become drinkable.

The Uruguayan taste Just as they struggle in Madiran to tame Tannat's tough-as-old-boots structure, so they do in Uruguay. The wines can show quite pleasant, violet-scented, berry and chocolate fruit, but there's always the wall of killer tannin to circumnavigate before you get to it. A helping hand from a jolly plump grape such as Merlot or Grenache would be of enormous benefit, but so far few have followed such a route.

Where next? Stay in South America to see what the Argentinians do with another variety from **Southwest France**, namely **Malbec**. Or head to Tannat's homeland and try the improving wines of **Madiran**.

Australia

G'day
Best-known wines Penfolds' Grange, Jacob's Creek red...

"By the year 2025, the Australian wine industry will achieve $4.5 billion in annual sales by being the world's most influential and profitable supplier of

branded wines, pioneering wine as a universal first-choice lifestyle beverage... Australia has an opportunity with its innovation and leadership to drive the global wine industry much as Japan did with cars." (*see* below.)

The two "Best-known wines" on the previous page go a long way to explaining Australia's phenomenal success since the mid-1980s. One is a limited-production wine selling for the same price as first-growth claret, the other a much cheaper high-volume product, yet both illustrate the two best aspects of Australian wine, namely flavour and reliability.

Both also come from large companies. In other countries, big is usually not beautiful, but Australia is different. The four largest producers – Southcorp Wines (which produces Grange), BRL Hardy, Orlando-Wyndham (Jacob's Creek) and Mildara Blass – produce 70 per cent of the country's wine, with several of their wines ranking among the very best available. Just as importantly, these four companies, though rivals, get together with other people in the industry to discuss how they can work together for the benefit of Australian wine.

The most obvious fruit of these pow-wows is a document called *Strategy 2025*, a 30-year blueprint for the Australian wine industry from which the above quote is taken. The mission statement is: "Total commitment to innovation and style from vine to palate." It would come as little surprise to see it continue, "To boldly go where no wine-producing country has gone before, to seek out new drinkers in distant galaxies and say, 'G'day mate, fancy a drop of Shiraz?'"

Pie in the sky? We're going to have to wait until 2025 to find out. So far some of the initiatives outlined in the document – which, really should be called *Wein Kampf* – are on target, others are not, but it does give the Aussies something to aim long term, which is what they currently need. The adulation which Australian wines have received in the last 15 years seems to have started going to a few heads, and we've seen some wines soar in price. This has been due partly to a succession of small vintages in the early 1990s and increased worldwide demand. However, the important aspect of value for money (which was what won the Australians so many friends in the first place) does, in some cases, seem to have been forgotten.

That said, Australia remains a source of some of the world's most energetic red wines, whatever the price you pay. In the near future, new vineyard plantings will mean that lower-priced wines should be either better or cheaper – and sometimes both – than they have been for a few years. And even with the price rises, some of the top wines, especially old-vine Shiraz, remain good value compared with what other countries have to offer. Thankfully, the attempts at elegance which marred so many wines in the 1980s have been abandoned, and the producers are now not afraid to make rich, ripe and burly reds. Shiraz leads the way with Cabernet Sauvignon not far behind, and there are also enthusiastic noises being made by Grenache and Mourvèdre, also known here as Mataro. Cabernet Franc and Merlot are beginning to appear as single-varietal wines, but usually they are blended in with Cabernet Sauvignon. Producers in warm regions have mostly given up on Pinot Noir, but the variety is finding a home in some cooler spots.

Each week sees two new wineries established, and each year sees vineyards appearing in regions where previously there were none. Occasionally you worry that some Australians are beginning to take themselves too seriously and are turning into Californians, but a glass or two of sparkling Shiraz usually sets your mind at ease.

Where next? See specific entries for **Adelaide Hills, Barossa, Clare, Coonawarra, Hunter Valley, Margaret River, McLaren Vale, New South Wales, South Australia, Victoria, Western Australia** and **Yarra Valley**.

RECOMMENDED PRODUCERS
Chard Farm
Felton Road
Gibbston Valley
Giesen
Neudorf
Pegasus Bay
Mark Rattray
Rippon
Danny Schuster
Waipara Springs
Waipara West

New Zealand

Dashing up the learning curve
Best-known wines Hawke's Bay and Waiheke Island Bordeaux blends, Martinborough Pinot Noir

New Zealand reds used to fall into the "let's-be-polite" bracket. The wines, with their weedy, vegetal flavours and aromas were patently the result of underripe fruit, regardless of whether the colour was wishy-washy or not far from black. That was Phase One. Phase Two came about when those who had been making the underripe wines decided to either abandon them altogether in favour of white varieties. Some altered their ambitions from making a Cabernet Sauvignon with a touch of Merlot to making a Merlot with a touch of Cabernet. Others spent more time in their vineyards in order to get riper and more concentrated fruit.

The quality improved enormously, and the best winemakers turned out wines any country would have been proud to claim as its own. Yet everyone nodded to each other and said that red wine was all very well, but that New Zealand's forte was its white and sparkling wines.

They hadn't bargained for Phase Three, which we're in now. Today, red grapes take up over a quarter of New Zealand's

vineyards, and while a lot of this is Pinot Noir destined for sparkling wine production, most of it is used for table wines. New red wine vineyards are popping up at an alarming rate all over the country, from Waiheke Island near Auckland in the north where Cabernet is king to Central Otago, home to some of New Zealand's finest Pinot Noir. In Hawke's Bay, the country's most important red wine region, red grapevines are being planted at twice the rate of white ones. If this carries on, there may come a time when it is red wine rather than Chardonnay and Sauvignon Blanc for which New Zealand is best-known.

Most of the red wine comes from the North Island, with only Gisborne not producing in any great quantity. The Bordeaux grapes rule in the regions around Auckland, especially Waiheke and in Hawke's Bay, although here strides are being made with Syrah. At the southern end of the island, Martinborough can also turn out a good Bordeaux blend, but Pinot Noir is the real strength.

In the South Island, Marlborough is definitely white wine territory, although Merlot, Pinot Noir and even Syrah have been used to good effect. To the northwest, Nelson has a few Cabernet vines, but the best wines so far have been Pinot Noir, especially that of Neudorf. Pinot also does well in the regions around Christchurch, especially in Waipara. Cabernet will ripen, but only in the best sites, which many producers prefer to keep for their Pinot anyway. In the most southerly wine region in the world, Central Otago, once again it is Pinot Noir which grows surprisingly well, producing the intensely perfumed wines of Rippon Vineyard. Newcomer Felton Road has already shown that Rippon's success with Pinot is not a flash in the pan.

Where next? See entries for **Auckland**, **Hawke's Bay**, **Marlborough** and **Martinborough**.

RECOMMENDED PRODUCERS

South Africa

Beaumont
Boplaas
Bouchard-Finlayson
Buitenverwachting
Die Krans
Goudini
Groot Constantia
Hamilton Russell
Klein Constantia
Spice Route
Steenberg
Swartland Co-op
Du Toitskloof
Whalehaven
Zandvliet

Getting there

Best-known wines Kanonkop Pinotage

"I don't give a **** what anybody thinks about my wines… I like them and think they are damned good. I am not going to change my style for anyone." Unless, dear reader, you are built like a brick privvy, the ex-Springbok rugby player-turned-winemaker who uttered those words is rather larger than you, and not to be argued with. His sentiments may have been voiced more forcefully than those of other South African wine producers, but underneath, many feel the same. Yet they also feel offended when outsiders don't rate their wines as highly as they do themselves.

While South Africa's best wines are getting better and better, most have a long way to go before they will catch up with rivals in Australia and California. High acidity, fruit flavours which are not fully ripe and hard finishes are common in too many wines. The South Africans claim that they are making wines in more of a European style than a New World style, but surely they should just be letting their own vineyards and grapes do the talking. Many winemakers have learned their trade in that haven of top-quality reds, Germany, and you get the feeling that they are more interested in making their wines conform to certain statistical analyses than in actually making them pleasant to drink.

Anyone who visits the wine-growing regions of the Cape will realise straight away that most places are prime red wine country. Unfortunately, the vineyards are heavily biased towards white grapes. The most widely planted varieties used for quality reds are Merlot, Cabernet Sauvignon, Pinotage and Shiraz, yet these four among them can only muster 12.5 per cent of the vineyard area.

Another blow is that many vineyards have been terribly afflicted by viral diseases, which, apart from shortening the lifespan of a vine, also affect its ability to ripen. For varieties such as Cabernet Sauvignon, which is a late ripener anyway, the effects are disastrous, and have been all too evident in the wines. The fruit flavours are baked and raisiny, yet the tannins are coarse and green, which doesn't make for very pleasant wines.

SOUTH AFRICA ○ Johannesburg

Cape Town○

The viral problem is being addressed, although the plant nurseries are struggling to keep up with demand for "clean" vine cuttings. Producers are finding that replanted vineyards with improved clones ripen up to six weeks earlier. Also, several sites which used to be considered unsuitable for red grapes are now fair game for Cabernet and Co. Cabernet Sauvignon is the most widely planted red grape, performing at its best in Stellenbosch and Paarl Constantia, often with Merlot by its side. These regions are mostly too warm for Pinot Noir, although the coastal parts of Stellenbosch have had some success with the variety. However, Pinot seems to have found a home down in Walker Bay, although the number of producers there is tiny. South Africa's own grape, Pinotage, is currently enjoying something of a revival after years of being considered fit for little beyond cheap jug wine. The best versions can be excellent, and age as well as the Cabernets. In the 1980s, the Australians would have felt under little threat from South African Shiraz, but today's fresher, more complex wines are far better.

The Constantia region is making a name for its white wines, but the reds, usually Bordeaux blends, can also be very good. Inland, Worcester, Robertson, Olifants River, Klein Karoo and Swartland are hot and dry, and are the sorts of places which the Australians would transform into irrigated oases of easy-drinking Shiraz and Cabernet Sauvignon. So far, the South Africans have yet to follow their example, but the occasional blend of Cinsaut and Ruby Cabernet can be enthusiastically juicy. The high point of these hotter regions is in Calitzdorp in Klein Karoo, where Die Krans and Boplaas make some of South Africa's finest "ports".

Hopefully the next edition of this book will detail the huge strides South Africa's producers have made in the first decade of the new millennium. Already new wineries are popping up throughout the country. New grape varieties are already being planted – there's Nebbiolo in Constantia, Mourvèdre and Malbec in Paarl, and Barbera in Durbanville near Stellenbosch. And the number of producers expanding their horizons by working vintages in other parts of the New and Old Worlds shows that many in the Cape *are* beginning to care about what other people think.

Where next? Chile and **Argentina** are the competition, **Australia** and **California** remain a leap ahead. See also **Paarl** and **Stellenbosch**.

Highlighted section shows where the key wine areas are: Olifantsrivier, Piketberg, Swartland, Tulbagh, Paarl, Durbanville, Worcester, Constantia, Stellenbosch, Robertson, Swellendam, Klein Karoo, Overberg

Index

PICTURE CREDITS:

Front cover: Steven Morris Octopus Publishing Group Ltd; Joe Cornish 2–3 top, 10, 23, 25, 46, 55, 57, 120, 152; James Johnson 34, 35, 68, 85, 93, 98, 102, 111 bottom, 113, 127, 138, 140, 157; Jason Lowe 21, 59, 87, 115, 137; Richard McConnell 15 top, 29, 75, 81, 91, 109, 134; Steven Morris 4, 53, 64, 70, 77, 150; Alan Williams 2–3 bottom, 16, 18, 30, 43, 44, 45, 49, 71, 83, 96, 100, 101, 105, 106, 111 top, 123, 125, 129, 130, 142, 145, 148, 154. And many thanks to Seagram UK and the ICEP Portuguese Trade and Tourism Office for their kind contributions. Seagram UK 2 top, 20, 52, 88; ICEP Portugese Trade and Tourism Office 9, 69, 117